Praise for *What's Left of Us*

"The story of one man's struggle to pierce through the lies, pain, and shame of a harrowing past. Farrell's writing is blunt and honest; there is something heroic in his attempts to salvage a productive life from the ruins of abuse and addiction. A stunning piece of work."
— T. J. English, author of the national best sellers *Havana Nocturne, Paddy Whacked,* and *The Westies*

"In the stripped-down, busted-and-back voice of a man with absolutely nothing left to hide, Richard Farrell gives us this deeply moving tale of addiction and redemption. *What's Left of Us* is a rush of blood to the head and heart, the kind that only true art can deliver."
— Andre Dubus III, author of *House of Sand and Fog* and *Garden of Last Days*

"A work of compelling honesty. The writing is so powerful, so brutally sure of voice and experience that the reader is immediately jolted straight into the hellish existence of addiction. An amazing story not just of survival, but redemption."
— Mary McGarry Morris, author of *Vanished* and *Songs in Ordinary Time*

"It is hard to explain how a story so filled with pain and chaos can leave you rejoicing. It is a testament of Farrell's stunning writing power that he carries you on this roller-coaster ride of ugliness and beauty. Don't miss it."
— Phyllis Karas, author of the *New York Times* best-seller *Brutal: the Untold Story of My Life Inside Whitey Bulger's Irish Mob*

"A wild ride from start to finish. Riveting."
—Chris Cooper, Oscar-winning actor

"What's Left of Us is Richard Farrell's true-life account of his struggle to come to grips with his father's destructive love. The story sears itself into your heart and doesn't let go."
—Anna Hamilton Phelan, screenwriter of
Girl, Interrupted, Gorillas in the Mist, and *Mask*

"How Richie Farrell survived his life, I'll never know. That he was able to write about it with such honesty and emotion and without any bullshit at all is a miracle."
—Scott Silva, screenwriter of *8 Mile*

"Richie Farrell's raw and visceral writing grabs you, slams you into the soul of an addict, and doesn't let go until you experience the courage it takes to wage a life-or-death war against your inner demons. It is absolutely breathtaking and inspirational."
—Harry Ufland, producer of *The Last Temptation of Christ, Not Without My Daughter,* and *One True Thing*

"Alternately heartbreaking and heart-stopping. I couldn't put it down." —Dorothy Aufiero, producer of *The Fighter*

RICHARD FARRELL

WHAT'S LEFT OF US

CITADEL PRESS
Kensington Publishing Corp.
www.kensingtonbooks.com

CITADEL PRESS BOOKS are published by

Kensington Publishing Corp.
119 West 40th Street
New York, NY 10018

All Kensington titles, imprints, and distributed lines are available at special quantity discounts for bulk purchases for sales promotions, premiums, fund-raising, educational, or institutional use. Special book excerpts or customized printings can also be created to fit specific needs. For details, write or phone the office of the Kensington special sales manager: Kensington Publishing Corp., 119 West 40th Street, New York, NY 10018, attn: Special Sales Department; phone 1-800-221-2647

CITADEL PRESS and the Citadel logo are Reg. U.S. Pat. & TM Off.

First printing: July 2009

10   9   8   7   6   5   4   3   2

Printed in the United States of America

Library of Congress Control Number: 2009923863

ISBN-13: 978-0-8065-3074-1
ISBN-10: 0-8065-3074-X

For my Dad

There is no such thing as a normal life.
There's just life. Now let's get to it.

—Doc Holliday to Wyatt Earp
moments before the gunfight
at O.K. Corral.

Acknowledgments

I'd like to thank my mother who survived this war along-
side me and encouraged me to tell my story. Melissa Hardy
whose love gave me a son, Aidan, and the courage and in-
spiration to move on with my life. To my children, Jack, Rick,
Will, and Siobhan, who forgave my sins. And finally, to my
agent, Emmanuelle Alsplaugh, and my editor, Mike Shohl,
who believed in my ability to write this story.

Breath of God

The Acre wasn't pretty. You'd never see it on the post-cards sold at the corner drugstores in downtown Lowell, Massachusetts. The Acre wasn't big. Nobody had grass in their front yards—just black tar that formed the alleys separating the houses. The Acre wasn't rich. Most families had only one set of good clothes set aside for Sunday's Catholic Mass. The Acre was entirely segregated from the rest of my birth city. But it was still the best section of Lowell to grow up in if you were Irish.

The Acre was nothing more than a two-mile triangle of Irish who had formed a wall of self-protection. The homes were mostly triple-deckers—cold-water flats. Irish families had settled in Lowell years before to work in mills or build canals. All of them had escaped the horror of starvation on the streets of Ireland and found their way to Massachusetts. Compared to the Irish Famine, Lowell offered a promise of prosperity.

Smack dab in the middle of the Acre stood St. Patrick's

Church where my uncle Joe Farrell had hoisted the steeple during the Roaring Twenties. It was the same St. Patrick's Church that my grandfather, Richard Farrell, checked the doors of every evening at midnight as he walked his beat as a Lowell police officer, the same St. Patrick's Church where my father and mother brought me and my brother every Sunday as kids, where I'd received the blessed sacraments of Baptism, Confession, First Communion, and Holy Confirmation.

St. Patrick's School was directly opposite the church's parking lot. Two generations of the Acre's children had been educated there, from poor to poorest. It didn't matter how much money you had. There were only two prerequisites— you had to be Irish and Catholic. It was staffed by Notre Dame nuns who were known for their propensity to ask questions after they'd already used the ruler on your knuckles. The principal, St. Claire Joseph, expelled me in the seventh grade for entering after hours because my friends and I had to use the bathroom.

Adam Street cut a line down the center of the Acre and separated the school from the North Common. The North Common was the place where my father forced me to practice walking heel to toe so I wouldn't be a cripple. For the Irish elders who'd sit for hours on a warm summer night talking about the old days, it was more than a giant park. It was their St. Steven's Green in Dublin. In the early days, the North Common hosted football games on Sundays in the fall. Two to three hundred people would show up to watch the Irish kids play the Greek kids who had settled in the lower Acre. It was always a bloodbath. There was no football, just full-contact tackle with an old gray sweat sock stuffed full of leaves.

But by March 1987, the Acre that I remember was no more. The Irish moved out in the seventies. Some became educated and wanted more for their families. The majority was swallowed up by "white flight." They moved their families to predominantly white suburbs not more than a few miles from the Acre. Then Puerto Rico began importing their criminals to Lowell. The Acre was poor, old, and close to downtown—the perfect place for drug trafficking and prostitution.

I am a heroin addict. My life is limited to three concerns. The first thing I gotta figure out every morning is how to get a bag of heroin into my arm no more than ten minutes after I wake up. If I fail, I'm dope-sick. The cramps inside my lower stomach go on a full-scale attack. I can't stand. I can't walk. The diarrhea squirts out like a water hose. But I'm damn good at getting high now. I hardly ever stay dope-sick long.

The second issue is drawing a "hot shot" or a "beat-bag." The majority of heroin in Lowell originates from New York City. Puerto Rican gangs bring it here by the kilo. The drug dealers on Adam Street who package the heroin from one-pound bricks into grams and half-grams are no Einsteins. They cut the heroin or add fake shit to stretch quantity for profit. Some dealers cut it in half and double their money. Most use quinine, which gives the bitter taste, and an Italian baby laxative called Manatol because its fine white granules have almost the identical weight of pure heroin.

So picture this, four or five Puerto Rican males in a poorly lit room with the combined education of maybe the eighth grade, whacked on heroin or cocaine, drunk on port wine, with about fifty or sixty small piles of white powder lined out on an old door top propped on two twenty-gallon plastic paint containers being used as a cutting table. You don't have to be a fuckin' rocket scientist to figure out they ain't gonna be able to get the proper distribution of cut to heroin every time. Too much pure heroin in a half-gram package equals a "hot shot." You're history, because five minutes after the rush your heart stops. Too little or no heroin in a half-gram package gets you dope-sick.

But my major concern on Adam Street is "cotton fever." I'd rather be dope-sick all day than get what the Puerto Rican junkies down here call "cotton shot rush." It's when a dirty piece of cotton fiber used to filter the heroin makes it into your bloodstream. The sweats and shakes that ransack your body are nothin' compared to the fire under your skin. I've watched junkies do everything imaginable, cry hysterically, beg to die, boot two additional bags of heroin and overdose just to kill the sickness. A doctor in the emergency room once told me it comes from bacteria or fungus on the cotton, and not the cotton itself. To me the argument is pointless, you get "cotton shot rush"—it doesn't matter where it came from.

Heroin is not a cold-shake like cocaine. The impurities used to cut heroin need to be cooked off in boiling water before you shoot it intravenously. Down here we all do it the same: bite the heroin package open carefully, taste it, gag or dry heave on the bitterness, empty the heroin into a cooker (either a spoon or the bottom of a tonic can), draw 50cc of water into the syringe, fill the cooker until the heroin drowns, and light a match.

After you see tiny bubbles dancing in the cooker you

place a small sliver of cotton or a piece of a cigarette's filter into the liquid. With one hand firmly steadying the cooker, the tip of the needle is guided into the cotton or filter with the other hand. The plunger is moved upward slowly by biting firmly on the tip and moving the head upward. If all goes well the syringe fills with about 20cc of heroin. The task of hitting a good vein is next. And nobody down here takes the time to wrap a belt around their arm and whack the skin over a vein. That's fuckin' Hollywood. If you make it to where I am—you're an expert at veins. After contact, you watch your blood snake into the syringe, you pull the trigger, hot liquid moves quickly up your arm, your heart tingles, and you feel an immediate rush of adrenaline guzzle your brain in one swift sip.

From there it's a crapshoot. Most addicts don't carry sterile cotton balls or Q-tips in their back pockets. If you're lucky you have access to a clean filtered cigarette. But most of the time you have to find a cigarette butt on the ground, in an ashtray, or a garbage barrel. "Cotton shot rush" is a perfect example of life as a heroin addict. You live for the moment. If it happens, it happens. But there is no mistaking it when it hits. Ten to twenty minutes after you pull the trigger it whacks you like you're in the third day of the flu virus. The ears give it away: if they start to ring, you're fucked. Pressure begins to mount on each side of your temple like a vise squeezing slowly together. Sweat pours off your brow, but at first there is no temperature associated with it. The shakes progress quickly to trembles. Chills hit immediately after and the body's temperature spikes to over 102. Sometimes the brain fogs and things appear that aren't there. I'm not sure why some cases are more extreme than others. On occasion it can last only an hour; most times it resolves it-self within twelve to twenty-four hours. But if the bacteria takes up residency in your heart and you don't seek medical attention, you're dead. I roll the dice about a dozen times a day.

Each morning I do what all the other runners down here on Adam Street do: I lurk in the doorways, dodge the police, jones, and wait for addicts to drive up and buy their morning dose. Now Adam Street isn't safe. And only one rule counts—the strong survive. The drug trafficking goes on all night long without a break. There's routine police surveillance, nothing big though. Every shift the cruiser drives by to let us know they know. But for the most part the drug trade is in your face twenty-four hours a day, seven days a week.

I wasn't always a homeless, jobless, low-life heroin ad-dict. Once I was a good kid, an altar boy for Father Mul-doon right here at St. Patrick's. I went to the YMCA as a young boy and played basketball, baseball, and football. And I was a pretty fair student—but school bored me. I think it had something to do with the fact both my parents were teachers.

When I was thirteen, my family moved out of the Acre into the wealthiest section of Lowell: Belvidere. Dad wanted the best for his kids, and the Irish no longer owned the Acre. All the old Irish families had moved to the suburbs or bet-ter sections of Lowell. The Farrells had become engulfed by "white flight." My dad said the Puerto Ricans would even-tually overrun all of the good old Irish neighborhoods.

Our house was very modest compared with the houses on the hill behind us. The view from the back porch of our brand-new home was a sixty-room castle belonging to a billionaire, Mr. Lions. He lived with his wife, a chauffeur, two maids, a cook, and a groundskeeper. To the right of the castle was a forty-room-plus mansion owned by Dick Donahue, a former legal counsel to President Kennedy. He lived inside with a beautiful wife and eleven children. Every morning, I'd look out the bathroom window as I peed. No, we weren't in the Acre anymore.

My brother, Sean, and I had it all—friends, a giant yard in which to play tackle football, and five-speed bicycles. Sean was ten and a half months older than me. We were Irish twins, born in the same year. I was born with cerebral palsy. Or that was what my parents had been led to believe.

Back in 1956, Doctor Griffin, a specialist at Children's Hospital in Boston, told Dad I'd never be able to walk normally. I'd been a breech birth; my feet came through the birth canal first. The doctors told my father and mother that several minutes without oxygen had caused permanent damage. They said the muscles in my right arm and right leg would atrophy unless I exercised them daily. They said I had cerebral palsy. Dad couldn't accept any kid of his being a "cripple." He forced me to run every day. And five days a week, I'd exercise with free weights in my basement—just to be "normal." By the time I got to high school the sport headlines of the *Lowell Sun* read, CRIPPLED AT BIRTH: FARRELL NOW GRID STAR.

My parents were both teachers. Mom taught sixth grade at Edith Rodgers Junior High School in Lowell and doubled as a waitress, carrying trays in the evening at Valley's Steak House in Andover. Dad taught Honors English at Lowell

High School, and every Tuesday and Thursday he taught English to the Puerto Ricans who had come here for a better life.

They both worked two jobs so Sean and I would have more than they'd had in the Acre. Sixty hours a week for each of them so we could live in a white split-level home with a brick front and a two-car garage—Dad's side had an automatic door opener—all sitting on a quarter acre of land in the best area of Lowell.

I cannot pinpoint any one incident that brought me back to Adam Street. I'm not entirely sure how I went from being a well-off Belvidere kid to a homeless addict. All my dad ever wanted out of me was to play football for the Fighting Irish at the University of Notre Dame. It was his dream that drove me from my early teens into my last year of high school. I became a football star for my Dad. But an illegal chop-block one Saturday afternoon in late fall ended that dream. My team was about to defeat the state champions. There were under two minutes left on the clock. They had possession of the ball. My coach signaled me to blitz the quarterback, not allow him to set up and complete a long pass downfield. I anticipated the snap of the ball, shot the gap, and was in their backfield untouched. But three things happened at the exact same split second: my left hand reached for the quarterback's shoulder, my right foot planted firmly on the turf, and the helmet of the fullback trying to block my clear path cut out my right knee from the blind side. *Pop!* Like giant overstretched elastic, the insides of my knee exploded.

After that day, I had seven knee operations to remove torn or floating cartilage, one operation after another, in an attempt to correct complications from the previous one. Those surgeries introduced me to prescribed pain medication. I fell in love with what those little pills accomplished inside my head. All my pain, emotional and physical, disappeared.

I had let my Dad down. I had let myself down. But it didn't matter while I was high on pain medication. My mornings began with pain pills and my days ended with them. I was physically and mentally addicted.

From there, my life aimlessly bounced around until I fell into an exploding real estate market of the early '80s. In no time at all, I was worth half a million dollars by the time I was twenty-one—owned a two-family rental unit, a two-family owner-occupied in Belvidere, and an eight-acre farmhouse in Pelham. It seemed I had everything, and no excuses. But the injuries from football got me addicted to drugs, and the night I watched my father die, and everything else that happened, sent me on a path to heroin.

"Yo, yo! Heroin, cocaine. Dimes and nickels."

Ten or twelve Puerto Ricans surround an oversized, sparkling-green, new pickup truck. I sit, too dope-sick to fight through the crowd. At this point I know my addiction is overtaking me. No longer can I get by on shooting two or three bags a day. Now I need a bag of heroin every two to three hours just to keep my muscles from cramping into a thousand small knots. Everybody's pushing and shoving to be the first to sell a bag. The competition is cutthroat. You see, the dealers sitting comfortably upstairs in the houses give us a free bag of heroin for every five bags we sell. A bundle of heroin, ten bags, costs the dealers one hundred bucks. The runners sell it on the streets for thirty dollars a bag. I once saw a guy stabbed smack-dab in the middle of his eye in a pushing match to sell a thirty-dollar bag.

"Richie Farrell? I'm looking for Richie Farrell!" A little round squash of a head pops out the window of the truck. A white guy.

"Richie, man, the man axen for youse," one of the junkies yells.

I stand up in the doorway, a little shaky. My eyes don't want to focus.

"Beaver?" My eyes adjust slowly to the light. "You crazy bastard. What you coming down here for?"

Robert Billson is his real name. He's maybe fifty-five—a skinny, bald, tough little prick with pointy buckteeth. He played hockey at Boston University and then some professional in Canada. He and my dad taught together at Lowell High; that's how I know him.

I know why he's come and I'm kind of glad to see him. But I have to act for the boys. I have to pretend I'm angry. This is my turf, my life, and Beaver's new truck and white skin threaten my survival.

Beaver is a born-again Christian, but not really. I mean he believes in Jesus Christ and all, but swears like a Hells Angel. He's the complete opposite of what you think a born-again Christian would be. Beaver is more like a guy you'd meet on the corner bar stool of a local bar complaining about everything that's wrong in the world. His wife, Inga, is Norwegian and the sweetest person I know besides my mom.

He has two grown sons. I'm convinced that after my dad died two years ago, Beaver took me on as some kind of penance for the sins he committed raising them. He and my dad were a lot alike really, cut from the same cloth. Both of them could explode in an instant. One second you'd see a saint; blink your eyes and there'd be Lucifer.

"Richie, I'm going to a meeting and wanted to bring you!"

"A meeting," I say. "What kinda meeting?"

"Meeting!" Somebody in the crowd begins to taunt.

"Well, it's just a bunch of people sitting around talking."

Beaver looks a little nervous. I have to figure a way to get us out of here without him getting robbed and still be cool.

"No, no thanks. No meeting, but you can buy me some food and a beer."

I wink at Beaver and walk swiftly to the passenger door. It's cool to go with somebody for food. The Spanish churches in the area always come by with their vans, pick up a group of us, take us back to their churches, and preach the Gospel while their women feed us. I can't understand a lick of Spanish, but the rice and beans are good.

"Drive."

Somebody kicks the side panel of the truck and an almost-empty beer can bounces on the seat of the cab behind us. Beaver's face tenses; he shoots glances from one side to the other.

"Drive," I say in a careful but determined voice.

"Those fuckin' scumbags. Who the fuck do those no-good scum-sucking cowards think they are?" Beaver says, driving away.

I want to tell him, "Beaver, one of them killed two men in Puerto Rico, the other raped a twelve-year-old girl, and another cut out a white guy's tongue for calling him an asshole." But I don't. It's not good for your health to talk about these things to anybody.

"Beaver, you gotta be careful down here," I say. "These ain't nice people. Where we going?"

"Church, man." Beaver's eyes begin to smile. "Praise the Lord!"

"Sure, Beaver, Alleluia."

"Shit."

Beaver reaches for a tape on the seat next to him and jams it into the deck. Some holy music. It makes me sick. My head starts to pound, like a balloon inside is expanding and contracting.

"We are a new generation, the chosen people." Beaver sings off key, making it twice as hard to listen.

The church is in Littleton, a suburb southeast of Lowell, a half-hour drive away. Am I glad when we pull into the parking lot. I'm so car sick, the nausea is starting to overtake me. The moment the door opens I puke my most recent beer all over the side of Beaver's new radial tires.

Beaver lets me use his handkerchief, and then I follow him to the door, down the back stairs, and into the basement. Shit, more singing. Only this time there are twenty or thirty white people who look just like Beaver. Fine-looking people who just have something in their eyes, something that says, "I'm not all there."

"Sit down up front, Richie," Beaver says.

No, no, I can't sit up front. But I do anyway—right next to Beaver. This lady, about seventy, with jet-black hair, stands right in front of me banging and shaking a tambourine. Inside my head, it sounds like whips snapping against my eardrums. Every couple of minutes, between songs, she wipes away a line of black sweat dripping down her forehead. I can't tell whether she uses shoe polish for hair dye or whether her face is just dirty. My eyes can't focus on the others. I try, but I want to crawl up inside my ass and die.

Finally, the music stops and Beaver walks up to the front and stands silently while he reads his Bible. Nobody speaks. I think about running for the door. But I'm too sick, so I pray to the God I had learned about at St. Patrick's School.

"Please, God. Get me the fuck out of here," I say quietly.

"Praise the Lord," Beaver yells.

"Praise the Lord," the people yell back.

The bells in my head start to ring again. Somehow I know God isn't going to answer my prayer.

"Alleluia! Alleluia!" they volley back and forth for what seems like ten minutes. Every once in a while I hear an, "Alleluia, Jesus!" And then they start another round of "Praise the Lord." The old lady starts jumping up and down, and a round guy with a short-cropped, gray crew cut strums on an old wooden guitar. His horn-rimmed glasses are too small for his head and sit halfway down his earlobes.

"Stand up, brother," somebody says.

But by this time, I can't see a thing and I'm bent over in a fetal position. I don't know who grabs my arm and pulls me to my feet. It just comes, the moment I stand up. Projectile vomit.

"Praise the Lord!" the old lady shouts.

Beaver comes to my aid with a towel somebody has thrown him. I open my eyes long enough to see the guitar player trying desperately to wipe my puke from his strings.

"Please, please." I try to speak.

"Come on, brothers and sisters," Beaver says. "Extend your right hand to this young man. Let's come against those demons, in the name of the Lord."

One more time they chant. The room starts to spin and the whole joint smells like regurgitated beer. I fight not to vomit, gulping and dry heaving. They pray so hard they don't hear me scream, "Shut the fuck up." The old lady keeps smiling and wiping away the rivulets of black running down her face. All I remember is losing everything, feeling like my guts are coming out of my mouth, and then I hit the floor. God has answered my prayers—everything goes black.

I wake up three feet from the ceiling in somebody's top bunk. I could swear my aunt Phyllis has just left the room; it's weird, like when you aren't sure whether you're in a dream or reality. Aunt Phyllis was blood. She gave me my first blow job when I was twelve. She's dead now, but I often dream of her lips.

"Good morning." It's Beaver's wife, Inga. I guess I've been dreaming. I have no idea how long Inga has been in the bedroom watching me sleep.

"Where's Beaver?" I ask.

"He's in the prayer closet, Richie. He's been praying for you all night. You've been quite sick. You've slept almost an entire day."

"The prayer closet? Where's that?" I ask, climbing out of bed and jumping to the floor.

Inga is tall and stately looking with a jaw that reminds me of Kirk Douglas's. She's in her early fifties. The gray in her hair has turned it a different shade of blonde. And even after twenty years in this country, she still has a Norwegian accent. I start to get dizzy as the blood rushes from my head. Inga grabs me and holds me close. I see real motherly compassion in her eyes. But she's also extremely good looking. I'm thirty and right now twenty years isn't so far apart.

"Are you okay, brother?" Beaver says, dashing into the room.

I move away from Inga quickly, a little embarrassed, void of any thoughts or feelings. Beaver takes my arm, helps me down the corridor, and sits me comfortably at the kitchen table, where coffee, juice, and pastries are already waiting for me.

"Come on, Richie, eat. You'll feel better," he says.

I want to but can't. My body is beginning to jones again. My gut wants a nice rainbow bag of heroin, not cheese Danish, cranberry nut bread, or croissants. I sip the coffee and the orange juice, which hurts the back of my throat.

"Can I call your wife, Richie?" Beaver asks. "Let her know you're okay? Where you are?"

"Na, na," I say anxiously. "She don't give a fuck. Oops, sorry."

Inga snickers and tries to say something, but Beaver cuts her off. I swear she's going to make a joke about Beaver's foul mouth. He is the only one allowed to use that language in the sanctity of his house. Everybody else who cusses is a sinner.

"Richie," Beaver says seriously, "your wife loves you. She is just very, very hurt by your actions."

"Fuck her," I grunt. "Oh, shit."

I've done it again, slipped up. I don't even think about it. Inga bursts into laughter and has to leave the kitchen. Beaver's squash turns pink and his lips pucker.

"Come on, now. Don't be an asshole," he says in a coaching way.

"Beaver, do me a favor. You're a great guy. I appreciate everything you're trying to do for me. But leave her out of it."

I can feel myself getting hot. The muscles in my calves begin to spasm, and if they could talk they'd be crying for heroin. I have to make a plan; otherwise I'll soon be dope-sick and nobody will be safe.

When I get dope-sick, I turn violent. And I'm scared where that violence could drive me. First a cold sweat turns the hair on the back of my neck into a dripping mop. Then I get cramps in my stomach, aching mad, screaming for somebody to help. A knot twists my calf muscles into a gnarly ball on each step. Tighter, tighter—holding, squeezing my sphincter muscles so I don't shit all over myself. And the whole time knowing that giving in will end the riveting, twisting, gnawing fire in my large intestine.

"Why, Richie? Why leave her out? She's your wife, the mother of your children."

Beaver's preaching now, getting defiant. Just like my dad. I remember a Good Friday when I was eighteen. I'd just come home from a workout at the YMCA. Only moments before, Dad had woken from his daily afternoon nap. He was tired and grumpy—sitting at the kitchen table eating gingersnaps and chasing them down with Moxie, a tonic Dad always said you needed to acquire a taste for. But I never understood how anybody would want to learn how to drink something that was comparable to mixing molasses and kerosene. I opened the refrigerator door without speaking—nobody talked to Dad unless he talked first.

"You go to Confession?" he grunted.

"No, I believe my sins are between me and God," I responded, gulping from a gallon of Lipton iced tea.

I was stupid. I'd let my guard down. You never took Dad out of your peripheral vision. Seconds later he tackled me on the kitchen floor. We wrestled for a good five minutes. He wanted to murder me over Catholic ideology. Each time he swung the Moxie bottle at my head, it spilled suds all over my favorite Fighting Irish T-shirt.

Beaver's ranting and raging forces me to remember who I really am. Now I have the excuse I need to inject a bag of heroin into my bloodstream—to kill the pain of remembering that I've let down my family. Each sip of coffee is just a reason to scan the room, looking for something, anything small, I can slip into my pocket. Something I can pawn that'll be worth thirty bucks.

"Please, Beaver," I say. "I don't want her knowing nothing. She's outta my life."

"And the kids, too?" he asks.

That hurts. I love my two boys and I hate my wife, Louise, even more because she can have them. I cry every morning and evening when I think of them and I'm not high enough to forget.

"Well?" I shrug. "Life sucks, right, coach?"

Right there in front of me, with Jesus hanging on the cross off the kitchen wall, Beaver goes ballistic. He throws a half-drunk coffee toward the sink, splashing coffee all over the red-checked wallpaper.

"You stupid motherfucker. You don't get it, do you, son? You hate, son. You need the Lord Jesus Christ to fill your heart with love. Don't you understand, asshole? He's the only one who can free you of that bondage of hate and heroin. You must die and be born again!"

Beaver jumps up, runs to the sliding-glass door, and almost separates the door from the runner. He pushes the screen out trying to open it and takes off, as if he knows he has to get out of there or he'll kill me.

I guess the Holy Spirit has changed Beaver. My dad

would have punched me in the face. I don't even look up. The guy might be out of control, but he's the least of my worries. I'm jonesing big time and any minute now all the rules are going to change. Anything and everything is fair game.

The bathroom is the first place to visit. Every house has leftover pain medication. Nine times out of ten, somebody's gotten hurt once and the doctor's prescribed Percodan or even Tylenol with codeine. Sane people, most of them, follow the directions: take one every four hours for pain or as needed. In that case, there's always some left over in the medicine cabinet. The pills are my only answer. They'll calm the jones so I won't do anything bad. They'll save me, Beaver, and Inga until I get a bag of smack. I figure if Beaver is anything like my dad, I have about twenty minutes before he turns back into a quiet, loving man again.

I hear the shower running when I'm halfway down the corridor to the bathroom. The door to the bathroom is open. I have to take the chance. Inga sings softly but loud enough to cover my footsteps. I'm in luck; she has the water scalding hot. The steam is so thick it forms a large cloud that seems to swallow the solid glass door. I'm safe. I cannot see her so I know Inga won't be able to see me.

The medicine closet over the sink doesn't squeak. My eyes scan it quickly as Inga's voice sounds like an angel's behind me. If Beaver comes back, I'm dead. Shit, a hit. I slip a bottle of Percosets gingerly into my hand. I don't bother risking shutting the door, just glide gracefully out into the corridor. There are six pills left out of twenty-four. Jackpot. I pour a glass of water at the kitchen sink, see Beaver heading out of the shed in his backyard, swallow all six, and hide the empty bottle behind a cookie jar on the counter.

"Richie!" Beaver begins fixing the screen back on the runners. "Still sitting in the kitchen?"

I swallow a few gulps of cold coffee and nod my head as I watch him trying to bend the bottom runner back so it will line up with the screen. Inga has returned in a pair of white tennis shorts and a T-shirt. Her hair is wrapped in a towel. She cleans the table, smiling and singing the same tune.

"Richie, I've been thinking and praying out there." Beaver has finished the door and pulls a chair next to me at the table.

I nod, waiting both for him and the Percs to kick in.

"Richie, first I must apologize for my behavior. Okay?"

I know what's coming. Standard script in lunatics. My dad was the best at it. He was an English teacher, brilliant at manipulating language to deflect the awfulness of violent deeds he'd committed against his family. Like the day he caught me thumbing a ride when I was fourteen. He used duct tape to tie me to a kitchen chair and cut me with Mom's electric carving knife, because he "loved me." Said there were a lot of bad people in the world. Wanted me to know what the "boogie man" would do to me if he picked me up thumbing.

"But God just spoke to me out in that garden shed," Beaver says.

Inga stops the water to listen but doesn't turn. Beaver has trained her well—like my mom. When Dad spoke the Red Sea parted.

I wait, praying silently for bells to go off in my head, for that rush of adrenaline when the Percosets hit my heart.

"Richie, God told me that you need to know Him. He said you need to ask Him into your heart and ask Him to set you free of the double H: heroin and hatred!"

Just then, at that precise moment, my prayers are answered. The Percs kick in. A direct hit to the heart. Alleluia! My fingers and toes tingle, adrenaline races up and down my spinal cord. My eyes seem to float inside my head and nothing else matters. The Percs do the job but they surely can't match the heroin rush. Nothing can. Heroin is like licking the breath of God.

"Richie?" Beaver asks. "Would you like to ask Jesus Christ into your heart? Would you like to die and be born again?"

Inga turns and walks close to the table. At that moment, I don't care how many times I'm born. She's extremely sexy, I'm high, and I don't have to feel anything. I think she knows I find her attractive.

"Sure, man. What do I gotta do?"

In a quick sick instant, I hope it has something to do with climbing back into the womb. Maybe I can go back and fix everything I've fucked up. Do it right. But it's only a flash, and somehow I know that won't work.

"Well, brother," Beaver says, "just say a few words."

I start thinking, Wow, magic words, man. That's what I need—magic! But actually, nothing matters to me right now except how to keep this buzz going, how to stay like I am at this very second—without a feeling or care in the world.

"Sure, I'll say the words."

Inga spins around and reaches slowly for my shoulder. Her fingers are so warm and soothing to the touch. Beaver stands up and starts pacing around the table. I want to start laughing. I always smile or laugh when I'm nervous. But something makes me think of Dad and the night I killed him— his face, the instant he died, his bluish-green glowing skin, and his crimson-red blood-filled eyes. I start to cry.

"Praise the Lord! Rejoice in His Name!" Beaver shouts.

"Oh, yes, Father God, thank you, Jesus," Inga whispers with conviction.

"Are you ready, brother? Do you want to be set free?" Beaver asks.

"Yes," I manage through the tears.

"All right, Richie," Beaver says. "Just say what I say. That's all you have to do."

I can't hold back the image of my dad there on the kitchen floor, the single teardrop slowly forging its way down his cheek. The Percosets aren't strong enough. I feel like my insides are leaching out through my tears.

"Jesus, I'm a sinner and I need you to run my life."

"Jesus, I'm a sinner," I repeat. "Please help me."

"Alleluia, Jesus." Inga begins to cry.

"Jesus, come into my life and fill me with your Holy Spirit," Beaver continues.

"Jesus, I need your spirit," I reply.

And that's it. Something splashes across my face. A gust of country air bursts into the room and moves the wind chimes hanging on the wall ever so slightly. It feels like hot oil running across my chest, moving slowly down my stomach. It burns. In an instant, I feel straight. Shit-scared. My eyes open wide. Beaver starts laughing, like he knows what's going on. Inga says something, but I can't hear her. I stand, thinking maybe I can outrun whatever is happening to me.

"Oshka belgh haver opsa shennna goosgkle jubler crumster domenisca," I shout.

"Come, Holy Spirit," Beaver screams hysterically.

Every cell in my body tingles. And then, somehow, I leave my body. Or I just can't feel the weight of it. I know it's there, but it's as if all I have is a brain. Memories of my dad race across whatever space I'm in, as if they are happening at that instant: my childhood, my brother, Sean, football, Dad's funeral, all of it crashing through me in a split second. Then, the feelings come back in only my fingers. Somebody is choking me. I can't swallow or breathe. Beaver continues smiling and Inga cries.

"Help me!" I beg.

"Keep going, brother," Beaver says. "Don't worry; it's only the Holy Spirit."

"Praise you, Jesus Christ. He's been touched by your Spirit," Inga yells.

Somehow I pick myself up off the kitchen floor. My T-shirt is soaked through with a sweet-rancid body odor. I feel good, like every tear has wiped away years and years of bad memories. It's like being locked up, released, and then running full-speed into an endless green field filled with bright yellow daisies. There are so many new feelings, I don't know which one to explore first. Something truly has happened to me, but have I been touched by the Holy Spirit or the Percosets? Maybe it was a combination of a Higher Power and an opiate derivative.

"You're free, Richie!" Beaver speaks, interrupting my reverie.

"What happened?"

"The Holy Spirit set you free, Richie!" Inga says.

"Yeah, but what the hell was that language? What came out of my mouth?"

"You spoke in tongues, Richie!" Beaver says, clapping his hands and dancing around the kitchen.

I don't really care if they're telling the truth. All I know is that something inside of me feels different, as if it's a spring afternoon, the birds and flowers are singing praises to the end of winter and I'm standing under a waterfall. I feel cleansed. My mind stops spinning. I feel secure for the first time in years, but is it real? Will it last?

"Richie?" Beaver asks. "You want to go tell your wife?"

I don't even have to think twice. What do I have to lose?

"Sure."

Then, in the bathroom, while I'm splashing cold water on my face to clean up for my visit to Louise, I see Inga's solid 14-karat gold charm bracelet with her children's birthstones. And I have no choice really. I have to take it.

Born Again

Beaver takes the old, long, roundabout way into Low-ell. Country roads, miles and miles of trees, and the hand-built stone walls that the Minutemen hid behind to shoot at the British during the American Revolution are now surrounded by huge white homes with sprawling front yards. We don't talk, but the countryside brings me back to the first time I ever laid eyes on my wife.

I was twenty-four. Louise was eighteen and had recently graduated from high school. I'd bought a restaurant and bar in Haverhill, Massachusetts, from the proceeds of a life insurance policy my grandmother had left me, and she walked in. The parquet floor had recently been installed. The glue wasn't dry and this striking, long-legged brunette walked across the parquet, stopped, and asked for a job application.

Louise Grandstorm was full Cherokee Indian—tall, dark, with legs that climbed gently to a kick-ass mother of all asses.

But the thing that took me by surprise, the thing that floored me, were her lips—plump, sensuous, dripping hot, pinkish-red, purple lips. I remember the first words she spoke to me: "Can I fill out an application for a waitress?" Her tongue slowly glided over her upper lip and I was mesmerized. I felt weak in the knees. I wanted to make love to her standing up, right there on my new parquet dance floor in front of everybody.

Two weeks later, we were together, planning the rest of our lives. Oh, God, I miss those days. We'd make love in the morning, before the shower, after the shower, for lunch, or for no reason at all. We were in love back then and at the very least, nobody can ever take that away from us.

It was the years after the first one that killed us. I'm not sure what specifically changed. We did everything together. We worked together in the restaurant and bar and never paid our bills. We drank and screwed on the bar stools every night. The place shut down in less than a year. I drank White Russians for breakfast and ate Valium for lunch. I was twenty-six, she was twenty. It was 1982 and nothing but the moment mattered.

The eighties came on hard. The real estate market exploded. We bought two income properties: a ten-acre farm in Pelham, New Hampshire, and a two-family home near Shed Park in Lowell, plus a brand-new maroon 190D Mercedes-Benz. Then I fucked up everything. It was right after my sons, John and Richard, were born when I met Melissa O'Brien. She was a real estate agent in Pelham who kept me up-to-date on cheap land for sale.

I never went looking for sex—it was an opportunity and I wasn't in the habit of turning down opportunities. We'd driven to a ten-acre plot of land for sale, drove right over the rough terrain, and walked the perimeter. She wore a white see-through skirt so short I could see the bottom cup of her ass. She bent over once to pick up her pen and it was over. In a heartbeat her underwear hung on several blades of high grass and we fucked madly under the blue sky.

Things had changed between Louise and me after the children were born. I missed those passionate, mind-blowing fucks where the top of your head blew off and you couldn't move for twenty minutes after the climax. I'm not sure whether it was the responsibility of kids that killed those moments for us or whether we began to take each other for granted.

Not too long after we moved to Pelham, I got in over my head financially. I couldn't handle the mortgages. I panicked. I became convinced that if I burned the house down, the fire insurance on our farmhouse would give me and Louise a new beginning. I was sure they'd never be able to prove I did it.

"They have to catch you with the match," I told myself.

The main house had been built some time in the 1840s when cornstalks were used for insulation. Our advantage was that the electric stove hadn't been properly installed. The undersides of the electric burners were too close to the wooden structure holding the stove together. I'd actually discovered it by accident. Forgot I'd put tea on and went outside to push John in the swing. When I came back in the smell of burning wood filled my nostrils as the kettle whistled. I opened the cabinet under the stove and discovered the opportunity for what my dad called "Jewish lightning." Dad always said that Jews never lost money. He said they'd burn a place to ashes and collect on insurance. Smart Jews.

As part of our routine, we always sanitized John's and Richard's bottles every week with boiling water. That morning would be no different, except that afterward, I made sure that Louise took the boys in her car and headed to Haverhill to see her parents. I'd timed the burners in a few test runs and I figured that we'd need 90–120 minutes to get clear of the house. I was correct almost to the minute. Louise left at 9 a.m., and the house was fully engulfed in fire at 11.

The police suspected arson but could never prove it. Somebody called the local police chief and alleged I was involved in crime. Bullshit. Sure, I knew guys who were criminals—old friends I'd grown up with in the Acre—but they were petty thieves and had nothing to do with the farmhouse. They weren't involved in organized crime.

So much for new beginnings. I've never been so wrong in my life. Just two days after deciding to burn down our old farmhouse, Louise found out about Melissa. The police chief and state fire marshal couldn't get me on anything. The arson investigator had not found any accelerants. But they knew what I did. So for revenge they ratted me out. The pricks went to my mother's house, where we were living temporarily after the fire, and asked Louise if she knew about Melissa. They hated me. They thought I had money and you didn't have to be Sherlock Holmes to find out I was screwing the best-looking girl in New Hampshire. The chief was an ex–FBI agent whose ex-wife had accused him of molesting their three-year-old daughter. The state fire marshal was a former drunk who flashed Louise his ten-year medallion from Alcoholics Anonymous. For some bizarre reason, he assumed that would win her sympathy, that she would open up and spill all like at an Alcoholics Anonymous meeting.

From the moment Louise found out about Melissa she held me hostage. The affair was the seed for a hatred she refused to let go. She brought it up daily; threw it at me like it had happened yesterday. And the pain on her face when she talked about it—I knew she lay there at night picturing the act in her mind. I don't blame Louise for kicking me out.

I never meant to hurt her the way I did. If things had been different. . . . If I hadn't watched my dad die, if I hadn't become a useless junkie, if I hadn't turned into a horrible excuse of a dad myself, if I hadn't screwed Melissa all over town, I would have loved to have lived happily forever in a not-so-large, yellowish house with a white picket fence, two cars, kids, dogs, and a two-week vacation. I think I could have really loved her, if there is such a thing.

All of a sudden, Beaver's car slows in the city traffic and the old mill towers rise out of the horizon. Beaver senses my anxiety as we drive through the old Acre neighborhood. We pass Mrs. Courtney's triple-decker. In my head I replay Mary Beth Courtney jumping off the back porch and breaking her leg. In slow motion, I see a movie of my life growing up Irish Catholic in the Acre. I can see Dad holding my mother's hand as they strolled lovingly in the North Common. I can see my brother, Sean, being beaten up by Bobby MacIntyre. I wished I'd jumped in and kicked Bobby's ass. Not because I could have, but because it would have saved me from Dad's beating for watching it happen. This was life in the Acre. One second everything around you would be in perfect harmony, peaceful and serene, and then without warning or reason the world would explode.

And that's when I see Paddy's Convenience Store, where

my mother's father, my grandfather John Slavin, used to take me for donuts when I was seven.

"Beaver? Can you stop there for a minute? I need to grab a drink before I face Louise."

He looks confused. I know he suspects I'm up to something. Shit, Paddy's is now a Hispanic store with some real characters, junkies that haven't showered in days, hanging out front. It no longer sells donuts. Now it's a variety store for the police and a drug den for us junkies. He stops anyway. I think he wants to believe the Holy Spirit is stronger.

Inside, I trade Inga's gold bracelet for a bag of dope, a fresh needle, and a can of warm Pepsi. Beaver is waiting for me, reading his Bible. I actually feel bad about getting high after all he's done for me. In fact, even though I've been a junkie for some time, I can't recall ever feeling this bad. I really hope the guilt doesn't interfere with my high, though.

Beaver drops me off a few houses away from my old house, where Louise and the boys are now living, post-fire. I guess Beaver knows I need a few moments to compose myself. Or maybe he's nervous, too. He's probably wondering about me. Am I really born again?

"Thanks, Beaver."

"Richie, remember, God is with you now. Things are different. He'll get you through it. Trust in Him."

I watch him drive away and for a split second want to run after him. But something, maybe my kids, forces me to walk toward the front door. First, though, I hide the needle and heroin in the bushes around the side of the house.

Louise never let me come home again after finding out about Melissa. My mother backed her but secretly loaned me money she thought was going for food. Of course, I used it for heroin. I haven't seen the boys much. I missed them at Christmas; Louise wouldn't allow a visit. But I sneaked into Mom's house through a cellar window on New Year's Eve and watched them sleep for a while. They slept in the basement. I'd grown up sneaking in and out the same window. I was a pro at going undetected.

Dad always told me time would heal everything. But he's wrong. Time away from my boys doesn't stop the anxiety attacks. In fact, it is the time away from my boys that only forces me to shoot more and more heroin, desperately trying to banish the overwhelming visions of John and Richard playing alone in my mom's carpeted playroom.

John was a truly inspiring baby, four weeks late after three false-labor runs. Jibs, we called him. He was born with a defective heart valve. The doctors said if it didn't adjust itself in forty-eight hours, he'd be airlifted to Boston for open-heart surgery. My dad gave me some prayer to Mary about penance and I taped it underneath John's incubator. Dad said the prayer had never been known to fail. I desperately wanted to believe that—and it worked.

John is four now: tall, white skin, dark Indian eyes, and strawberry-blond hair with floppy little locks. His eyes sparkle with elation whenever he sees me, and he usually bolts toward my legs and straps his arms around them in a death grip.

Richard, or Ricky, is a completely different baby. He looks just like Louise—dark complexion, beautiful lips, high cheekbones, and an attitude and a half. He's only two, but demands your full attention. When he was a baby, he was colicky. Every night after supper and right before bed, he'd get bad gas. Cry, scream, and holler. I remember putting him in the old baby carriage and pushing him around the block. It was the only thing that calmed him down. I think the sound of the wheels on the cement lulled him to sleep. If a neighbor started speaking to me and I stopped walking, Ricky would scream again.

As I climb the three front cement steps, I'm scared. I wonder how Louise and the boys will react to seeing me standing here. But I'm more frightened, I think, of seeing the kitchen floor where Dad died, naked, his face green, yellow, and blue. My mouth is dry and tight, and my palms feel clammier than usual. Dad has been gone only a little over two years.

"Daddy, Daddy!" John shouts.

Louise's eyes go cold. The depth of her hatred is so great that she looks nearly evil when she sees me. She looks as if she wants to slam the door in my face.

"Please," I beg. "Can I come in?"

The tension is cut only by John at Louise's legs, fighting desperately to open the screen door. I see Ricky behind Louise's right shoulder. He stands bent over on the top step, trying to get a better view of me around Louise. Believe me, the smile on his face is worth the anxiety. When I smile back he shoots me a little wave.

"Daddy! Daddy!" John screams.

"Please, Louise. One more time, let me see them one more time. I promise not to steal anything."

"One more time? One more time?" she says sarcastically. "That's you, Richie. One-More-Time Richie."

But she lets me in, allows me to take the boys downstairs to the playroom as long as I promise to "stay out of her sight." At first it's spooky. Mom has done the playroom over with fresh orange-brown carpet and new greenish-yellow floral furniture. The Ping-Pong table is gone, but otherwise it's the same room. The same place where my friends slept over on Friday nights and we played Ping-Pong until three in the morning. The same place where my dad caught me masturbating over the *Sports Illustrated,* Swimsuit Edition, and then forced me to tell Father Dan at Confession.

First Ricky, John, and I play Superheroes. Ricky is Robin, John is Batman, and I'm the Riddler. John finds a long, black towel and holds it around his neck as he springs from couch to chairs. I have to quiet them a little. Louise would throw me out if she knew I was letting them jump on the furniture. Each bounce on the new springs ends with Batman issuing another order to Robin. They finally catch me and arrest me near the back bookcase. I'm thrilled to stop. I'm out of shape, tired of running, and my right knee is beginning to swell.

After an hour, Louise comes in and announces they have to bathe and go to bed. Ricky grabs my right leg, hides from Louise, and squeezes tight. John sits on the floor and explodes in tears. Of course their reaction only gives Louise more reasons why I'm not a good role model in their lives. Still, she agrees to let me stay and put them to bed. But I'm not sure I can make it that long. I'm beginning to jones again.

"Well, boys," I say, untying my wrist where they handcuffed me after the arrest.

"Dad!" John begs.

Ricky keeps hiding between the V in my legs. Louise is beginning to get that "fuck you and die" look in her eyes. A look she'd never had the first year of our marriage; a look, in fact, I'm sure I'm directly responsible for. By fucking Melissa

I lost my right to be a husband and to wake up in the morning with my beautiful little boys.

It's time to go. I don't want them to see me dope-sick. I don't want the boys to have lasting memories of their dad sweating and breathing heavily. Besides, I want to leave Louise as peacefully as possible.

"Okay, boys," I tell them. "Here's the deal. You guys run up there and hop in the tub. I'm going for a quick walk, and I'll be back in ten minutes to tuck you in."

The kids are rounding the corner before I even finish getting the words out of my mouth. Louise knows why I'm going for a walk, but this time she doesn't seem to care. For an instant, only an instant, we hold each other's gaze. And I can see that despite all the damage, no matter how deeply buried, love is still there.

I retrieve my needle and the bag of heroin from the bushes. But they aren't bushes anymore. I remember planting them with my dad one Saturday in April when I was a teenager. We planted seven evergreen trees that day along the southern side of the house. They were only three feet tall and we spaced them every ten feet up the property line.

Now they are twenty-five-feet tall and form a complete wall between our house and Mr. Murphy's house next door. I feel like I'm in a time tunnel. I sit, lean back against the foundation, and try to find a good vein. I look under the back porch and see the remains of the hole I dug as a kid to keep my frogs in. I remember the day when my father said I couldn't keep them anymore. He said I had to throw them back in the pond at the end of our street. He said it was costing too much to refill the hole with water every day. I remember stealing my dad's lighter fluid, filling the hole, and lighting them up. I should have thrown them back into the pond, but for some sick reason I wanted to hurt them. After all, Dad told me he loved me, and I loved these frogs, too. I could see their bugged-out eyes looking at me, not even trying to escape that fiery hole.

Now I find a good vein and pull the trigger. Nothing.

"Shit!" For some reason there's no rush. No high. No peace. Maybe it's the Holy Spirit. Maybe it's being born again? I don't know. But one thing I do know is that I don't want to live like this anymore. I want to kill myself; end this existence.

I remember Father Turnbull telling us in the sixth grade at St. Patrick's that suicide is an unpardonable offense against God. "Damned," he said, "you'll be damned! Never even allowed into Purgatory." But how could I believe a priest who brought young boys up to his room to do sit-ups in their underwear? He never asked me to go. I think my dad scared him. Besides most kids he picked for sit-up detail were shy and from broken homes. Turnbull was no dummy. He picked his victims carefully.

Inside, my boys wait for me to tell them a bedtime story. John used to like to hear the one about Barney Fife, but I wasn't talking about Don Knotts's character on the old Andy Griffith television show. Barney was a make-believe character my dad had invented for my brother and me. Dad told us Barney had fallen into the foundation as they were pouring it. Dad said he was so vicious, none of his fellow workers would pull him out. So Barney walked the house at night, mean as could be, but without any power. My stories were just creative versions of Barney's plight. But Ricky is still too small for that tale; Louise would kill me if he had nightmares.

Louise tells them I can stay only five minutes. My mom gave them my brother Sean's room because it has two beds. Louise sleeps in my old bed. They'll be all right, I tell myself. They're young. In a few years they'll forget about me. I've already messed up their lives but at least I won't play a significant part in their becoming young men. The good news is I'll never get the chance to screw up their lives like Dad did mine. They won't have decades of violent memories to destroy them.

I decide that if I do find the courage to end my life, and their suffering, I want their last memory of their dad to be one of song. So we sing the "Ants Go Marching" and "Row, Row, Row Your Boat." Ricky can't keep it going and John gets mad. But they're so tired that ten minutes later, they're asleep. Before leaving, I get on my knees and put my face on the pillow next to theirs. I whisper how much I love them. And how I'll always be watching them. I try to leave but collapse on the floor.

Louise finds me crying there on the floor between their beds. She picks me up, a little angry but also a little confused.

"Richie? Come on, you'll wake the boys," she says.

I'm a mess and for a moment she almost hugs me.

"I'm sorry, Louise! I'm sorry, John! I'm sorry, little Ricky! I'm sorry!"

Chapter 3 ....

Boots

I haven't seen my boys in almost two weeks. I can't face the thought of being alive all day. Last night, I stayed on the fifth floor of the Butler Mill building with Nicky and Joey—two of my junkie friends. It's the oldest and most structurally sound mill in the city. There's an art to what we call "milling." First, keep moving—never stay in the same place more than two nights. And second, be gone by morning light. Due to recent pressure from the local merchants and the city council, the Lowell police routinely search the old mills, trying desperately to rid the city of human decay.

Nicky is Greek, square jawed, six feet, broad shoulders, with pitch-black, shoulder-length hair. He admits to being nearly forty, but after eighteen years of shooting dope, you never would believe him. He looks at least fifty. At eighteen he was a Golden Glove champion and got an invitation to the Olympic trials; he still has the tattered, faded letter crumpled and shredded in his wallet.

Joey is a small kid, Italian, about twenty-four with a hump back. He was in a motorcycle accident; he hit a tree doing ninety on his honeymoon. Joey's back was broken and his bride killed instantly, decapitated. I never hung with these guys growing up in Lowell. Nicky is one of those Greek kids whose family lived in the Acre, while Joe hails from "Little Canada," a Franco-American section of Lowell that borders the Acre's north perimeter. Us Belvidere kids never venture far from our turf.

The three of us don't have much in common other than Lowell and the condemned mills. Heroin unites us.

Me, I just turned thirty last week. Ten years earlier I was on my way to the University of Notre Dame. I was once a warrior, six feet tall and 235 pounds. I could run on the edge of the wind. Now the only thing left from my past is my faded, navy-blue jacket with a gold football emblem on the front. Both elbows in the leather coat are shot, holes clear through the inside liner. But it's the only thing I have to keep me warm.

Nick and Joey are still asleep on the wooden floor, huddled close together like lovers trying to keep warm. The third floor is two football fields long and empty except for the enormous mahogany beams held in place by a solid oak post at the center, six inches thick, petrified, hard as pure iron. The mill is stark, desolate. The only hint of the mill's industrial past is the set of four-inch holes staggered every six feet where black metal bolts once anchored the looms to the floor.

One, two, three, four . . . I don't wanna live no more.

The sun rising over the tree line shimmers off the

Merrimack River, casting orange-yellow light onto the broken, brick mill buildings surrounding the city of Lowell. It is early spring, 1987; trees are sprouting buds even as snow from a late winter storm begins to melt.

In the 1830s, Lowell was the birthplace of the Industrial Revolution in America. In the nineteenth and early twentieth centuries, hundreds of smoke stacks saturated the inner city with a fine, white ash as rural and immigrant teenage girls came to the city to better their fortunes, operating giant looms for not even a dollar a day. But by the 1980s, the great mill buildings of Lowell were nothing more than a haven from the cold for heroin addicts, crack heads, and prostitutes. The mills had shut down. Industry had moved south to take advantage of cheaper labor and no unions. Lowell's economic base, like other mill towns in New England, went the way of the buffalo.

"One . . . two . . . three . . . four . . ."

I sing our song four or five more times, gradually getting louder and louder until Nicky's eyes open. At first his jaw gets tense and he looks confused. But once he's focused, he smiles.

"Josepe, Josepe, get up, my friend; our brother is calling the end. One . . . two . . . three . . . four. I don't wanna live no more," Nicky sings.

Joey recognizes the song even in a semiconscious state. After all, he's been the key promoter of the scheme. We took an oath about a month ago, agreed to one rule—all three of us have to go along with the killing. We've all tried to go straight. Between the three of us we must have entered a dozen different rehabs. In and out, in and out; we just couldn't do it. We certainly don't want to die of AIDS or worse, dodge that bullet and become a lifelong junkie. After seeing my kids, I just know. It's time to go. But it takes time to build the courage to die. Today seemed like a perfect day to die. I'm not sure why, nothing special happened to bring the three of us to an agreement, it was one of those things. All the stars lined up.

Most think suicide is the last act of a coward. But for those facing it, quite the contrary. Yes, it's difficult leaving your children. It takes me a long time to confront the fact that my kids will have to live with that legacy. But how would they live with the legacy of their dad walking the downtown streets of Lowell in a worn-out football coat and worn-out sneakers, the toes exposed? Out of sight, out of mind, is how I see it. At least they won't be haunted by what became of me. They won't have to see me degraded and pathetic. That alone gives me the courage to continue, to succeed.

"Richie, no bullshit?" Joey asks.

"I'm ready," I say.

Joey lets out a howl, rockets to his feet, his pants wet and his crotch soiled. Together, we sing and dance around the center post like children in a nursery school. But then, slowly, emotionless, one by one, we stop, fold up our blankets, and walk without speaking toward the stairs. It's time.

Outside, the sidewalks are covered with slush and the cold bite of the morning air makes the skin on my face feel tight. The hole in the bottom of my Converse sneakers sucks in an entire puddle. Nicky is the only one with new boots. Stolen. He walked into Kmart, put them on, and walked out.

"Nicky, I never got my boots," I say.

"You won't need them after today, Richie," Joey says.

"But I want my feet warm one more time."

"You're fuckin' chickening out," Joey whines.

"Fuck you. I'm sick of you, Joey. I'm going to do it so I don't have to see your fuckin' face anymore."

"Come on, Joey, don't sweat it," Nicky says. "We'll go to Kmart, I'll put on a pair of new shoes for Richie, and walk out with a VCR. Richie will have his new shoes and we'll have enough money to sing the song one last time."

"Sure, but I just don't understand the new shoes," Joey says.

I glance at Joey. He looks pathetic. Part of me wants to drill him and the other part of me wants to hug him.

"I just want to die with new shoes, Joey. My father always said if you want to judge a man's life, look at his shoes. I want them to find me with new boots."

"Enough already, let's go get it done," Nicky says.

The sidewalks in downtown Lowell are crowded with business people on their way to work. I spot Paul Georges, the vice president of Central Bank, fumbling with his keys and coffee as he tries to open the bank's doors. He spots me first, actually, but turns away as soon as I make eye contact. Seven years ago, he gave me loans for income property. In fact, he'd tried to warn me about becoming over-extended financially. But today, Paul doesn't dare acknowledge me. To most Lowellians, I'm a ghost. At first, the "look right through you" stares and the whispers bothered me. But after my first bag of heroin of the day, I stopped caring. Today, the only thing I care about is scoring a new pair of warm boots, shooting two or three bags of knockout dope, and dying.

When we get to Kmart the door is still locked. Nobody

talks. Joey sits on the base of a ten-cent, automatic rocking horse. Nicky stakes out the situation through the window. I look down at my big toe sticking out through the hole in my sneakers.

"Nicky," I say, "shouldn't we wait till later, you know, when there are more people?"

"Piece of cake, Richie. This will be my last and greatest boost."

It takes raw talent to be good at boosting. Stealing is one thing, but picking up a TV, a VCR, or a set of golf clubs and walking out the front door is an art. I'll tell you, not many people have the balls to get away with it. Nicky has the face, though, the "I'm doing nothing wrong" smile.

"I just hope he doesn't get caught over the shoes," Joey says.

I go inside two minutes after Nicky. Joey stays outside, his appearance far too hideous: the soiled pants, greasy hair, and hump back would call attention to us. Somebody might call the cops. My job is to run decoy, look suspicious, draw all the store detectives to me. We know the layout, each department. We've studied it, committed it to memory. Nicky heads for the shoe department. I beat it for the men's clothes behind the cash registers, away from the front doors, and begin to count out loud. When I reach one hundred, the games begin.

"What are these clothes?" I shout. "Who makes these? Are they made in the USA? Nothing's made in the old USA anymore."

I could feel them closing in—the people who think I'm crazy, and the others who want to get a look. It's working;

I'm succeeding. We're a team, and precision and timing are so important.

"Excuse me, is there something I could help you with?" asks a wide, white lady in a pink dress.

"Made in America, nothing's made in America. Why don't you sell American clothes here? The sign says you sell American-made clothes!"

I've got her now. This patriotic bullshit always works. But now I have to turn up the juice.

"Sir, excuse me, you're going to have to be quiet or we'll have to ask you to leave."

"Quiet, no way! I'm an American! This country was made by the people, for the people, and under the people."

Somehow that doesn't sound right. But the four or five store detectives closing in on me don't seem to want to correct my take on the Gettysburg Address. Out of the corner of my eye, I see Nicky's back heading for the front door, his body slinking side to side like he's had too much to drink or his shoes are too big. But the best part is, everybody is watching me.

"Sir, it's time to go," says a muscle-head with tight black pants.

"Okay, you Commie bastard. But it's people like you that make this country so fucked up."

As Tight Pants and a redhead with firm breasts escort me to the front door, I want to thank them for being Americans, because without them my new boots wouldn't have been possible.

Nicky and Joey are waiting around the corner on a park bench when I catch up with them. Joey is holding the VCR box close to his chest, just like my first football coach had taught me to hold the ball so I wouldn't fumble. Nicky is on the edge of his seat, rocking back and forth, anxious, wanting desperately to get to the pawn shop before we're spotted.

"Nice boots, Nicky," I say.

"Let's go," Joey says. "We don't have time to change shoes now."

I don't argue. It wouldn't be fair for Nicky to walk back in my ratty sneakers. I can wait until we score the dope and get down to the business of the day.

"I can change quick if you want, Richie," Nicky says.

"No, that's okay, Nicky. We don't have the time."

"Come on." Joey stands and almost falls over. The hump in his back seems bigger now and his feet can't hold him. Nicky looks away, pretending not to notice. I feel worthless.

And right then, it hits me—the three of us are useless. We don't deserve to live.

"Joey, let me carry that for you," I say.

Reggie, the asshole at Friend's Pawnshop, gives us only a hundred dollars for a three-hundred-dollar VCR. He knows us, knows we're junkies, and knows the machine is hot. As long as we get enough heroin to go through with it, there's no sense complaining about the money.

The walk up Adam Street is quick. Nobody talks. The sun is getting higher in the sky and feels bright and warm on my cheeks, almost like it's beckoning me. Hookers and junkies line each side of the street hustling, arguing, everyone looking to get high. I know them all, every last one. I shot dope with the guys and protected the girls, but at that moment they might as well be mannequins. The only thing that means anything to me is singing that song.

For one hundred dollars we can buy a bundle—ten bags—of almost pure heroin. Because of the way it's packaged, in half-inch, heat-sealed, plastic bags with red, yellow, green, and blue stripes—they call it Rainbow. It's badass stuff. One time I overdosed on half a bag. For sure three and a third bags will do the trick.

We stop in front of St. Patrick's School, across from the dealer's house. Hector is his name, a crazed, quick-tempered Dominican.

"Richie," Nicky says, "take the money."

"Don't get beat," says Joey.

"Not today, guys!"

Everybody beats everybody down here. They sell bags of baking soda or vitamin B if they think they can get away with it. Once they beat me, but never again. I immediately went to the Giant Store, a place in the Acre that sold everything, and bought a toy gun. It was an authentic-looking 44 Magnum; a replica of the one Clint Eastwood used in the movie *Dirty Harry*.

Outside in the parking lot, I tossed the bag, tucked the gun under my belt, into my groin, and walked back to the house. For about an hour, I waited and watched from an alley about twenty yards away from the doorway that led to the dealers who had beaten me. After the cops circled, I knew I had at least an hour before they returned. It was time to make my move. In a full gallop, my left foot blasted the cheap lock holding the door secure into several pieces. A half dozen Dominicans panicked as the door flung open and I pulled the 44 Magnum into their view. I moved with an insane burst of adrenaline. Several hit the floor, one attempted to run but I tripped him, booted him in the face and upper chest at least a dozen times. A young girl started screaming in Spanish. I knew enough to understand what she was saying. She was begging me not to kill him. As a compromise, she ran to a bedroom and brought me a brick of their heroin, ten bags of the good stuff. Since then the Latinos have called me "Loco."

Two sharp knocks on the door. I can feel somebody inside watching me. Seconds go by, and then I hear the sound of dead bolts, maybe six or seven, being undone.

"What's up, my man?" Hector asks.

The open door lets out the smell of frying fish, probably carp, a scavenger fish these people caught in the Merrimack River. A little boy who looks too old for a diaper sits at the kitchen table. Hector is small, stocky, with lunatic, black eyes. He has a scar stretching from his right ear across his cheek, the mark of a prison rat, somebody who squeals to save his own hide.

"Bundle of Rainbow," I say.

"Oh, you like the 'bow, man. You like getting fuck-upped."

I nod.

"Careful with this shit, man. Shit'll kill ya."

I pay him one hundred dollars for our lives, ten bags of pure heroin, and he tosses me three new needles for free. He goes to open the door, but I don't follow. Instead, I bite the corner of every bag. He doesn't turn, expects it. Heroin is cut with quinine and has a bitter taste. A taste you could never duplicate, especially to a junkie.

"I'll see ya tomorrow," Hector says, and closes the door.

"Been nice knowing you, asshole," I whisper.

The closest mill is fifty yards, no more. But it's in seriously bad shape. Young kids are always going in on a dare and falling through the floorboards. We decided to go back to the

Butler Mill. It is only two blocks farther and it's the cleanest. Who knows when they'll find us?

"Now is everybody sure? No second thoughts?" Nicky asks.

"I'm ready," Joey blurts. "How about you, Richie? You're not going to chicken out again?"

Somehow I've always been the one to find something to live for. I think Nicky asks me for that reason. I also think something inside of Nicky wants to live as much as he wants to die. He knows life would be better if we could walk away from heroin. But it's too damn hard. We've all heard the numbers in rehab—less than 5 percent ever make it back to a comfortable, normal existence.

"First I have to try on my new boots."

"Fuck the boots," says Joey.

"No, no, I promised Richie the boots," says Nicky.

My sneakers are so cold and wet, my feet feel warm and tingly. The socks are sticking between my toes and smell like Swiss cheese. I lace one boot at a time, no socks, dry feet, warm and secure.

"Hurry up, Richie," Joey yells. "You're stalling."

I stand up and walk back and forth, proud, like I've won something special and am showing it off to the world.

"How they fit?" Nicky asks.

"Too big; I'm going to have to bring them back," I say, winking at Nicky.

"One . . . two . . . three . . . four . . . ," Joey starts, "I don't wanna live no more."

It's time to get serious. Nicky glances at me and begins to sing. Before long, I follow. There will be no chickening out today.

"Okay, who's first?" I ask.

"I'm going first," says Joey.

"No," Nicky says. "Let's all go together. We'll all fire the trigger at once."

"That sounds good," I say.

"No, I'm going first. I want to pull the trigger first."

"We do it all together, Joey, or we don't do it," I respond.

"Fine, give out the bags and let's make some cookers," Joey commands.

Heroin has so many impurities and you have to cook it before you can shoot it. You have to burn off the poisons or it will kill you. Funny that we can die on any one shot of uncooked heroin. We're planning to die for good today and still we're doing things by the book. Death is one thing, but how you die is different. We want to go from pure heroin, uncontaminated euphoria instantly spinning to death.

We use the bottoms of Pepsi cans as cookers. Coke cans are no good. Somebody at Coke must have had a junkie for a son and found out that heroin addicts use cans for cooking, because Coke made their aluminum porous when hot. The heroin leaks right through. The funniest thing is to watch a sick junkie running around cupping his hands under a Coke can bottom, trying to save whatever he can. It happened to me once.

We each grab an empty Pepsi can from the stockpile we've saved in an old canvas bag, squeeze the can in the middle to make a crease, and fold it back and forth, faster and faster. My can gets warm from friction, cracks on one end of the fold, and begins to break apart.

"Shit," I scream. While I'm pulling the can apart my thumb gets in the way and is lacerated below the knuckle. Now blood streams down my forearm and covers the top of my new boots.

"Use this rag," Nicky says. "Tie it tight. Let me see it."

"He did it on purpose, Nicky. He's trying to chicken on us."

I wrap it tight and wipe my forearm on my dungarees above the thigh.

"You know, Joey, if you weren't going to die, I'd whack you right now."

"You're a real tough guy, huh, Richie?" Joey responds.

"Why do you have to be such an asshole? I mean, right to the end."

"Okay, guys." Nicky jumps in. "Let's sing the song."

"One . . . two . . ."

"No, I'm not singing the song with that fucking ass-wipe, Nicky," I say.

"See, Nicky, Richie is a coward."

Now, I'm pissed. I want to pull the trigger myself, shoot him up, and put the little miserable humpback son of a bitch back in hell where he came from. I hate Joey then, because he represents everything bad about Adam Street. We're all junkies, but Joey's disposition reminds me how far down in the gutter I am. He isn't a nice guy.

"Nicky," Joey says, "I'm going anyway, and I'm going first."

He's already heated three and a quarter bags in the Pepsi can cooker, drawn it into the needle, and is searching for a good vein.

"No," Nicky screams. "All of us together."

But it's in, the blood registers, and Joey pulls the trigger. He looks at Nicky, then me, his eyes roll backward, and he collapses in a heap in front of us. We don't speak. Nothing to say. Nicky is next.

"I love you, Richie," he says with a hug. Steps back, jabs, pulls the trigger, smiles, and hits the deck.

Both of them are lying there, dying. Joey looks so peaceful—no pain. One bag would get you high. Two bags would get you so high you might overdose. But three and a quarter bags will slow your heart down to a perfect stop. Only a "cocktail" or a shot of adrenaline to your heart can bring you back. That would be an option on the street, but nobody knows we're here; by the time they find us it'll be too late.

I begin to sweat. My palms and forehead drip.

The blood from my thumb begins to trickle again down my forearm.

I glance out the window toward the Acre.

I see my dad.

I see my mom crying after Dad shattered her wrist with the telephone because she mistakenly paired a dark blue sock with a black one.

I have two choices—run or die.

Like a doctor performing microscopic surgery, I pour the contents of the rainbow bags into my cooker. With my good hand, I reach for the bottle of water, insert the syringe, and draw up about 20cc. I squirt the water into the cooker, watch it slowly move across the white powder and turn to liquid smoke. I reach for Nicky's lighter, flick it on, and move it evenly back and forth under the cooker until the heroin begins to bubble. The smell is sweet and it makes my stomach turn. I steal one of Joey's cigarettes, bite off a small piece of the filter, and spit it into the middle of the burning liquid.

It's time. I can't believe this is the way Richie Farrell is going to die.

Nicky or Joey haven't moved for a good five minutes. At best, they're brain dead. I hold the cooker up close to my mouth with my bad hand, put the plunger end of the syringe between my teeth, aim the tip of the needle into the center of the cigarette filter, and pull the plunger back with my teeth until the filter goes dry. I have 10cc. My filter grabs everything that isn't pure heroin. My heart races and I get a hard-on. But this is better than foreplay. I'm finally in control. I throw away the cooker, shake the syringe up and down, and tap the top.

"What the fuck do I care about air bubbles killing me," I say quietly.

I alternate arms daily. If not the veins will collapse from overuse. Or worse, you'll get an infection under your skin. And if it manages to creep into your blood supply, you're cooked. Junkies die. Shit goes right to your heart. Shuts you down; usually it's a fatal case of cotton shot fever. Yesterday was right; today I'll fire into my left right below the bicep. Both arms look like dartboards. But, out of nowhere, a huge, unfucked-with vein pops out in the middle of my forearm. It'll be a clean hit. One, two, three, and everything will go silent.

"Cheer, cheer, for old Notre Dame. Wake up the echo cheering her name."

I insert the needle—there's a little sting—pull back on the plunger, and a dash of red-blue blood snakes up the middle of the clear liquid. A direct hit. Nothing left to do.

"Shake down the thunder from the sky . . ."

I squeeze.

". . . and although the odds be great or small, old Notre Dame will win over all."

Everything goes warm. I sit down. The room begins to spin. I remember my father dying. I see Joey and Nicky asleep. What would I say to my father? Joey looks so much like LeBeau, the little French guy on *Hogan's Heroes*. Brightness and brightness. I feel safe. I remember, Dad never let me watch *Hogan's Heroes*, said it was Jewish propaganda. I see Dad lying on the kitchen floor, begging for his pills. But he's laughing.

"Dad, the Jews didn't kill Jesus," I call out. "He killed Himself. *Hogan's Heroes* was just a kids' show, Dad."

"He's coming back."

"Blood pressure, eighty over sixty."

"Pulse, fifty-one."

My father begins to disappear. He's crying. I watch him turn away and I see purple-blue stripes up and down his back. It's the first time I've seen him in pain. Dad coined a term for them: zebra stripes. It was one of his favorite punishments: bruises and welts from a leather belt being swung ferociously at the meat of your hamstring, right below your ass.

"Nurse, go tell the police this one's going to make it, too."

The room is a mush of green cinder blocks, silver instruments, and people in white hiding behind masks.

"Sir? Do you know where you are?" somebody white says.

"He has stabilized."

My throat is scratchy. There's a tube through my mouth into my stomach. I couldn't talk if I wanted to.

"Mr. Farrell? Is that your name? Nod if that is your name."

I nod.

"You're a very lucky man. Some young boys were checking out the mills and found you. The paramedics were able to save your friends also."

I'm happy Nicky has survived but secretly I wish that little bastard Joey had bought it. He's irredeemable and it would have been a blessing for his family. Not that I'm any better, but Joey's a pathetic waste of human life. I actually love him and want him to die to end his misery. I know that may be a direct contradiction—but I do love him. We were soldiers in the same war zone. I don't know what to think about living. Part of me is pissed and another part of me feels like I've just won a million dollars on a scratch-ticket Bingo.

I know the cop right away when he comes in. Inspector Foley. A fat, Irish bastard with green teeth and bright red cheeks. He was one of the first on the scene the night my father died: December 4, 1984. The paramedics were taking Dad out on the stretcher. Dad's arm swung limp as they carried him down the stairs. Foley walked right up to me, locked eyes, and said, "Maybe I can't prove it, but you had something to do with it."

"Well, well, Mr. Farrell, wouldn't your uncles be proud of you," he says, shaking his head. "What a sight! Richie Farrell half-dead, butt naked on a metal bed in the emergency room."

My dad's brothers, Uncle Jack and Uncle Richard, had been police officers on the Lowell force. Jack died of a heart attack the day he retired. Richard died one night in his sleep—also a heart attack. Foley looks fatter than the last time I'd seen him and his tie is covered with coffee stains. But one thing is the same—his rancid breath. "Fuck you," I say. But of course, with the tube, he can't make out the mumble.

"When can he be moved?" Foley asks one of the doctors.

"After he's been stable for one hour."

"Good, we'd like to transport him for the three o'clock session in district court. He's got no outstanding warrants but his buddies are going away for a small vacation."

A nurse with chocolate-brown eyes starts working on the tube in my mouth. She's beautiful, even under the mask. I can see my reflection in her eyes, and it's not make-believe. I'm alive. I can tell she thinks Foley is an asshole, too.

Somebody starts talking; sounds like a doctor but I cannot see him."The paramedics on the scene stopped some light bleeding and shot him with what we call a 'cocktail' after they found a slight pulse. The saline combination immediately counteracts the heroin. So if there is no brain damage, and his condition continues to improve, he'll be good as new in about an hour or two."

The voice is coming from over the brown-eyed nurse's head, and the tone is raspy and echoing, like a slow-motion tape recording playing again and again.

"Okay," Foley says. "Thanks, Doc, I'll get some lunch in the cafeteria and check back in an hour or so. See ya, Richie boy."

I watch and listen to the clock tick for about an hour. Every ten or fifteen minutes the nurse or doctor comes by, checks my blood pressure and pulse, or reads my chart. Then, just as I'm nodding out, the good-looking nurse with compassionate eyes starts fooling with the tube down my nose.

"Richie," she says. "My name is Thelma; I'm going to remove your oxygen tube. It may be very uncomfortable."

I nod.

"The doctor will not let me give you Valium. That cop, well, I guess you have to go with him soon. I'm sorry."

I wink and I see her white mask move forward. She's smiling. Man, is she beautiful. Women. Shit. Now I'm real glad I'm not dead. I never met a hot woman I didn't undress in my mind.

"Ready?"

She peels the tape holding the tube off my nose with great care, so she doesn't hurt me. Nobody ever does that. Most people rip it. They always say it doesn't hurt when it comes off fast. I've felt this before, in the fall of 1975, the time I'd shattered my nose playing football. The doctors packed it with gauze and for two weeks I had to breathe through my mouth.

Next she begins pulling the tube. It feels like a snake, or a rope. I hate the sensation. I shut my eyes and pray. Without thinking, I bite down on the inside of my lip until I taste blood pooling under my tongue.

"Almost done," she says.

"Is he ready yet, Doc?" It's Foley, sticking his red face in where he shouldn't.

"First, I'm not a doctor, and second, please stand away while I complete this procedure."

"Oh, picky, picky, she must like you, Richie. Listen, honey, this guy you're infatuated with is a good-for-nothing junkie sociopath. How does that strike you, honey?"

She looks a little startled, like she's had a revelation, or maybe she's beginning to wonder if Foley is telling the truth. But I wink and her eyes come alive again.

"Listen, honey," she says, sarcastically. "Go see the doctor. You'll need his authorization to move him."

When the end of the tube squirts out, I feel like I've been healed. Fresh oxygen filters down my nose, burning the membranes inside my throat. I'm overcome with gratitude. Thelma has given me a reason to live.

"Thanks, Thelma," my voice squeaks.

"Would you like to sit up?" she asks.

"Sure, but—"

"Okay, Farrell, the pampering is over," Foley interrupts. "The doc has signed off. You're in my custody now. Sit up."

He grabs me by the shoulders and forces me upright. A big clot of phlegm drops from my nose into my throat, and I entertain the thought of spitting in Foley's face. But that would be a bad move.

"Do you understand suicide is against the law in the State of Massachusetts?" Foley smiles. I guess he thinks it's funny. But the funniest thing is the fact that Foley really thinks I'll answer him. He grabs my wrists one at a time, and squeezes the metal cuffs to the bone.

"I got you this time, Farrell," he says.

Thelma has removed her mask. I can tell she wants to wish me luck. We share a glance at a distance and she walks out of the room. Foley grabs my left elbow and yanks me toward the exit.

"The lifers at Walpole are going to love you. You're going to spend a lot of time on your knees."

Lowell District Court is jumping with nervous energy. Foley ushers me into the courthouse through the back door. Smoke billows out of the lawyers' sitting room. Police officers dressed in three-hundred-dollar suits line the old brick corridor. Most chat with district attorneys about getting their stories straight in front of the judge. Some make deals and others laugh about their war stories. But all of them stop for a second to see who Foley is bringing to lock-up.

"There he is, Mr. Notre Dame."

"Foley, you caught Jesse James."

The police like to make fun of me because I've told everybody I played football at Notre Dame. Only the junkies and hookers from the street bought the story. It was easy to bullshit them; they didn't grow up with me. The police knew my family. Nobody who really knew me believed my lies. But at this point, I don't care about their opinion of me. With my new shoes and the reflection of myself I saw in Thelma's eyes, I feel quite confident.

"Hey, hey, here come the Irish," I snap back.

Foley goes to open the door to lock-up, but I stop. He looks at me inquisitively. I'm shocked by the tone of my reply to those cops. I realize that my words carry an edge of something I haven't had in a long time—pride. I'm not sure why, but the fact I survived gives me a sense of accomplishment. It's weird, but somehow I feel like I'd beaten Foley at something good. He removes my cuffs and sits me down without a word.

I've been here a dozen or so times before. Most of the early trips had been for kids' pranks, like the time we ordered two hundred dollars' worth of pizza from five different take-out restaurants and had it delivered by five different cab companies to the Mulligans, who lived in a house directly across the street from us. There were six boys, all crybabies, momma's boys. The old man was always blaming things on me. Me and a friend, Artie Fosse, hid in the bushes about ten feet from the guy's front door. I would have gotten away with it, but Artie split himself in two laughing. It was funny, five cabbies standing on Mulligan's front walk, holding boxes of steaming pizza, and demanding money. That had been a long time ago, when even old Judge Cowdrey snickered. But times had changed, old Judge Cowdrey was retired and the offense I might be charged with is a little more serious.

There's another big difference today. I'm alone. Mom is not sitting next to me, reassuring me everything will be okay. All the prisoners in lock-up go before the judge in the first call, about ten o'clock; most of them are new arrests. The second call is for any cases that have been agreed upon by the defense and district attorney handling the case, and the third call is mostly old cases or pre-trial hearings. All the prisoners have been sent back to the Billerica House of Correction or released. It's a good bet I'll be the first one to see the judge.

I hear the key opening the door.

"Richie Farrell."

The voice is a little familiar. Dan Callahan is the public defender. We weren't friends; I knew about him. My dad had him in English class at Lowell High School, and to top it off, he's a big Notre Dame fan. Dan is in his midforties with a small frame, yellow-white hair, and freckles that he's had since childhood. I like him.

"Hi, Dan."

"What happened?"

"What can I say?"

"Richie, the judge will have to follow the law and send you to a psychiatric hospital or a detox for evaluation."

"Listen, Dan, I don't care. I want to live. I'll do anything. I don't want to live like this ever again. Something happened to me on the floor inside the old mill. I don't know what it is. I woke up. There is a reason I woke up."

"Okay, Richie, slow down. First, we'll go in, I'll tell the judge a little bit about your past and suggest he sends you to Lowell Detox for ten days."

"Thanks, Dan!"

There's no need to ask Dan what detox involves; I'd been to Lowell Detox several times before. But Dan goes through the steps anyway. He explains how the first two days the doctors there will be able to help me with my drug problem. How they'll wean me off the heroin first. But then he tells me about this psychiatrist there, Dr. Levine. Says I'll have to talk with him for seven days, every day. He stands up and rings the bell so the court officer would let him out.

"How long, Dan?" I ask.

"Ten minutes," he says, looking at his watch.

Two court officers bring me before the judge in shackles. I guess they think I'm dangerous. Maybe I am. But I don't feel humiliated this time. Everybody knows I've tried to kill myself. I can see every eye, every face in the joint. They all read the same way—"poor bastard." But what they think doesn't matter to me today. The judge is Neal Walker, a big man with an even bigger head, known for his compassion toward drug addicts.

"Mr. Farrell, please stand," says the Clerk of Courts, a round, bald-headed man seated right below the judge.

"Your honor," Dan Callahan jumps in. "I've spoken with Mr. Farrell at length, and he will do anything the court asks to prove himself."

I am not convinced Dan really believes in me, but he's doing a kick-ass job convincing the judge. He explains how

I come from a highly respected Lowell family. He relates how I was a remarkable athlete, injured my knee, and became addicted to prescribed pain medication. Judge Walker shifts his body, almost comes to full attention as Dan explains about the night I found my father dead. He goes on and on how traumatic it was for me. How my father was lying unconscious on the family's kitchen floor when I discovered him. Dan is animated, using his arms, showing the judge and courtroom how I compressed my father's chest trying to revive him.

The courtroom reminds me of St. Patrick's Church on Holy Thursday. I was an altar boy back then, and all the pompous asses would parade around in colored garments and big hats, while swinging chains with burning incense. I have to be careful; Judge Walker is watching me think as Callahan makes his pitch. I think he's trying to look into my soul, trying to find the truth, to make a judgment. I've always thought how hard it must be to be God, to make all those decisions about so many lives.

". . . I recommend and the prosecution finds no exception, that Richard Farrell be ordered to Lowell Detox for a period of seven days. At that time, the doctors will be able to help him with his chemical dependency and Dr. Levine, the county psychiatrist, will be able to evaluate him for the court."

Callahan sits down, the prosecutor has nothing further to say, and Walker and the round, bald man whisper at the bench. I look around at the brick walls and wonder if I'll make it. So many times in my life I've tried to be normal. It's so hard to change when you've destroyed so much of your life.

"Richard Farrell, please stand." The round guy again.

Callahan stands with me. I feel comfortable with him standing next to me. I'm not alone in the courtroom. I give him a nod and he winks with both eyes.

"Richard Farrell, you are hereby ordered to Lowell Detox for a period of ten days, at which time Dr. Levine will conduct a psychological evaluation, and you will be ordered to return to this court upon your discharge. Do you understand?"

"Yes!"

But I'm lying. I don't understand. I have no fuckin' idea what's going to happen to me. But my stomach and lower back are beginning to speak to me. One thing is certain, I'm gonna have to kick heroin.

The drive to the detox center goes by in slow motion. I sit in the back of a police cruiser and watch Downtown Lowell move slowly through memory. My dad held my hand at that same bus stop outside the same Wentworth's Five and Dime store. Each image is cut into half-inch squares by the wire mesh separating me from the driver. I'm classified as "a danger only to myself," so only one police officer has been assigned for the transfer. He never turns; he never speaks. I can see his cotton-white hair under his faded-blue cap. He's a veteran. I'm sure he worked with Dad's deceased brothers, Lt. Jack Farrell and Officer Richard Farrell. I recognize him. In fact, I'd helped his son after he made my team in Lowell Junior Football League. I'm sure that's why he doesn't turn around to converse with me.

I'm scared. Zillions of thoughts are jumping around in my skull—I'll have to face my children, my wife. I've never thought of being successful at living straight before. Shit,

I'd been all set to die this morning. I'm not sure about this Levine guy. I can't help but think of Nicky and Joey. It's going to be tough for them—kicking heroin in prison is something I wouldn't wish on anyone—not even Joey. But maybe three months away will allow him to get some help.

Nicky has a few more warrants—all for shoplifting. He'll do at least six months and the first thing he'll do when he hits the street again—heroin. But if it weren't for him, I wouldn't have these new shoes. I miss him. Nobody else in this world would have understood why I would want to commit suicide in new boots. But he did.

Joey and Nicky each died separately and alone of a heroin overdose the first day they were released from the Billerica House of Correction. The paramedics saved Joey's heart with another "cocktail." But his brain was mush—Joey's mother turned off the machine keeping him breathing. Nicky was found sitting on the ground outside the Rainbow Cafe—his favorite Acre bar. It was a warm night in early fall. The cops saw him sitting there on several of their rounds. They knew him. He was a fixture; sat there every night. His eyes were open—fixed on the old Acre's North Common.

He'd been dead for hours.

Chapter 4 ....

The Coke Bottle Crucifixion

I'm no rookie here. I've been to Lowell Detox at least a half dozen times for heroin addiction. The staff knows me on a first-name basis. Today is different—previously I'd admitted myself.

Nothing is ever constant at the detox. Like the city of Lowell, the building seems to decay more with each visit. Today the smell of grief is rancid. The front desk area is dilapidated. Large chunks of grayish-white paint peel and blister off the walls. Behind the bubbled hanging paint, half-inch cracks form spider veins that never let you forget how far you've fallen.

The cop takes the shackles off my ankles while a dozen inpatients with pin-striped bathrobes and orange smiley slippers cram into the hallway to get a peek. It's a big deal—a cop, the head doctor, and a fuckin' addict in leg irons. I say nothing as Dr. Levine evaluates my medical condition. He tells Mrs. Kay, the head nurse, I don't need to be locked in isolation. I guess I don't look much like a killer.

Mrs. Kay admits me to the ward. She'd been head nurse at Lowell Detox since the place opened thirty-five years ago. She has to be seventy-five now; walks slightly bent over and drags her right shoe. As she hunches over, sorting medication, I notice two little squares of gray duct tape holding her RN hat tight to her yellowish-white, thin hair. Mrs. Kay doesn't look up.

"I hate the ward," I whisper so she can hear. But she already knows and smiles. It's her payback for seeing me again under these circumstances—her way of punishing me for not staying straight after my last visit. I'm stoked; only thieves and incorrigibles are placed in the ward. "The single rooms are all full up," Mrs. Kay says, gleaming.

My neck's on fire. I'm better than the ward. There are absolutely no private moments in the ward. I couldn't masturbate myself to sleep like I'd done countless nights before in one of the four private rooms. No medication these retards could give me would put me to sleep faster than jerking off to my favorite sexual memories.

"Look what we have here! Farrell's back. Yup, Richie Farrell is back." John Hardy steps into the front desk area to take Mrs. Kay's instructions. He's been the head day orderly here for as long as I've been visiting. He's thirty-five-ish, five feet six inches, balding, and overly self-conscious about his freakish purple, pug-nose. He lifts weights and wears shirts a size too small in an attempt to offset his low self-esteem. We have a long, outstanding, mutual disdain.

"Hey, it's Arnold Schwarzenegger!" I respond sarcastically. "You put up one eighty-five yet? That chest of yours is looking fucking huge."

"One eighty-five. Bullshit. I warm up with two forty-fives and two thirty-fives—two oh five on the bar."

His little pencil neck lights up like a Christmas tree.

"Holy shit. Two-fucking-oh five. Your heart is gonna pop right out of that shirt."

Hardy's trying to get me to my destination quickly. He's never won with me. Back in the day I could drive up 350 on an incline bench press and he knew that. I hesitate as he rushes me through the doorway. The room is thirty feet by ten feet, with six beds and six, five-feet-tall silver-gray age-beaten lockers. The brick walls are pea-soup green, the white ceiling is shrinking and fading away, and the tile floor is dark green with black dots.

"You know the drill. Eight days in paradise. Any open bed is yours," Hardy recites before heading out.

The longest permissible stay for all patients is seven nights. The first day, Orientation Day, doesn't count. Discharge is actually on the ninth day before noon. Once you complete the program, you have to be out at least seven days before you can come back. For most patients, Lowell Detox is a revolving door.

For me, it's a flophouse for quitters who need a breather before we go out and do some more dying. I choose the bed at the far end, next to the window and the radiator. It's the only window in the ward, single pane, the old kind, big, maybe six feet if I stand on the ledge. Icy air rushes through a long crack partially covered with gray duct tape.

I have two roommates, Dr. Tim Adam and Mike O'Brien. I know Doc. He's a crackpot, but I like him from the get-go. Adam is a regular at Lowell Detox—held some kind of record, something like twenty-eight times in four years.

Doc Adam, I guess, is in self-proclaimed hiding—from himself. He's sixty-five, crippled from arthritis in his left knee, and almost legally blind in both eyes. He wears horn-rimmed glasses with lenses as thick as old Coke bottles. His round, fat face sits crookedly, almost uncomfortably above a swollen red neck. Except for the white scraggly hairs over each ear, he's bald. His nose is thin with a bump in the middle that flattens out toward his nostrils. Doc Adam tells everybody he's a pioneer in research pertaining to the body's immune system. He'd conducted studies for Harvard, where he taught medicine for ten years. Said he also practiced at Mass General Hospital for twenty-five years until the Medical Review Board took away his license.

Supposedly, Doc had come up with this theory that AIDS is a man-made virus. He reportedly told the press that the CIA was experimenting with chemical warfare in Africa and something went out of control. On a previous admittance to Lowell Detox, Doc told me somebody slipped acid in his tea and he had a bad trip. They locked him up for six months and the Review Board ruled him incompetent.

"Richie, I'm glad you're back. I have to tell you something in case they kill me," Doc says as if he's about to tell me I have cancer.

"Doc, this is Richie's first day," Mike said. "Keep it simple. He's still sick."

I shoot a sudden, inquisitive look toward Mike. I bite my words. I want to tell him he's gonna get slaughtered in here. Mike doesn't even know me and he was coming to my aid—to save me. Like he wants to be my friend. This is a fuckin' war zone, buddy. You don't make friends here.

"I just wanted to tell Richie where it was hidden, you know, in case, you know, Mike, if they get me."

"Doc, who is going to get you?" I ask.

"Richie, forget it, get some rest before the chow horn," Mike said.

"No, who's after you, Doc?"

At first I'm interested, but then I get nervous. My diarrhea begins to bubble like hot water. The fever chills bend me over in pain. I need to get high. I want to die. I cut Doc off and bolt out of the room.

An hour later I come back to the ward and Doc is gone. Mike is sitting up on his bed reading the Bible. He starts alluding to scripture. Out of the blue, he tells me a punk murdered his entire family. I can't listen. It's most likely pure bullshit, ordinary detox dialogue. But it's impossible to get past how much he doesn't belong. Mike is a virgin. This is no place for him. He should have been sent to a plush rehabilitation hospital like Hazelden in Minnesota—a place where rich people go and make up stories about how tough they were on the streets. Inside here—there are no more tough guys.

Mike says his daddy owns the largest private insurance company in Boston. He calls it "fatherly instinct" to hide Mike in Lowell Detox. Says his daddy knew filling out a health insurance claim for alcoholic treatment would ruin Mike's future in the insurance industry; he'd be a marked man. So Daddy called a friend, a congressman, who pulled some strings and had Mike stashed where nobody would find him.

Mike is a Christ who has trouble carrying the cross. Thirty years old, handsome, blond with steel-blue eyes, perfect features, Yale graduate, president of Daddy's insurance company, beautiful house in the country. Mike had everything. Then one Monday night while he and his friends drank beer and watched the Jets destroy New England on the big screen at Johnny's Bench (a sports bar in Lowell filled with Christs), some fucking maniac kid rang his front doorbell. His wife believed the kid's story about the broken-down car and opened the door. The kid never used the phone, but he did tie her to their bed and when he was finished killed her with Mike's pillow.

But this kid didn't stop. He found the baby when he was searching the house for valuables, filled the tub with warm water, and submerged Mike's sleeping three-month-old. Mike found his wife nude and his daughter floating. He dragged them downstairs, lit a fire, and held them for hours. When he called the police in the morning, they arrested him. Three days later they found the kid and let Mike out of jail. He says that was the day he jumped into a bottle of whiskey.

I find myself listening, almost feeling bad. Could it be true? Nobody speaks the truth in here. But he's reading the fuckin' Bible. This guy believes in something. I ask him how long it has been to see if he knows details. But he doesn't answer. Instead he confides in me, asks me to promise I will not tell Mrs. Kay. I shrug and Mike takes it as yes. He admits that the first thing he'll do after leaving this place is drink. Got it all planned out. Buy a fifth of Jack Daniel's and slug it down. I believe him. He says the whiskey is the only answer to washing away the vivid memory of his baby floating in the bathwater.

The chow horn sounds at the front desk and like smoke filtering down a corridor, the warm smell of French fries slides under the door and into the ward. I feel sleepy, but it's mandatory. I have to eat.

"Mike," Doc calls from the other room. "Get up, come on, let's be first in line." Mike jumps out of bed, throws on his slippers, and races out the door before I could even ask his daughter's name.

I follow Mike to the small cafeteria, get a coffee, and sit down next to Doc. Crazy Mary is at the table, a nymphomaniac cokehead who knew Doc was a medical man and wouldn't leave him alone. She's obsessed with the four oozing sores on her face. Doc turns to me and whispers, "She's probably HIV positive." But he couldn't tell her. Mike sits next to me. You can sense he hates Mary. His plate is piled high with dark brown overcooked chicken tenders swimming in ketchup. He tells us he grabbed a couple of extra for Doc.

I finish my coffee and go get another cup, a bittersweet, special mixture of coffee beans and saltpeter the doctors prescribe to curb libido. Nobody says much at the table. And then, Rick, the orderly with the harelip, pops his head in the far door and yells, "Ten minutes to clean up." Rick's the other day orderly. He does what he's told and minds to himself. In fact he's the only one of these orderlies who never looks down or judges the patients here. It might be the harelip; maybe he thinks he's impaired like the rest of us.

"Leaving tomorrow, Mike?" Rick asks.

Mike doesn't answer; he shakes his head, the whole time surveying the twenty-seven patients sitting around with their faces stuck to their plates.

I can't believe how different we all are, yet we share common ground: killing pain, terror, suffering, pretending; and our insidious blue-and-white, pin-striped bathrobes—the hospital pants with the crotch wide open, and the orange-and-black foam slippers with raised imprints of a smiley face across the instep. A face making it impossible to look down, a face reminding me I have nothing at all to smile about.

"I'll clean up," says Doc. He loves to keep his hands busy, picking up ashtrays, sweeping the floors, or cleaning the trays and plates after chow. He tells me it helps him not to think. I have a half hour to shave, shower, and get my vitals checked.

Back at the room, Mike sits on his bed. I think he's praying; his face is covered by his hands and he rocks back and forth. I move on my toes quietly to my locker and pick out a towel, a razor, and a small, clear plastic packet of enema soap the nurses gave us as a substitute for shampoo.

I shake my head. This place gives me access to razor blades and I just tried to kill myself. But I cannot have a bar of soap because it can be used as a weapon. Mrs. Kay has outlawed any and all bars of soap. All because once, years ago, this Hells Angel put a bar of soap inside his white athletic sock and turned it into a nunchaku, a weapon used in martial arts. He swung it around and around with such intensity he almost killed a kid. I mean what is the chance of that happening again? People kill themselves every day with razors. Nothing makes sense to me anymore. Now I have to wash my face with liquid soap that was originally intended to be squirted up somebody's ass who hadn't shit for a week.

There are two bathrooms on the floor. The one near the front desk has three showers and four toilets and is only for men. The other bathroom is at the far end of the long corridor outside my room. It has a single shower and toilet, and there's no sign on the door, but women have the first right of use.

Outside my door, the corridor is narrow and dark, illuminated only by the light filtering through the glass in the bathroom door. I glance at the door across from the bathroom—Dr. Levine's office, my savior, the county's headman. Tomorrow will be my first session with him. And I'm sure I'll pay for his saving me from jail. I can see it now.

"Tell me about your dreams," he'll ask.

"Well these giant, freaky frogs chase me every night," I'll say.

"Do they have any significance?" he'll ask.

And then probably I'll have to tell him about the frogs and how I gassed them when I was eleven. And Levine will probably tell me it's their ancestors chasing me to get revenge. But he'll be wrong. Their revenge is the fact that they can enter my dreams.

I stand at the bathroom door for a second before I turn the doorknob, listening for life or the shower. Not a sound. I go in, lock the bolt, and switch on the light. The entire bathroom floor, walls, and ceiling are covered with small white and black tiles. The fluorescent bulbs in the overhead light fixture illuminate everything in the room like a white-out. The smallest cracks in the floor tile are transformed into deep ruts. Patches of air particles dance together; the room seems to breathe, like the light has given the room a life of its own.

I feel the way I did in the confessional booth when the priest pulled back the shade and I could see his face, but he couldn't see me. I was safe: I could lie, or I could tell the truth. I yank at the yellow-white shower curtain, ripped in more than a dozen places, stinking from the mildew cling-ing in large clumps to the lower half. The drip, drip, drip of the old, wooden, cracked water tank hanging on the wall over the toilet reminds me of my grandfather's house. I stretch my towel over the top of the radiator cover, turn the hot water on high, and hang my bathrobe and hospital pants on the hook on the back of the door.

The scalding water brings relief to the muscles in my neck and shoulders. I push my head under the flow of the water and cover both ears with my fingers. My eyes shut; I don't feel trapped or scared, or even concerned. I'm inside my head and my eyelids become a movie screen projecting the past. I see Dad on the floor—cold, blue, dead—and I want to cry, but I'm safe, and I never cry when I'm safe. I open my eyes and reach for the bag of enema soap, which resembles a package of soy sauce from a take-out Chinese restaurant. I bite the top and squeeze out about a quarter's worth in my left hand, put the rest in the soap dish, and work the lather into the hair on my head, under my arms, and between my legs.

The cramps in the back of my thighs and calves feel like the large knots in the rope at the old YMCA gym. I rinse myself, turn the water off, and step out of the shower. The mirror is clouded from the steam. I can't see myself, but the little water beads on the glass bring back a message somebody had written in yesterday's steam. It says, "Jesus died to kill the pain. Mi . . ." The words are right across the middle of the mirror and it appears the signature wasn't finished because the author ran out of glass, but the "Mi" has to be Mike. Unless, maybe "Mi" is the start of a new sentence. On top of Jesus' name is an arrow pointing toward the heavens.

In a heartbeat, this airy feeling comes over me, numbing my lips and making my skin tight. Little goose bumps run up my arms. I grab my towel off the radiator cover and tie it around my waist; it's hot and soothing, and the heat penetrates my hips.

The steam that stops the mirror from doing its job has all but gone and so has the message. I lay my razor on the white porcelain sink, but it slides forward and bounces off the tile floor. There are four bolts fastening the sink to the wall, and the top two are exposed about one inch. The gap causes the sink to angle down, like somebody had sat or stood on the edge.

I turn the hot water on, splash my face, squeeze the rest of the enema soap into my palms, and lather it on my face. My razor is ultra dull, but a warm shower before a shave always makes the task easier. Each pull of the razor cuts another line of white soap off my face until I am completely exposed. It's the same face I had as an adolescent, and the same face I've seen in all the papers and on television. But now it looks different—old, wrinkled, worn. My eyes are still green but they don't sparkle, and the whites have little squares of yellow in the corners. My blond mustache has grown many white hairs, far too many to pluck. The scar on my right eyebrow is bright purple and the hair on the sides of my head, over my ears, is almost completely gray. And I am only thirty years old.

I look right into the middle of the mirror, into the green crystal eyes staring back at me. "What happened to Richie Farrell?" Once upon a time I was a football star. Six feet tall, 230 pounds, and I could bench-press four hundred pounds. "How did I wind up in this fuckin' dump?"

I guess I was destined for this the day I was born. But things really fell apart when Dad died three years ago. My aunt Helen, the nun, said I killed him. She wasn't even there the night he died. Somehow Sister Helen believes I was the reason for my dad's anxiety. Because I ruined the Farrell name, disgraced him in the City of Lowell by constantly being in trouble. She said Dad was a proud man and couldn't live with the embarrassment. The pain of it all destroyed his heart. Fuck that, he died of a heart attack. That kind of bullshit really pisses me off. The only thing Dad was embarrassed about is the fact I never got to play football at Notre Dame.

I splash cold water on my face to close the pores and on the white porcelain to rinse away the dead hair. The hair is caught in the whirlpool and the sink slurps loudly before everything rushes down the drain and disappears. The knock at the door is more like a timid, meek tap. I think it's one of the girls.

"Who is it?" I say.

"It's Mike. How much longer you going to be?"

"Hold on a second, I'm finished."

I slip on my pants, put on my bathrobe, struggle with my smiley-face slippers, and snap my head up and down three times to loosen my hair. The bathroom is beginning to clear. All the steam once trapped up near the ceiling has disappeared. I notice a thick black pipe about ceiling level, running over the sink into the shower. In the middle of the pipe, somebody has tied the arm of a white-and-blue-striped hospital robe, one end is knotted and the other hangs down only inches and is ragged and frayed.

Mike taps the door again. I don't want to open it, but I do. Mike walks past me and turns on the shower, his face as white as fresh snow on a country field, his blue eyes swollen almost shut. I close the door behind me and start to walk back to my room. The corridor is darker than before; the pupils in my eyes haven't adjusted to the difference in light.

Halfway down the hall I hear the latch click on the bathroom door. I stop, listen, and wonder if Mike is the author of the words on the mirror.

Doc is in the dining room limping around, mopping the floor. "Hey, Doc," I yell loud. He flinches; the mop bounces out of his hands and ricochets off the floor tiles. He goes for his horn-rimmed glasses with both hands and forces them close to his face. At first he's mad that I've scared him, but then a smile turns his whole face warm.

I ask him what happened to his wheels. He gives me some story about how dangerous the back stairs are. Something screwy, he was helping a visitor carry flowers, tripped, and had to jump five stairs to the ground.

"Sprained both ankles," he said. "Richie, you going to group tonight?"

"It's canceled, Doc."

"Richie"—he pauses, bends down, smiles, and reaches around for the mop stick—"Mrs. Hart would never cancel group. She loves to play God."

"Hey, Doc, I'm worried about Mike. What do you think? Is he all right?"

"What, Mike? He's just anxious about going home tomorrow."

I bum a cigarette off Doc and go back to the room. Eva, the cleaning lady, is in the room emptying the wastebasket next to my bed. She's close to thirty, overweight, and a little retarded. Her hair is a natural orange, and she has an under-bite that causes her chin to stick to her chest. She wears a two-piece pink uniform with pants at least three sizes too small. And when she walks, her ass resembles a sack of live cats on their way to the town dump. Doc warned me about her hanging around the shower. I think, tomorrow, I'll drop my towel purposely in front of her, but her eyes are so crossed, she'll probably never realize.

I have fifteen minutes to brush my teeth, get my vitals checked at the nurse's station, and be on time for group. I take a couple of deep draws on the Marlboro I bummed off Doc, think about Mike's wife, his kid, my father, my kids, and the bathroom down the hall. I pinch the hot head off my cig and stick the remainder behind my ear.

The corridor leading to the front entrance smells like ether, hot air, and disinfectant all trapped in a tunnel with no exits. When I reach the front desk, Mrs. Kay, the head nurse, is all alone getting the medications ready, filling tiny clear cups that hold white tags with patients' last names. I purposely whack the hand holding my toothbrush against the counter to announce my presence, but Mrs. Kay doesn't acknowledge me.

"Mr. Farrell, step in the door up to the sink, brush your teeth, use the comb, and sit on the chair when you're finished."

While I wait in the blood pressure chair, I can see through the double doors to the recreation room. Everybody is watching *The 700 Club*, a religious show the orderly switched on. Mike is back from the shower, dressed, and sitting on the edge of his chair, rocking on his toes. His elbows are resting on his knees and his head has dropped forward into the palms of his hands. Doc sits next to Mike, nonchalantly inhaling a Marlboro while Crazy Mary sits sideways with her mouth flapping in Doc's face.

"Put your left arm out," Mrs. Kay says.

Like a robot, I roll up my robe and extend my arm. The

black band around my biceps pinches tighter and tighter as Mrs. Kay squeezes the black rubber bulb. I can feel my heart pounding in my left hand.

"Mrs. Kay, I'm worried about Mike," I say. She pays no attention, pretending she can't hear with the stethoscope balancing from each ear. Her eyes and ears zero in on the blood pressure gauge, watching and listening for the first and the last beat. Her eyes shift to the chart on the desk and the pressure releases in my arm. "Mrs. Kay," I repeat. But before I can finish, she picks up a thermometer, snaps it back and forth in the air, and shoves it in my mouth. She jots something down in my chart and says, "Mr. Farrell, I would spend your time here worrying about you. Now go get some rest. Tomorrow, when it is mandatory for you to attend the morning meeting, you'll be free to discuss any issue you have." I lower my head, and when she finishes, walk into the rec. room and sit down in the chair next to Mary.

Meetings are optional the first day. It's called transition time—a time to sleep, to mend your body physically and mentally for a week of treatment. But whoever set the rules had no clue about heroin withdrawal. If they'd had a clue they would have understood the anxiety the second day is two hundred times worse than the first. And the third day is the day the knots turn into a thousand tiny super-tight clothespins pinching your calf muscles and lower back. My best bet is to go back to bed. I didn't have to be in the rec. room but I couldn't rest with the visions of Mike hanging himself in the bathroom.

"Doc, I got to tell you something about Mike," I whisper.

"What's going on?" Mary butts in.

"Mary, can you get lost?" I say. She gives me some space. I return my attention to Doc.

"Doc, I found a message in the steam with an arrow pointing up."

"A message in the steam?" Doc asks.

"What did it say?" Mary blurts.

"Mary, shut the fuck up, or I'll pop that giant zit on your nose with my fist," I say firmly.

"Fuck you," she replies.

"You'd love to, Mary," I say, running out of patience.

"What did the message say?" Doc asks again.

"Something about Christ, but the arrow pointed up to a pipe, and something like a bathrobe was tied around it, and the sink was loose," I explain.

In the distance, I can hear Mrs. Hart's voice coming from the corridor. Doc was right—she's never late.

"Good morning, group," says Mrs. Hart. "How does everybody feel on this wonderful day?"

Nobody answers her. Gloria Hart is a moron, a recovering alcoholic, and a counselor all in one. She has pock marks on the bridge of her nose, a space between her upper front teeth you could fit a good size cigar in, and the makings of a pretty fair black mustache. Born with some rare deformity, she has two shriveled arms, about half normal size. They hang awkwardly out of her dress and the pinkie finger on the right hand twitches when she becomes excited. Curious, I want to ask her how she sits at a bar stool and drinks, or how she wipes herself, or how she gives herself a good scratch.

Mrs. Hart walks into the rec room, past the pool table and four large windows covered with wire mesh, turns off the TV, and sits down in one of the green vinyl chairs that forms a giant circle around the room.

I hate any kind of organized meetings, but the court has ordered me to be here and this is better than jail. And the meetings are mandatory. Mrs. Kay has worked it out so if you don't go to meetings you won't get your anxiety medication for the day. It is a step meeting, twelve steps to recovery, she calls it. But I never can get past the first step. The one that says we are powerless and only God can bring us to our senses. There is no God. And if there is, He has a lot of fucking explaining to do.

"Our Father, who art in heaven . . ." Mrs. Hart leads with prayer and everybody joins in, even me, just in case.

"All right," she says. "Today, why don't we discuss issues that bother us? Mike, you're going home tomorrow, so why don't you start?"

Mike stands up and for a moment, he looks like he's going to cry and laugh all at once.

"Hi, hi, my name is Mike." His voice is loud and crackling.

"Can you start again," Mrs. Hart says. "Take your time and speak a little softer."

I'm not sure what's happening, but it appears that Mike is changing character right in front of us all.

"My name is Mike, and I'm an alcoholic. I'm scared. I'm scared to go home. My father is coming for me in the morning, nine a.m. sharp, so I have to begin the charade, acting brave." Mike's chin begins to pulse and his eyes dance all over the room.

There are twenty-seven addicts in the circle. Nobody is happy. We feel safe, I guess because we're all sitting in the same shit. But there isn't enough hope in the circle to light a candle.

"It's okay to be scared, but why don't we discuss your fear. Maybe the group can help you," Mrs. Hart says.

"I, I don't want to leave," Mike says, whimpering. "I'm safe here. My friends are all here. I can't get by without Doc."

"Well, what are your plans when you arrive home?" she says. "Are you going back to work, and are you going to continue with your meetings while you're at home?"

"I'm president of my family's insurance business, the automobile division. My division processes claims—death and bodily injury. I'm not up for that."

"Is there anything fun about the job?" Mary jumps into the conversation and Mike's face goes blank. I can see his mind fixing on to the past. Then his teeth gleam, and his eyes sparkle. He starts laughing, a deep, round laugh, the kind that boomerangs, contagious, and suddenly everybody in the room is laughing.

"On the back of our accident forms, we have a space where we ask the insured drivers to summarize the details of their accidents in the fewest possible words. Every year, my secretary compiles the most interesting and I read them at our office Christmas party."

"Can you recall any, Mike?" says Doc.

"Please, tell us some," says Mrs. Hart.

"But I might laugh and spoil the punch line," he says.

"Go for it, Mike," Doc says.

Mike sits up straight, spits in his palms, rubs them together, runs his fingers through his hair, stands up, takes off his coat, and loosens his tie.

The whole group sits on the edge of their chairs as Mrs. Kay pushes the chrome-plated medication cart from patient to patient.

"Let's see," Mike says. "Oh, yes, I told the police I wasn't injured, but on removing my hat, I found I had a fractured skull."

Four or five of us laugh but mostly only to be polite.

"Wait, wait, how about this one? I pulled away from the side of the road, glanced at my mother-in-law, and headed over the embankment."

Doc comes unglued. He bends over, head up, mouth open, yet nothing audible comes out of his mouth. But he is wheezing and I can clearly see every one of his dark yellow, tobacco-stained teeth. His glasses ride the peak of his nose like a cowboy on a wild bull, and a small line of drool seeps from the corner of his mouth. I start laughing at Doc until my side feels like it has been pierced by a sword. Mrs. Kay continues with the meds, concentrating on her responsibilities like a world-class athlete standing in a coliseum, unaffected by the cheers of fifty thousand people. She stops in front of me and hands me a Dixie cup full of water and four yellow Valiums.

"Saves me a trip to your room," she whispers. Everybody in the room is in hysterics. I cup the pills in my palm and throw them into the back of my mouth. And as I inhale the water and pills, Mike delivers the knock-out blow.

"Oh, oh, yes, I got one," he says. "I saw a slow-moving and sad-faced old gentleman as he bounced off the roof of my car."

Water, pills, and Dixie cup explode from my lips, and needless to say—Mrs. Kay catches the water. Her eyes dart wide like she's been struck by lightning. And a tiny bead of water drips off the very tip of her nose. But that's the least of my problems. The sudden burst of laughter has caused me to fart. And it isn't dry. My bowels piss putrid water that runs into my slippers.

I couldn't help myself. The way Mike said it; I could see the old guy in my mind bouncing off the car. Mary falls off her chair onto the floor rolling, squealing, and snorting like a whore in a porno film. Mrs. Hart's little finger is going crazy flicking back and forth, and Mrs. Kay looks up and watches. For a quick instant, I think, I've witnessed a miracle—an actual laugh from Mrs. Kay. But she turns on a dime, bends over, and pushes her cart out of the room.

None of us care; we all want Mike to go on and on. It's the first time I've seen twenty-seven addicts laughing back at their orange smiley-face slippers.

"Here's one," Mike says. "A truck backed through my windshield into my wife's face."

Suddenly, without any warning, Mike's mouth opens and he stops. The silence is sharp, penetrating like a razor's edge cutting up the middle of my back. Goose bumps chase one another down my forearms, my stomach turns sour, and my body temperature drops twenty degrees. Mike's face loses all color, and the momentum in the room stops short like it's run full steam into a brick wall. Doc looks up and sits back quickly in his chair. Silence swallows the group, and Mary, still on the ground, moves on her side to find Mike's face.

"Mike, are you all right?" I say. But he doesn't answer, just wails like a newborn baby boy who has just been circumcised. "Mike, Mike, it's okay, Mike," I say louder. But it's too late. Nothing can stop his killing pain, cutting and twisting and ripping and turning, until he chokes and vomits what seem to be whole sections of his heart.

Doc stands and limps around the circle emptying all the ashtrays into his ashtray, and limps behind the pool table and vanishes out the back door into the dining area.

"Who would like to continue?" Mrs. Hart asks feebly.

Nobody's buying because Mike owns the floor.

"My little girl was so cold. I held her tight against my chest, close to the fire. Her little hands were blue and hung back like the arms on the frog puppet sitting on the top of her crib. I just wanted her to breathe, to breathe, to cry, to be warm. I wanted to put her to bed and rock her one more time. I wanted to see those blue eyes smile."

Soiled pants and all, I get out of my chair and kneel down before him. "Mike, it's going to be all right," I say. But it's too late; he takes off out of the room.

"Mary, what would you like to talk about today?" Mrs. Hart asks with a phony half-smile, her tongue flipping up and down from lip to lip.

"You're kidding, right?" Mary asks.

"No, the group must go on," Mrs. Hart says. "Mike is going to have to deal with his problems or he'll never get better. We must move on."

Mary sits back on her chair and all of us, without exception, want to get high one more time.

"Hi, my name is Mary and I'm an alcoholic. My uncle and father took turns with me when I was twelve," Mary says. "Daddy told me if I told, he'd kill Ma, and when I got to be thirteen, I sold my body for drugs, and it didn't bother me one bit."

Mrs. Hart asks me twice to share my experiences and hope. But legally I'm not at the meeting; I should be in bed. Mrs. Kay's rule, I don't have to speak on the first day. Each time I avoid eye contact, staring down at the two faces on my slippers, pretending not to hear. She goes around the circle, forcing, prying, and everybody has a war story.

Murph, a black Marine sniper whacked out from Vietnam, has cold black eyes; one of his upper front two teeth is missing, and all he talks about is death and killing.

"Charlie was like slow-moving cancer," Murph says. "Once he grabbed on to you, he just never let go."

Depot Annie, I like her the best. She is an old lady with gray hair and broken teeth, and she usually falls asleep in the cafeteria snoring with her head tilted back and mouth wide open.

"My husband left me fifteen years ago. Run off with this young girl. My kids were all grown up; I was all alone—gave up my life for him and the kids. Now my kids won't even visit me; say it was my fault."

Twenty minutes later, Doc and Mike still aren't back, and when I pick my head up off the floor—Mrs. Hart has me in focus.

"Mr. Farrell," she says, "it's your turn to share." I suck my lips together like a fish, rock back and forth, thinking about how much I would tell them.

"My name is Richie, I just thought I farted. But instead I shit my pants. I'm going to clean up. Besides my turn to talk nonsense doesn't arrive until tomorrow."

"Mr. Farrell, I could argue—you show up, you speak."

"My name is Richie; I'm a drug addict. I don't have any hope for you, mankind, or anybody. The best I can do is talk war stories, and they're not going to help anybody. There's already enough pain in these four walls to cripple this entire city."

I scan the room slowly, deliberately, like a TV monitor in a padded cell. Mary picks away at the sore bleeding over her left eye, and Murph fusses about some young kid he blew away twenty years ago. Mrs. Hart's little miniature hands hold the clipboard against her chest, and Mrs. Kay stands by the front doors writing notes in somebody's chart. I wipe my face with my palms, force my head straight up, groan, and curse the Lord.

"If you people think for one moment that hearing about my misery will make your misery any easier to handle, you're a bigger fool than me. I'm no cherry when it comes to detox; I've been to these self-help meetings before, heard nightmares, cried, hugged hurting strangers, and no story I ever heard took away the sight of my father laying there stone cold dead. No story I ever heard at one of these groups ever helped me forget the fear and trauma I suffered the day my dad beat me with a fence post. Hey, even Mike's story, his wife and daughter."

Frozen fear. "Oh, God! Mike!"

A picture-perfect vision of Mike hanging in the bathroom jumps me. I have to move now, get out of this room, and save him. I should have seen it earlier. My mind zeroes in on the torn robe cloth wrapped around the pipe in the bathroom. I remember the words in the steamed-up mirror. Mike's chair is empty. Adrenaline rushes into my stomach, and before I have time to think my feet sprint toward the front doors. "Mike! Mike!" I scream. Mrs. Hart drops the clipboard on the floor and leaps to her feet.

"Mr. Farrell, come back here!" she yells. "Sit down or I'll have you sent back to the judge!"

I'm not concerned at all about getting tossed into jail. My mind focused only on Mike and the private bathroom at the far end of the dark corridor. Although I've had seven knee operations, my legs can still motor. In fact, once I get up full steam, not much can stop me. Rick, the orderly, hears

Mrs. Hart's calls for help and rounds the door from the corridor almost at the exact instant I make my cut and turn down the same corridor. Poor bastard never had a chance.

All I did was lower my shoulders two inches and my velocity and leverage cut him down like a wrecking ball. His shoulders bounce off the front desk and he skims into the air like a flat rock skipping across the water. He hits Mrs. Kay on the phone at the front desk like a linebacker creams a running back at the goal line. Out of the corner of my eye, I see them both crashing, rolling on top of the medicine carts, legs and arms flailing, medicine and supplies scattering everywhere.

I'm on my toes; my arms swing tight to my side like pistons in an engine; my head is leading, six feet in front, stretched out like a sprinter. The drive of my legs pushing off the cold tiles tears the bottoms out of my foam rubber slippers.

"Code Red, Code Red!" blasts the intercom system. Code Blue means there is a medical emergency or somebody's heart has stopped; Code Red means somebody snapped.

The brightness of the corridor changes quickly to dark gray, and the door to our room pops out in front of me. I cut hard on my left leg, flying sideways through the air. I flash back to my Dad on the sidelines screaming, "Dig in!" I can see pay dirt at the end of the corridor, light filtering from the bathroom. Halfway down I hear the sound of running water in the shower. Digging and driving, harder and harder with each step, I yell, "Mike! Mike!" My heart pounds against the muscles in my chest and I can't help but see again the picture of my dad lying on the kitchen floor—the skin on his face, green, black, and yellow-blue.

Light peeks through the half-inch gap at the bottom of the bathroom door. The tiles at the foot of the door are illuminated, bright, and only steps away. Still moving full speed, I know coming to a sudden halt will blow my bad knee. Both heels brake; pain shoots up the back of my right thigh; my eyes water; and I can hardly stand straight. My body ricochets off the old brown door, and the wood splits right up the middle. At first I'm scared to turn the doorknob, but then I see three hospital security guards, running after me with nightsticks they carry in case of these violent situations. I have little choice now. Over the years I've found heightened reality is like water—it finds its own level.

"Hey, asshole," says the guard out front. "What the fuck you doing?"

He looks scared, only a kid, and goes to raise his club. But I hit him with a forearm shiver and put him down like he was shot. The two behind him stop, backpedal, and halfheartedly make a move for their nightsticks.

"I'm going in that door," I tell them, pointing, pausing to let them see how serious I am.

Nobody moves, so I step back and boot the middle of the already cracked door with my bare foot. Wood splinters fly everywhere, trapped steam rushes out of a man-sized hole like smoke billowing from a burning building.

All I can see are bare feet dangling from a cloud of white, wet steam about eye level. The two guards behind me freeze when they see the shadow. One gets on his radio and calls for Code Blue. I jump through the hole and support his legs, trying everything to take the downward pressure off his neck. His skin feels like hot ice: it's so hot it's freezing cold. I have to get him down and jump-start his heart.

"Get the Doc," I say to the guards. "One of you get the Doc in the ward at the end of the hall, and the other one come in here and help me get him down."

When I step sideways to let the guard take one of his legs, my right foot crushes something sharp, and blood oozes from the top of the paper-thin foam smiley slippers trying to protect my toes. Any pain is camouflaged by the throbbing ache in the middle of my knee. The sound of metal and glass grinding against the tile floor gives me chills. It's as if time, past and present, are blurring together. My arms loosen from his legs and fall free. I look up. The steam has nearly settled; his face is now visible.

"No, no," I whisper. "It's Doc."

A thin, solid red line of blood runs from my foot into the drain. In shock, I pick up my leg, look down, and see the source of the killing pain. Doc's bent pair of horn-rimmed glasses with thick, shattered lenses are resting in a pool of dark-purple, clotting blood.

Mike and I sit on our beds for a good hour without so much as a word or even a cry. We haven't received the official word yet. One of the EMTs who cut Doc down thought he felt a slight pulse. I want to tell Mike how I thought he was the author of the message in the mirror. But I can't find a way to begin. Finally, a little before 10 p.m., Dr. Levine enters the ward.

"Doc is going to be all right," he says.

Mike starts to cry.

"Dr. Levine, can't Mike stay a couple days?" I ask. "You know, after what happened and all."

"Well, what does Mike think of that?" he replies.

Mike doesn't give a flying fuck about anything right now. He's saddled onto the edge of a razor. He knows, any way he moves, he's fucked.

"Dr. Levine, my first session tomorrow, I'll let Mike have it. That's the least I can do. Maybe he can talk to you about everything, you know?"

"I'll go."

"What, Mike?" I ask.

"I'll leave tomorrow," Mike replies.

Mike stands and heads toward the front desk and we follow. Mrs. Kay is back to business as usual. There are no signs of any violence. Mike asks her if it would be all right if he takes a walk to the edge of the parking lot. She pauses. I think even Levine is surprised. She usually blurts out "No" to any request. Mike explains how he wants to look out over the Merrimack River as the moon shines down on the Hunts Falls.

Mrs. Kay nods. Levine asks if it would be okay if I accompany him. I hold the front door open. The fast early-spring winds whirl snow-covered leaves around and around. The cold, crisp, dry air stings the hair inside my nose. From the edge of the parking lot we stand, silently, watching car lights move slowly over the Hunts Falls Bridge.

I remember my dad brought me to these falls every Saturday when I was little. Dad and I would walk up river collecting old Coke bottles with long, thin necks. After we claimed six or seven bottles, Dad would toss them into the river's current and the necks would bob up and down on the surface. The objective was to break the bottles' necks with a rock and watch them sink before they went over the falls and shattered on the jagged rocks below. Tonight, I can't see the falls' raging white frost. But I clearly remember how the falls looked like a herd of charging white elephants.

Neither of us speaks. The cold is coming on hard. But it's a non-issue. Our bodies have become numb. Finally, Mike turns and I follow.

Dr. Levine has already headed home when Mrs. Kay orders me to shut the door. And when I get back to my room, three new recruits have been admitted. This skinny guy with a scraggly, gray-white beard and a black leather Hells Angels jacket has moved my blankets and sheets so he can have the window. I think about fucking him up—grabbing his beard and slamming his head against the radiator.

But I remember my dad telling me to choose the swords I fall on very carefully. These guys travel in packs. And more important, I'm only a silent tough-guy now—only in my mind. Besides, tomorrow morning will mark the first of my seven days talking to Levine about my past. I have to start with these psychological tests. Dr. Levine says my answers might help him figure out how the fuck I got here.

Chapter 5 ....

Official Day One: Morning

Mrs. Kay doesn't play games. It's 6 a.m.—sharp. Transition Day is over. The clock is ticking. Today counts and I'm dope-sick. The day orderly, John Hardy, stands over my bunk. My eyes try to focus on the tattoo escaping his tight, short shirt sleeve. He looks more afraid of me than I am of myself. Mrs. Kay's nose seems longer in the gray light, her eyes bloodshot. I swing my legs onto the floor and notice she's holding a rubber band tie-off, a few empty glass tubes, and a hypodermic needle to draw blood.

Immediately, I know what she's after. In the early '50s, the State of Massachusetts funded the detox to deal with the rising alcohol problem. But this is 1987—people are dying of AIDS. To most, just hearing the words "HIV positive" conjures irrational fear. Of course, the detox doesn't discriminate when it comes to uneasiness about a little bug that can take out the toughest. We're all fairly close together— sharing kitchen utensils and common showers. Therefore, anybody with holes in his or her arms the day of admittance is mandated to submit and sign off on an HIV test.

I'm petrified. I try to keep a good poker face, considering what it will take physically to resist. Rick, the orderly with the harelip, and another young kid I don't choose to know, stand in the archway of the door a few feet behind Mrs. Kay. I've been labeled dangerous. I want to tell John and Mrs. Kay the truth—I'm not a tough guy. I haven't been dangerous to anyone since my early twenties. I don't want an AIDS test because I may be HIV positive. I run from everything. I'm a coward.

I think back on one of the many days I was dope-sick. I was still with Louise and the kids. It was near sunrise. I drove from the farmhouse in Pelham, New Hampshire, squeezing my sphincter muscles until the urge to fart left me. If I could only hold out until the white liquid hit my heart—I wouldn't shit myself.

Adam Street was naked except for a grotesquely thin Puerto Rican kid in his early twenties. He had a teardrop tattoo under his left eye. He was Nieta—an extremely dangerous Puerto Rican jailhouse gang. Of course, I was driving a Mercedes-Benz and was built like a jock. He thought I was a cop. But I was jonesing, and I couldn't care less what he thought of me. I was a fucking warrior. Only my agenda mattered. First, don't give him the money and let him out of my sight. Second, bite the bag—make sure it's heroin. Third, get safely to the Burger King bathroom on Chelmsford Street to cook the heroin and stick the needle into my vein.

I motioned him into the car. He directed me to a house off Middlesex Street with hand commands. It was a predominantly Cambodian neighborhood. We didn't speak. I had a nine-inch screwdriver in the driver's side compartment of the lower door. My left hand never left the yellow handle. If he went for me I would have driven it right through his left eyeball without even thinking about it.

He left the car, expecting me to follow. One knock and it opened. The place was a shooting gallery. Wall-to-wall junkies sleeping on the floor. I followed him to the bathroom. The mold smell made me gag. He cooked a bag in an aluminum beer-bottle cap, shot it, and handed me a needle and a fresh bag of heroin. His eyes were pitch-black—emotionless. His purple-crimson blood was clearly visible in the bottom of the syringe—maybe a centimeter thick between the end of the needle and the black rubber stop on the stick-push.

I carefully poured the tiny bag of heroin into his cooker—grabbed a cigarette butt out of the ashtray on the windowsill, bit off a small piece of the filter, and spit it into the cooker. I thought about my little boys and what it must feel like to die of AIDS. I turned the cold water on, gathered 20cc of water into the syringe, shot it into the cooker, fired up a match, and watched it bubble. The Puerto Rican kid watched. He thought I was hesitating because I was a cop. He had no idea I lived in a half-million-dollar farmhouse with a wife and two children.

I didn't have a needle. Never kept them on me. Tossed even the brand-new ones. It was illegal. The last thing I needed was to get stopped and have the police find a hypodermic needle under my seat or in the glove box of my Benz. But this kid had three; all had traces of dried blood where the end of the plunger meets the needle. His blood didn't stop me. I collected the boiling heroin into the syringe, found a vein, pulled the stopper back, watched the blood register, and pulled the trigger. The warm rush of pure exhilaration wiped out any thoughts of what I had just done.

I sit quietly as Mrs. Kay finds my good vein on her first visit. Nobody in the room speaks as she methodically watches a fine stream of my thick, bluish-red blood squirt into the glass tubes. I hear the ticking of the oversized wall clock and the sound of the kitchen help preparing breakfast. It's time to pay the consequences for getting high with dirty needles. I have no one to blame but myself. For the first time in my life I know one thing to be certain. There's really no sense in me getting straight—only to die of AIDS.

Before Mrs. Kay leaves she checks my vitals. My blood pressure is 180 over 120. She hands me a sedative, two Libriums. It's normal to have a dangerous blood pressure reading while you're kicking heroin. But what Mrs. Kay's given me is the equivalent of taking two aspirin thirty minutes before you have a root canal. The Libriums will help calm my nerves, but nothing touches the pain of guilt and shame.

I could have saved my father's life that night on the kitchen floor. But instead I watched him die. That's the fuckin' vision that kills. It will not die; plays across the inside of my brain all day long. And it's like fifty times worse when I'm dope-sick. The diarrhea cramps, the burning aches, the calf muscles turning into oversized golf balls, always seem to overwhelm me with the memory of my dad, begging for help, holding his chest, struggling to breathe. I thought he was faking. But he wasn't. He had faked so many times before. I fucked up. I couldn't tell the difference.

One night, I came home trashed. I was eighteen. Could not even walk into the house. I bounced off walls and smashed my head on the floor. Mom heard me and tried to quietly guide me into the daybed downstairs in the playroom. Dad woke up and went ballistic. My mom always wore her hair in a ponytail. Dad took my mother by that ponytail and used it as a whip just to get at me. She flew ten feet across the room. He hit me once, a right hand to the temple. The crack to my head came at the same time Mom hit the floor and slid into the wall with her head.

I became an instant animal. Turned into a monster. Dad saw the look. "That's my fucking mother!" I screamed. Immediately, I was sober. Chased him up the stairs, through the kitchen, and almost had him going out the back door. Ripped his fuckin' T-shirt off. Mom jumped on my back, and that saved him from getting a beating in our house. But I tackled him in the middle of our neighbor's backyard. And just before my left hand connected with his jaw, he grabbed his heart, started to hyperventilate, and said he couldn't breathe. I couldn't see his eyes in the blackness, but he was crying, begging me to call an ambulance. Mom screamed when she saw Dad clutching his chest. Mr. McNally, the neighbor, had heard the commotion and had already called the ambulance and police. At the hospital they said there was nothing wrong with Dad's heart. It was an anxiety attack. The bastard got away with it. He was faking. I just didn't believe him the night he really died. And that is why I'm in love with heroin. It kills the memory of how I misjudged and it cost a life.

"Mr. Farrell, take a shower." Mrs. Kay brings me back to detox, and I follow her command.

I'm in luck. The shower is vacant. Pain pulsates in my lower back as I strip down. Naked, I stand in the middle of the shower and adjust the temperature. The hot water from the showerhead can't even mildly erase the cramping in the back of my thighs. I squeeze a dime's worth of soap from the enema bag and massage it into my pubic hairs. I don't have to meet Levine until 10 a.m., so I consider masturbating until the water turns cold. The soap-lather begins to build into rich, thick cream. I'm hard. Nothing can happen today that is bad enough to steal my visions of sex. There is no reality I can't escape with my hard-on. I think about Louise giving me a blow job, or me firmly biting her nipples as I slowly tongue my way down to her pinkness. I'm so close to firing out, but I can't let it. The pain will come back. I've mastered the art of going to the brink and slamming the door. I stop immediately, let it throb, hands off, and in seconds the urge to explode diminishes. The pain in my back is all but gone. The water begins to chill but the warmth in my loins overtakes everything.

I begin again. The slow touch forces me to whisper, "Fuck AIDS." I close my eyes. The backs of my eyelids become a movie screen. I watch myself separating Louise's lips with my tongue. Her tender, erotic moans overtake the shower water hitting the floor. My body adjusts itself and my face and tongue attempt to tunnel inside her.

I stop and start again and again. No pain. The water is ice now. Goose bumps race up and down both forearms. I can't see myself because the white foam from the soap has completely enveloped my groin. I recall her riding me inside the Mercedes, moon roof open, her head bobbing into the night air. I can almost feel her pelvic bone slamming mine. I cannot hold it. My legs tremble on each blast of relief as it exits and finds its way onto the floor. I watch the water corral it into a whirlpool and suck it down the stainless-steel drain.

Seconds later—the pain engraves itself into my back and legs. For some reason a faint hum rings in my left ear. A cloud of guilt immediately encircles me. Shame so immense it's difficult to breathe. I feel pregnant with the memory of my aunt's lips around my cock. I see myself standing over her sleeping on the couch, whacking off, cumin' on her bathrobe. What kind of person am I? My dad was right. He always said I'd wind up a sexual deviant—jerking off in a murky, dank cell.

Mike is gone when I get back to my room. He never even said good-bye. I wonder if I'll ever see him again. Why they wouldn't let him stay a few more days makes no sense to me. Rules are something I never pay too much attention to. Especially when it comes to common sense. But I'm in no position to barter. Mike and I had shared a moment of our lives most people can't even imagine.

I don't mean Doc. But rather holding death in our hands, an account of death so vivid it sears itself into your memory. It's a vision that remains regardless if your eyes are open or shut. We are kin to a memory that is now transparent. Mike and I have double vision: we're condemned to experience life with that moment as our filter.

The cafeteria is vacant. I can't eat. The thought of food turns my stomach. I pour a coffee but toss it into the barrel. The saltpeter in the coffee would thwart my bathroom delight. Back in the ward, I realize the Hells Angel has left, too. Went AMA—against medical advice. The turnover in here is better than 50 percent a day. But most patients last a few days, wait until they feel a little better, and hit the streets for another run. I can't blame them; I did the same on all my other visits. Now I'm relieved I don't have anything left. If I'd started something with this creep he would have come back with all his buddies.

I fold up my blanket and head back to the bunk next to the heater. I have an hour before my first encounter with Dr. Levine. I'm anxious about the unknown. Levine is Jewish and my dad taught me never to trust Jews. He said he never liked these therapist types; he said most of these guys have more problems than I do. Dad wouldn't say this, but I think "shrinks" are no different from Catholic priests. In fact the only thing that separates them is a white collar.

Seven days though—what the fuck can I tell him in seven days? I'm only thirty. Maybe I'll make it all up. Like I did every Friday morning in Confession when I was young.

Levine's office is exactly like the rest of this dump—black and gray floor tiles, green cinder block walls and barren, distressed ceilings. Levine sits gracefully behind a lime-green, metal desk. I watch him writing energetically, almost oblivious to me entering his office. A small radiant desk lamp illuminates his wedding band and casts a moving shadow on the wall behind him.

Levine's face is kind, and the lines around his eyeglasses tell me he must smile a lot. He's not a big man, but he's not a small man, either. Two distinct things about him really hit me as I try to figure out whether I should interrupt him. First, the veins on the back of his hands are crimson-purple targets—perfect for sticking needles. As a heroin addict, that's the first thing I look for when I meet somebody new. How are their veins? It's important. If you're dope-sick, about to gag your insides onto your lap, nothing means more at that moment than hitting an unfucked vein.

But what really blows me away is the fact that he's a Jew with a normal-size nose. Dad always said Jews had big, hooked noses because air is free. My father was dead wrong. Levine's nose is smaller than mine.

"I thought I was supposed to come here and talk," I blurt, and the quick, scribbling sound controlling the room pauses. "I have to sit here for seven fuckin' days and watch you write?"

"Mr. Farrell, please sit down." He removes his glasses, smiles, and closes the file he'd been writing in.

He attempts a joke. "Would you like the cold, rigid, metal chair or the solid, firm, wood chair?"

"I'll sit, but don't ask me to talk for hours a day, seven days straight right off the bat."

He nods, bugs his eyes, and tilts his head slightly to the right.

"What do I talk about?"

I've jumped the gun. I usually hold my cards close to my chest. Most of the time I go by the code—the first one to speak loses. Why don't I just sit here and refuse to speak?

"Whatever you want to talk about."

"Pussy? Can I talk about pussy?"

"If you want."

"Better yet, I wanna talk about the inkblot test you want me to take. I want to talk about the asshole who thought up the answers."

I never stop for a response. He's cool. I can't read his

eyes. But I can feel him trying to open my soul. It scares me a little. There's something good about Levine, something I just can't grasp.

"Who thinks that shit up? I mean for Christ's sake. Correct answers to ink spots on fucking white paper."

I can't go on. I freeze. Everything goes blank. All I can see is my dad on the kitchen floor. Nothing's moved. Nothing's changed. It's as if Dad is right there on Levine's desk.

"Richard? Richard?"

Levine's voice brings me back, but my lips feel numb and I can't remember anything I was saying. For an instant I don't recognize where I am. Dad's in my head again, dead on the floor. He fucks with me every day, like when I was a kid. Back then, Dad never warned me when he was coming; it's the same thing now. The only difference today is, he's not really there.

"The court has ordered me to evaluate you for the State of Massachusetts. It is my responsibility to sit here and listen only. It's totally up to you what you talk about."

"But I ain't got nothin' to say. You can't make me dredge up what I don't wanna remember."

My chest starts to get tight. Pins and needles take over my left pinky finger. My temples pulse, and the beat of my heart begins to compete with my voice.

"I'm a no-good, fuckin' scum-bag junkie, Doctor. I shot heroin so I don't have to remember. Right now, even thinking about going back, my inside is screaming like a blender at high speed. I'm afraid what I'll do."

The sound of the clock over Levine's head forces me to breathe deep. My neck begins to cramp. Suddenly, I feel a thick, suffocating smoke.

"Frankly, take me back and I could hurt you real bad. I wouldn't even know I did it."

Levine leans back as if to make himself more comfortable for a long car ride on a Sunday afternoon.

"Are you violent?"

"Violent? No. Maybe? I don't know. I don't want you to think I'm a tough guy, because I'm not. But when I get scared I feel dangerous. Something happens to my perspective of reality at that instant. Heroin removes the threat. If I'm not high, my moods change as rapidly as the tick-tock in that clock," I say, pointing over his head.

"How do you feel right now?"

"Crazy beautiful. Like crazy is the place to be. But that could change. I got a million and one voices, Doc. Diminished capacity—I can be a low-grade moron one minute. I can revert to my childhood, be like a thirteen-year-old kid, whine, cry, and blame. Or I can recite Shakespeare verbatim. I can dialogue with the best paper-assholes out there."

I get him on that one. He leans forward and opens the file in front of him.

"Am I being pellucid?"

No response.

"Or are you much embrangled at the present moment?"

Levine writes faster and faster. The sound of his pen overpowers the silence. I have this motherfucker. He'll be eating off my plate in a matter of seconds. I'm juiced.

"Clear or confused? Which one is it?"

"A little of both," he says, but I know he's lying.

"See Doc, you cannot even understand what I'm saying. How in God's fuckin' name are you gonna understand seven days, four hours a day? Which voice you gonna follow? You gonna evaluate the angry, desperate kid? What about the articulate, almost a genius, charmer? And whatever you do, don't forget the ruthless, deviant criminal."

"Well, if I find it relevant, I'll look at all three voices. Richard, you aren't the first heroin addict I've ever talked to."

"This is different, Doc. You have no idea what you're getting into. Day to day, you won't have a clue to what voice shows up. And as soon as you think you've captured it—the fuckin' voice will change right in front of your eyes."

Levine closes the file and grins, but only one side of his face moves. This guy is tough to read. Most people I'm straight with end their conversation pretty damn quick. Not Levine. I reach over and turn his family portrait into my view. Levine's wife and two sons all have strawberry-blond hair.

"Hey, Irish Jews. I got one of these pictures at my mom's house. Everybody smiles. Dad slapped the shit out of Mom twenty minutes before our picture was shot. Nobody knows, the picture never told. Mom's smile wrote history."

"Why don't we begin talking about what heroin does for you." Levine boldly removes the picture from my hand and places it carefully away from any possibility of discussion.

"Doc, heroin is like licking the breath of God!"

I decide to tell Levine what that really means, explain how it feels to actually lick God's breath. I had several shooting buddies on the streets. But Bonnie Wigman was my friend. She was beautiful, night-black hair, plump, delicious lips, and a tongue that could touch the tip of her nose. Bonnie was an HIV-positive prostitute who fucked a married guy to pay for her drug habit. She always made enough money for two bags. Whenever we were together she took care of me, but I'd never fuck her. She wasn't into that. She told me something about fucking guys for money took away her need for that. However, she got off sucking cock. I mean her pussy would explode with multiple orgasms the instant she felt cum hit the back of her throat.

I loved having my cock sucked. We were a tailored match for one another. The preparation and anticipation for what we called "licking God's breath" was intense. We never tried it if we were even remotely dope-sick. As soon as the heroin was divided and sitting ready in our needles I'd have a hard-on. She'd drop to her knees, aim my cock in her mouth, wrap her tongue around it but not suck, and find her favorite vein. I did the same. After she hit, her eyes would confirm I was ready. It was incredible what she did to me. She made love to it. The moment I'd feel the urge to cum, I'd fight to hold on. A few minutes longer. My leg muscles would tighten to rock. Bonnie would sense it and be ready. Finally, I had no power left and a millisecond before I fired my first blast, I pulled the trigger to my syringe. Bonnie followed. Nothing but groans and muscle spasms. The top of my head would almost come off. We licked the breath of God.

For almost ten uncomfortable seconds, Levine struggles for a place to go. He's obviously caught between not fully being sure if I'm finished with my story and attempting to find his place in my file in order to continue.

"So you believe in a Higher Power?" Levine asks.

"Heroin. I believe in heroin. Stickin' a needle into my vein, watching the blood register, pulling the trigger, feeling the warmth moving up into my shoulder, exploding, rushing as the white liquid hits my heart—it's better than having sex."

"When did you first take heroin?"

"You know that perfect fucking euphoria right before you cum, like the millisecond prior to the first squirt? Right when your head explodes. Doctor, you ever notice when you're jerking off how far and how fast the first squirt flies out?"

"Is that what heroin does for you? Are you saying it takes the place of masturbation?"

"No, jerking off is jerking off. Heroin is heroin. It's a toss-up. I love them both the same. I'm just trying to explain something here. You jerk off, right?"

Silence. I love to fuck with these guys. For some reason most of these shrink types think it's easy to get inside your head. But before it's done I'll own this motherfucker.

"Doctor, heroin is like having multiple orgasms for hours at a time."

"I understand, but can you remember the conditions of the first time you took heroin?"

"Yeah, I was addicted to pain medication, Percodan. I had three or four doctors who wrote me a scrip every month. Told them I couldn't live with the pain in my knees. You know, from all the knee operations, football ruined me."

Levine nods and I take a small beat, for sure he's gonna ask me about my football career. But nothing follows. He doesn't care. Levine keeps nodding as if he wants me to continue.

"My friend was a heroin addict; he met me at the hospital the night my father died. Heroin and Percodan are both opiates, either one will take you there. The only difference, one takes you to your destination in about thirty minutes, the other delivers you home in a New York minute. I had no time. My mom was on the fifth floor recovering from surgery. I had to tell her Dad was dead."

"You never experimented with drugs as a teenager?"

"I wasn't born a junkie. It wasn't my goal in life. I was twelve or thirteen when I did my first joint. I was a normal kid, did what everybody did back then, got drunk on Boone's Farm apple wine at thirteen. Puked and was sick for three days."

Levine removes his glasses and begins to massage his eyes. He moves his head with each rub, not in frustration but what seems to be pleasure. He pauses before his left hand slides down to the file on his desk. I watch his demeanor change as he painstakingly opens a large manila envelope in the open file he's been writing in. The natural hum of the office is swallowed by pages turning over and over as he reads. Levine shifts. His lips purse. Something changes. I want to ask what the paper says. What does he know that I don't? He doesn't look comfortable. Maybe he's going to tell me I hadn't dodged the bullet this time. I'm HIV positive.

"I have these guidelines from the Commonwealth of Massachusetts. They want answers to several questions. I don't like them. They are archaic. But my options are limited. There is no easy way to begin."

"Just hit me, Doc. To be honest, I'm relieved. I thought you were reading something bad about me."

"Your lawyer informed the judge the onset of your problems began when you discovered your father had died. The first batch has to do with trauma. I'm mandated to tape-record your answers. Okay?"

I don't answer. But Levine isn't expecting an answer. He pauses and inhales a slow, constant stream of oxygen. My nature is to fuck with this kind of nonsense. But I have a sense Dr. Levine legitimately likes me. He reaches over and pushes the thin white button on the tape-record machine. *Click.* Game time.

"Have you experienced an event that would be markedly distressing or a serious threat to your life or physical integrity?"

Why should I tell this guy anything? Every time I ever started telling anybody about my shit, they turn away. Hide their eyes, like they feel sorry for me or I'm a crazy motherfucker or something. It's like trying to tell somebody what shit tastes like. He'll never understand and I'm sure he's heard the bullshit before. I think it's always better to be sarcastic to these kinds of people anyway.

"No, I'm fine, Doc."

"The next question has four elements that need to be addressed separately. Is there one particular event persistently re-experienced in at least one of the following ways: 1.recurrent and intrusive."

Re-experience. Recurrent. I don't even know what's real. How can I even begin to answer that? Sometimes I think my life is one giant dream and someday I'll wake up and be me. I mean, did this really happen to me? Did my imagination create everything? I can't answer these questions. But it seems like Levine doesn't even care about my answers. I get a sense he believes the questions are idiotic and hates asking. He allows me about thirty seconds to answer, doesn't look at me, watches his watch, and goes on with the next question if I don't respond.

"Second part. Do you have recurrent distressing dreams of the event?"

Here it is—the dream question. I want to tell it all right here. Puke the vision all over Levine's desk. Get rid of it forever. But I can't tell him it's about these kelly green, giant frogs. And death. My father's death. Because I'm not sure what is real. All I know is these giant frogs chase me all the time. These frogs force me into this one room. They don't let me leave. I have to watch my father die over and over.

It's always the same. I wake up in my bed to the sound of the phone ringing and ringing on the kitchen wall. When I jump out of bed to answer the phone, I see the frogs. They're outside my window watching me. I swear a few of them gotta be ten feet tall and four feet wide. The closest one's eyelids are always shut, but they're transparent and he stares at me.

I run to the phone. It's my mom. She's calling from the hospital. She's just had a hysterectomy that morning and is still quite medicated. Her speech is slurred. I turn and the frog is still there—watching. Mom tells me Dad won't answer the phone at their home and she's worried. I glance at the frog and tell Mom I'll go right over to check on him. The second I put the phone down, the frog is gone.

"You don't wanna keep a record of what I dream about, Doc!"

I thought for sure I'd get a response with that answer. Nothing, not even a muscle twinges in his face. I want to reach over the desk and grab him by the throat and force him to look into my eyes. He's like all the rest of them, only concerned with getting the job done. I think if he really cared about helping me, he'd refuse to continue with this dumbass nonsense. The air in the room begins to sweat. My throat feels tight. Levine doesn't look like Levine. He appears to be melting. I can only hear a piece of his next questions. Actually, just one word, "flashbacks."

My flashbacks are worse now than the day it happened. I mean seeing yourself there again is tougher than the first time; you're outside lookin' in, every second is burnt in your memory. Problem is, the unknown is gone after the first time through. Regardless of the terror, there is no guessing to what is about to take place. You have to sit through the ending over and over again. It's like, fuck, hold on, here it comes again!

I want to cry. Even if I confided in Levine right now he'd probably just move on. Maybe I should blurt it out, knock him off his fuckin' chair. Okay, asshole, here is my flashback. My father is on the middle of the kitchen floor. He's naked, clutching his heart, turning blue, and begging for his nitroglycerin pills. I scream, *Fuck you and die.* And he does what I tell him. Maybe if I stand up, do jumping jacks, and whistle "Dixie," Levine will pay attention to me and stop reading.

Levine flips the page to the next question. But I can't hear a word he says now. I bend my neck forward toward the tape recorder. My ass rises a few inches off my chair; my body resembles a broken umbrella. The microphone is only a square inch big, and I'm so close I can kiss it.

"Fuck you!" I whisper.

I can't fucking believe it. I almost bust out laughing. Levine moves on like it was a perfect answer. We don't even hit a speed bump. In fact, I think I see his leg twitch as if to say, "Fuck, yeah!"

I decide to stand up and walk over and open the window. It's not an attempt to get his attention. I want to find out how far of a drop it is to the ground if I decide to jump. Levine begins to fidget as I move around his desk to return to my seat. He's uncomfortable with me at his back. I sense his eyes watching my feet, but he still refuses to look up. I watch him reading, flipping the pages, getting ahead of himself. I click off the tape recorder before I sit back into my chair. Maybe that's what the tape recorder is for—to listen when I'm not in the room. Levine reaches out and pushes the button back into record position.

"Finally, the last question and then we move on."

I lunge out of my chair and hover over the tape recorder. Levine's eyes freeze double-wide. He stops writing. But this isn't about Levine. I nod at Levine, try to give him a sort of confirmation—so he'll understand I hold nothing against him.

"No, asshole, this is the last answer," I yell into the tape recorder.

Levine clenches his eyes together. He reminds me of my son Ricky whenever he doesn't want to pay attention to correction. He'll put his hands over his ears and squeeze his eyes tight. As if to say, I cannot hear you or see you, therefore, you aren't there.

"I live under a toilet bowl, and every five minutes somebody new has diarrhea on me. I can only concentrate on deflecting the shit!"

And then, like God himself has reached his hand inside the room for me—I turn and head for the door. Levine readjusts his glasses, sits back, and watches me go. "Tomorrow, we'll begin again. Tomorrow," he says softly.

Chapter 6

Official Day One: Afternoon

Mary Hart forces me to attend a mandatory therapy meeting in the lounge with all the other patients. She comes right into my room. I've warned her to knock. Said I couldn't be responsible if she walked in to me beatin' the bishop. She's clueless. Consumed individuals like her only hear the music in their head.

"Do you play chess?" she asks.

"With myself," I reply. "It's the only thing that kills the pain."

The lounge could be the set from my favorite movie, *One Flew over the Cuckoo's Nest*. It's rundown and dingy, and looks like it hasn't been maintained since the building was erected in the 1940s.

I found out Mary Hart is fifty-five. She's been a group therapist only a few years. Today, Mary appears a little taller and wider—four feet eleven inches tall and about three feet around. Mrs. Kay told me Mary was born with radial aplasia, a birth defect where your arms and hands never grow. My dad called them candy arms. We all sit in a circle of chairs. I watch Mary Hart control the room. Her arms look like a separate entity, completely independent of her body. "How are you today?" Mary asks, and everybody has to talk.

Murph, forty, the black Marine painted with tattoos from his knuckles to the tops of his deltoids, tells stories about how he killed gooks in Vietnam in 1968. He tells Mary the eyes of his targets chase him in his sleep.

Crazy Mary, twenty-five, picks open sores on her face. You can always tell a coke whore by the way they pick at their face. Mary goes on and on about how her tongue translates into money on the street. "Sucking white stuff for white stuff," is how she puts it. Hart doesn't even flinch. Mary goes on about the married guys who come from New Hampshire, with baby seats in the backs of their cars, to get blow jobs. I want to break in and ask her how many she's fucked, how many poor wives are HIV positive in southern New Hampshire and don't know it? But Hart is staring me down and I'm supposed to speak next.

I refuse to talk and she gets shitty on me. Her disability stumps me. I think about making a comment; get everybody to laugh. I always tried to make sad, serious issues funny. But instead I drift away mentally. I can't help but relive what it was like growing up disabled. I feel a slight tinge of empathy for Hart because of my own crippled leg.

My father hated the fact that I was a cripple. The summer I was eight, he would take me out every Saturday morning and force me to walk the perimeter of Lowell's North Common near our home, past all the children playing and all the adults resting on the benches. I was embarrassed. "Heel and toe!" he'd scream. Dad was a soldier in Korea. He knew how to march properly. He'd won the Purple Heart over there. Told us a grenade went off in a jeep he'd been driving. Said he laid in a ditch with shrapnel in his legs, bleeding for hours. Brought me with him once to the VA hospital for his yearly checkup. I was young, maybe two. Doctor asked what was wrong with me. So the fuckin' moron doctor tells Dad to force my muscles to work. He says, "Teach him how to march."

"Mr. Farrell, if you refuse to talk, there will be consequences," Hart threatens as she interrupts my daydream.

"Oh, my God. Will I be in trouble? Like what will they do? Put me in detox?"

Now she's pissed. I've challenged her. Everybody in the room is uncomfortable. Murph gives me a nudge, moves his jaw toward the ceiling, and winks.

"It's tough at first, Richie." He knows my name. "But you get used to it after the first day. Just talk about how you got here today. Nothing too deep, we all gotta do it, man."

Murph's black eyes are softer today. You can almost see he was once human. I like him a lot.

"I smiled when my dad died. That's why I'm here," I say, slightly over a whisper.

"You smiled and that brought you here?" Mary jumps in.

"Shut your fucking mouth up you miserable zit-head. Let him finish," Depot Annie says sternly.

I want to laugh. Good old Annie has my back. Murph is amused and understands that that's enough to cut it for me. Mrs. Hart sits back—waiting.

"If I have to tell you what happened, I refuse to tell the watered-down version like the kid told in that bullshit story *Catcher in the Rye.*

"Now I'll be the first guy to say it, I've made some big mistakes in my life. It looks like I'm gonna be required to tell you about most of them later. But as far as I'm concerned, the only mistake that really counts was the one I made on December 5, 1984."

Something touches deep inside of me and warns not to trust everybody in the circle with all the information about that night. I can only see some of their eyes. A few are looking at the ceiling; some are so physically sick they cannot pay attention; one is snoring in a dead sleep; and this guy with a long, beaded, white beard is nodding out.

I start to remember for the first time in years the details of what happened after the ambulance brought Dad to the hospital. I only heard the doctor say, "passed away." I'd been with my dad on the kitchen floor. I watched his face turn blue-black, yellow, and gray. I knew what the doc was gonna tell me. But still, waiting for those words, waiting to hear it was like falling off a large cliff. You somehow knew the ground and impact were only seconds away.

He was my dad. What kind of asshole doesn't cry when his father dies? So I dropped my head into my arms. I wanted the Doc to believe I was hemorrhaging water from my tear ducts. The truth was I was trying to hide my smile. I was bubbling up inside. I wanted to jump through the roof. And it scared the shit out of me. It was awful. I couldn't help myself. I'm sure he saw me smile. It killed me so bad my voice cracked. I'm usually a great actor, but I couldn't fake tears. It took everything I had not to celebrate. Every fiber in my body fought the urge to run out the front door of that hospital shedding my clothes while dancing through the streets bare-ass. And the worst part was, I didn't want to feel this way. I wanted to cry; I really did. But Dad had taught me it was a form of weakness. He said crying was for skirts. It was a fuckin' horrible feeling, like I'd just run for a touchdown and beat the team single-handedly.

"My dad died on December 5, 1984," I start telling the group the story, figuring I could get away with a soft version of the truth.

"Was he a mean son of a bitch?" Depot Annie asks. "My father tried to rape me drunk. I would have loved to kill that son of a bitch."

"He was bad to my mom. She was upstairs in the same hospital where Dad was pronounced dead. She'd just had surgery that morning. I had to leave the Emergency Room and let her know. I couldn't do it straight. That was the very first time I ever stuck a needle in my arm. I called my friend McGinn. He lived close. I knew he'd come quickly."

I began to drift away, above my body. My voice kept going, telling the story, but I saw Mom in her hospital room. The sight of her lying in bed canceled my smile like I'd been whacked in the teeth with a Louisville Slugger. I couldn't let her see me smile. Mom knew everything. No matter how I hid my sheets as a kid, Mom always knew when I wet the bed. Even if I washed, folded, and put them back on before she got home. She knew.

"McGinn was a heroin addict. In Vietnam, he got whacked out on the stuff. Said it helped him not to think about the killing. I had to be high to tell Mom. I just watched her husband die on the fucking kitchen floor of their dream house. How can I tell her? What do I say?"

Murph is at full attention, and for the first time in a very long time—I am in full control. Something inside of me is very different. Suddenly, talking about the pain is killing the pain. It feels good. Maybe now I don't need to jerk off all the time.

"I never did heroin, but I ate plenty of Percodan and other prescription painkillers for my bad knee. McGinn told me Percodan was synthetic heroin made in a laboratory. But I was a coward; hated needles. I could've taken four Percodan. But that would have taken thirty minutes for my stomach to break down the pills and numb me. I needed to tell Mom before somebody else did. I had no choice."

"Excuse me, Mr. Pelletier," Mrs. Hart interrupts. She's upset. I guess she's had enough with the patient snoring.

I wonder where McGinn is today. He hasn't crossed my mind in quite some time. He was a short Irish kid with square shoulders. His hair was a mix of gray and reddish blond. I smiled when I saw his face close up. He stuttered; it was quite funny to watch.

"McGinn met me outside the Emergency Room. The bathrooms were right next to the information desk. A horse-faced nurse with red zits on her neck watched us suspiciously as we moved across the lobby. I didn't care if anybody thought we were fags for going in the bathroom together."

"Are you homophobic? Because most people who worry about other people thinking they're gay are either closet gay or homophobic." Crazy Mary breaks my train of thought with her commentary.

Murph is concentrating on our leader Mrs. Hart. Her aggravation turns the skin of her neck right below both ears fire-engine red. Old Depot Annie has moved to the edge of her seat. It looks like she's about to stand up and let Crazy Mary have it any second. To me, this is wonderful; the tension in the room makes me more comfortable. I dig this kind of shit.

"Mr. Farrell, perhaps you could use the word homosexuals instead," Mrs. Hart says.

"Me, what about Pick-Her-Face over there? I'm just telling my story like you asked."

"Richie"—Murph laughs—"just go on. This stuff goes on at every meeting. You just gotta go with it."

"I cannot remember where I was. But Mary, about being gay, I bet you've eaten more pussy than I ever have." I couldn't let it go.

Crazy Mary laughs, "You're right."

"That's enough. Continue." Mrs. Hart is done with all the bullshit.

"You were in the bathroom with your friend." Murph puts me back on track.

"Mcginn hit me in the shoulder muscle with my first shot of heroin," I continued.

I told them how it burned like a butcher's knife ripping through muscle tissue. I could feel its legs racing to my heart. Bang! Wicked explosions shocked me inside out. The top of my head, from my ears up, floated to the ceiling. It was good shit. He opened another bag of heroin, poured it into a spoon, squirted some toilet water into the white powder, and lit a match.

I told him my dad just died and I had to leave to inform my mom. McGinn didn't flinch. Like a surgeon; he never looked up—only continued with his prep.

McGinn found a good vein about two inches down from his wrist and fired. I asked him if he knew what I was supposed to do with my Dad's body. But somebody knocked on the door and I couldn't hear McGinn's answer. So after a minute or two, I left him sitting on the floor mesmerized by the tiny black and white tiles. I was as fucked up as he was, but my dad had died and I had something to finish.

All of a sudden, my throat begins to tighten. The oxygen in the room doesn't seem to go deep enough into my lungs. Doom grabs hold of me like a shirt three sizes too small. I try to swallow, but there is no saliva. Murph spots me going south and he takes several long, deep breaths trying to guide me. It wasn't that I was dope-sick. I was there again. I saw Mom through the crack in the open door. She looked so peaceful. Nothing like she looked like at home when I was young. Not that she was freaked out all the time. She always looked scared of doing something wrong. Her long white hair made the pillow look gray. The skin on her forehead blushed with fresh oxygen. I had to go in. I had to tell her.

I explain to the group how there was no good way to do it, so I yell it out. There was no warm-up at all. I didn't ask how she was feeling or if the nurses were treating her proper. I simply said Dad is dead. She went into a convulsion. Her whole body trembled furiously. I could see only the whites in her eyes. She was trying to get out of bed. Her mouth moved with no sound. I hollered for help. Two nurses came running. The chubby little one with the short hair didn't like me right off. She asks what happened. I tell her, Dad died downstairs. The older one grabs Mom's head and says she is in shock. The chubby one doesn't trust me. I can tell that she knows one of two things about me: either I'm high or I coldly blurted out the information about Dad's demise. Maybe even both.

Guess I shouldn't have told her like that. But I didn't feel that bad. Maybe because I was so high on heroin. I know this is selfish, but seeing Mom in shock was better than Mom seeing me smile.

The next thing I had to do was call Sean. My brother

and I weren't close, to say the least. Actually, we were born in the same year—1956. Like I said, they called us Irish twins. But I don't think being that close in age meant we were close emotionally.

I think that me being born with cerebral palsy had something to do with the fact he and I are only ten and a half months apart. And having two pregnancies so close to each other was probably a reason my mom was in the hospital in the first place. Dad never gave poor Mom's insides a chance to get back to normal. He was a sex junkie. I'll tell you about that later.

Sean and I were different kids. He was tall, dark, and thin. I was just the opposite. I'm not saying Sean was a pussy or anything like that. I'll just tell you when he quit football Dad bought him a skirt. I kind of felt bad for the sonuvabitch. Football is a stupid game. I wish I could have told Dad that before he died.

Sean left for the University of Notre Dame in South Bend, Indiana, when he was eighteen. He never returned. But that doesn't make him bad. Even Jack Kerouac didn't want to die in Lowell.

I looked slowly at each and every patient in the circle and realized they were at full attention. I felt like a priest saying Mass. It was like they were watching a movie and I was the screen. I took my time. I wanted them all to understand why Sean hated my father. I spoke about how Dad always threw money in his face. Told him it cost eighty thousand dollars to put him through Notre Dame. Dad said he worked three jobs!

Which was really bullshit. He played the horses and won, taught English at Lowell High School, and taught night school twice a week. It was my mother who worked three jobs. Anyway, what's funny is Dad had coached Sean for Notre Dame since he was six or seven. Now Sean can't leave the place. He works for them. Goes to all the football games and doesn't speak for days if they lose. Like Dad. It's funny how easy it is to become what you hate.

I asked the nurses working on Mom if I could use the phone. The older one didn't even look; she pointed to the phone next to Mom. I informed her it was long distance. Sean lived in Southern California. The chubby young nurse had just finished giving Mom a shot and kind of rolled her eyes. I wanted to ask her the last time she'd gotten the old whazoo, but figured I'd never get the phone.

She led me down the corridor with this pompous little gait. I wanted to shuffle behind her, mimicking. But my dad had just died. And I hadn't done a very good job telling Mom. I was really hoping Sean wouldn't be home so I could leave a message on his machine to call me. I knew he'd never get me at home and somebody else would tell him about Dad.

After she pointed out the location of the phone she suggested not leaving a message on his answering machine. It killed me, like I'd tell my brother Dad was dead in a message. Most chubby chicks kill me. My dad told me fat people have bad attitudes because they're trying to make up for the fact they can't get the fork full of food outta their mouths. Luckily, I didn't need to worry about leaving a message, since my brother answered quickly.

Past experience taught me to take a different track with Sean. I started with Mom being okay and out of surgery. He sounded a little anxious. There was some forced small talk and then a pause that lasted a good fifteen seconds. I knew he knew when I could hear him starting to cry. He was breathing in short, quick grunts. Cold sweat dripped in the dead space between my undershirt and armpits. The heroin forced my eyelids closed. I spoke softly and told him that our dad had just been pronounced dead at St. John's Hospital in Lowell.

My skin felt like it did after a severe sunburn. Suddenly, in the middle of a high-pitched wail, the phone went dead. Sean had hung up on me. And wouldn't you know, the chubby nurse had just come back around the desk. She was checking on me, like she was trying to catch me leaving a message on Sean's answering machine. I stood there, the phone still up to my ear. She had no idea Sean was gone. The urge to fuck with her didn't give me a warning. It was my nature. I was best at fooling people and pulling off practical jokes. And Nurse Ratchet, the little porker, was about to get hers.

As if I were in the midst of a long phone message, I turned slightly and went off on one of my finest stand-up routines I'd done in months. I began telling a dial tone that the nurse said I shouldn't do this but what the hell does she know? Said she's supposed to be a medical professional and she's fifty-nine-and-a-half-pounds overweight. Went on about how she can't even hold a diet and about why nurses are supposed to know how bad it is for your heart and all. It must have killed her when I asked what the hell could she possibly know about leaving messages on answering machines?

I wasn't lookin', so it surprised me a little. But that chubby little porker grabbed my hand and tried to rip the phone free. I struggled to keep the mouthpiece close to my face. The fat bitch was both strong and determined; however, I always finished strong. I held on to the phone like I was riding a wild bull. But wouldn't you know fate hit me hard between the eyes. The heroin had clouded my ability to reason. I failed to take into account the fact phones start to beep loudly when they've been off the hook more than a few minutes. So I screamed "Dad's dead" to cover my gaffe, ripped the phone violently from her hands, and smashed the phone back down into resting position to hang it up.

"Mr. Farrell," Mrs. Hart interrupted sternly, "is there a point here? I'm not sure if it is in the group's best interest to continue listening to your complete lack of human decency toward people who are trying to help you. I'm offended and I'm sure others must be, also."

"What? Wait a second, let me get this straight. You'll sit here for hours and listen to people fabricate stories and I tell it like it is and I offend you? This is like that show *The Twilight Zone*. Hold on, Murph, are you offended?"

"Absolutely, Mrs. Hart, so much so I think I'll never attend another one of your meetings." He winks.

"How about you, Crazy Mary, my stuff bother you?"

"Just the part about you wetting the bed when you were young. How fucking old were you if you washed and dried your own sheets before your mother got home?"

"And you, Annie?"

"Not at all, Richie, I want to hear more," she replies.

I take a long beat, trying desperately to recall what I actually said to offend her. But honestly, nothing comes quickly to mind. Mrs. Hart is looking at her wristwatch. She wants this session finished. Maybe from now on I'll make things up as I go.

Suddenly, my mind jumps and skips. I'm completely mocus. That's a term somebody made up. We use it to describe how it feels when nothing makes sense. Nothing adds up. Space becomes a silver-gray vacuum. Thoughts enter and exit before I have even an instant to comprehend them. The inside of my head is a washing machine on the spin cycle. It furiously pushes all of my thoughts out tiny holes in my skull. Thoughts, thoughts, and more thoughts, too many fucking thoughts; my head is going to blow off.

I feel like I did the night Dad died, trying to figure out what to do with his body.

I'd put Mom out of it. Sean was in San Diego bustin' his heart out. McGinn was downstairs on the bathroom floor. And Dad was ice cold someplace in a storage locker below with a tag on his toe. I thought about finding him. I wanted to see him without any strength or control. I wondered if his face was peaceful or still distorted like it was on the kitchen floor.

Walk, I thought. Keep moving. If I didn't the heroin would fold me into an accordion. I knew I had to get away from my mom's room quick or risk the chance of getting caught crying by the chubby nurse.

One floor down, I find the hospital chapel. Church was the place my dad always took me when I messed up. It wasn't a coincidence I wound up there looking up at the "Stations of the Cross." I never could figure out why Jesus would go through so much torture if He had all that firepower. There He was chained to a post while this muscular guy with a big head whipped His back. Never mind, but the whip's tails had chunks of glass and metal tied to it. I would have winked, signaled God, busted those chains, and watched that guy's ass fall off. Dad told me and Sean that Jesus did it for us. And I felt real guilty about that. If it's true and all. I won't speak for Sean, but I wasn't worth that kind of beating. In fact, there aren't too many people out there who are.

The best thing, though, about being in church, was that everything stayed the same. Right there on the wall, Jesus never moved. You could show up here a hundred times and that guy with the whip wouldn't be finished ripping away Jesus' back. That crowd of people watching Him die would still be just watching Him die. And when you got to the end of the stations, Jesus would still be hanging dead from that cross while Mary knelt crying.

And you know what else? In the twenty years I'd been coming here, she'd never changed her clothes. In fact, nobody was different. Nobody changed their clothes. The only thing different was you. And I don't mean you'd be older. I mean you'd be different. You might have a Yankee baseball coat on. Or you might have just wet the bed. Or maybe your best friend might have just hit a tree head-on. Or maybe you saw your mother and father wrestling with no clothes on.

Better yet, your feet might be wet 'cause you've been walking in a downpour, steppin' on and popping those big bubbles the raindrops make in the puddles. I really didn't understand it, but I'd guarantee it. You'd be different and Jesus would still be hangin' bare ass with Mary crying in the same goddamn blue smock.

Don't get me wrong, I like going to church. There should be more places where things forever stay the same. It's just all mixed up. It's a freakin' shame, actually. The things that should change stay the same. Jesus shouldn't have to take that pain forever.

Like I'm gonna have to always see my dad there on that kitchen floor. But I don't want to see that forever. I wanna see the time Dad carried me up the stairs to George's Pizza when I was six and had braces on my legs. Dad picked me up on the bottom of those steep stairs and carried me like a war hero into that restaurant. I wanna feel the strength of his biceps forcing the cold metal to pinch the skin of my calves. I wanna see every head turn in awe of Dad's stature. I wanna feel that safety like I see Mary crying and Jesus' stomach punctured and oozing water every freakin' time I walk in a church. I guess I could make my own Stations of the Cross. And each time I'd come I'd be different, but Dad would always be the same.

Anyway, I'll never forget what happened next. A middle-aged woman entered the church. Her eyes were bloodshot and an excess of hairspray had caused her jet-black hair to resemble a dirty mop. She walked right up front. Sat right next to Jesus hangin' dead while Mary cried. I watched her for a long time. And for some reason, I couldn't leave without at least seeing the color of her eyes.

At first, I knelt next to her. After a while I told her my dad always said things have a way of working out. It killed me when she said her ten-year-old daughter had just been diagnosed with leukemia. I wanted to tell her if she smiled it would be even worse. But she had chocolate-brown eyes like my mother and I knew she knew.

So I told her to get out of here. Said this isn't no place for her. Let her know everybody in here stays the same. She was surprised, because her tears stopped immediately. Maybe she didn't expect the truth. Most people don't like the truth. I warned her if she didn't get out right now, she'd never be able to. I begged her. At first, she froze, but I think the echo bouncing around the empty church frightened her. She began to run, tripping on the kneelers. She yelled for somebody to help her. I knew I wasn't the one to fear. But I was happy that I frightened her. She left the church. I knew if she stayed, she'd eventually smile and bad things would happen to her.

I sat in the church trying to clear my head for the longest time after the echo of her run and the slamming of the door left me alone. It was freaky; I thought for sure the priest would come and kick me out. It always killed me how they forced you to be quiet in a place where everybody's dead.

Finally I smiled. Out of the blue a blast of white light hits me on top of the head. And I realize the ultimate truth— in real life, Mary smiled when they took Jesus off that cross, too.

The chow bell rings and I begin to awaken from this half-dream, half-reality state of being that is holding me. I'm suddenly able to focus on my story. I wonder how much I told the group and how much was only in my head. But it's not important anymore. Everybody has a half hour to clean up and get ready for dinner—plastic chicken with ketchup and orange cheese. Nobody speaks to me as they leave the lounge. Not even Mrs. Hart. Murph places a warm hand on my shoulder and Depot Annie is crying. She reminds me of my mom, crying over television commercials. I tell her I'm really sorry if I offended her.

I wish I could get the fuck out of here. I hate remembering. It's hard knowing that one bag of heroin, one mile away, would help me forget it all.

Chapter 7

Day Two: Morning

It's 2 a.m. and my leg cramps refuse to let me sleep for more than twenty minutes at a time. Sharp, cutting, heroin withdrawal compresses my calf muscles into several knots the size of golf balls. I just finished jerking off for the tenth time since midnight. I'm completely dry, shooting blanks. The orgasms last only seconds and kill the pain for just one short breath. I cannot go on inside this fucking shit-hole.

"Heroin. I need heroin. Fuck this. Fuck this," I yell sharply into the cool dark air.

There is absolutely no point in staying here. All I do is talk about my past. I'm outta here tomorrow. I can't take another five days of this nonsense. My stories ain't ever gonna change anything I've done. What happened to me is "House Business." Dad said we don't speak ever about stuff that goes on inside the four walls of our house. It was his number one rule.

I followed Dad's rule the morning I gave the eulogy at his funeral. It was December 11, 1984. I had about twenty minutes before I met Mom at O'Donnell's Funeral Home for our last visit with Dad. I needed heroin and I couldn't mess around with "beat" bags. I grabbed a couple "rainbow" bags and bit the corner. Quinine! The bitterness flip-flopped my stomach. It was pure. The baby laxative was too easy to spot; it made you want to shit immediately. I needed two bags, cost me eighty bucks.

Lying was easier whacked on heroin.

Mom's long coat was purple instead of black. Her eyes sparkled with new life. I got a whiff of freedom from her erect posture. Sean cried near Dad's coffin and the rest of Dad's kin said one last "so long." Maybe it was the two bags of heroin I'd booted in Jimmy O'Donnell's bathroom, but Dad looked happy. I thought I saw him smile.

I asked Mom if I could take off his wedding ring before they closed the casket. Sean removed the Purple Heart and scapular of the Heart of Jesus pinned to Dad's chest. Mom didn't flinch. She was high on the pain medication the doctors gave her at the hospital.

Mom squeezed my arm tighter when they began closing the casket. Inside, William Farrell's space shrunk. My ears began to ring. I could have sworn I heard Dad humming the "Notre Dame Victory March." I remember thinking, Dad's got nothing left but different shades of darkness. And my last memory of Dad's face were the white vapors of darkness swallowing his crooked nose.

Jim O'Donnell said it was the largest funeral procession Lowell had had in over a decade. Outside, purple flags waved on the cars stretching almost completely around the North Common.

"Everybody loves a fighter," Mr. O'Donnell told Mom.

Sean and I helped Mom to the limousine as the mist carried the sound of all the Acre's ghosts past me. I heard stuff nobody should ever hear. It bounced off St. Patrick's School. Secrets my father swore me to. "House Business. What happens in this house—stays in this house," he said. "If you ever speak of it outside these four walls you're no longer a Farrell." And I heard Dad tell me one last time— "You're a Farrell. We are better. Don't disgrace us!"

"Jim, they're all here because they're scared not to be," I whispered to O'Donnell as he tried to close my car door. "He'll haunt every one of them."

I'd driven the North Common with Dad too many times to count. Today was the last time we'd do it together. Blue lights flashed from two cruisers blocking the intersection for Dad's motorcade.

Mom, Sean, and I were silent but I could read Sean's mind. Together we'd understood what terror was. Our shadows connected on Mom. The heroin forced me to slip my skin. All three of us knew that it was the end of everything we'd ever wanted or believed in. Right then, we knew the faking was history. And I think that's what frightened Mom the most. How would we go on without the lies?

The flower car turned onto Adam Street and the runners swooped junkies' cars as we drove close to the church parking lot. There was Hector, the twelve-year-old I'd just bought the "rainbow" off an hour earlier. His dad was in jail and his mom was dead of an overdose. He forced all the runners into a moment of silence when he saw me. I'm not exactly sure why he did it. It wasn't for Dad or the black stretch limousines that ran by here all week. Maybe it was a quick pause, acknowledgment that we shared a common bond in this war zone, a war that we fought because we had limited our choices.

Nobody came to St. Patrick's and threw money into the collection baskets like the Irish. But when the Puerto Ricans invaded the Acre, most of the Irish fled. It became too expensive to heat the space. The Irish had always filled the collection baskets on Sundays. Most of the Puerto Ricans slept in on Sundays. Church was now downstairs with a makeshift altar and a low ceiling to hold the heat. Mom had to pay Father Muldoon an extra two hundred and fifty bucks to use the upstairs church. But Mom had no choice. Sean and I had been raised upstairs. And Dad's funeral was huge. You can make people stand, but in a Catholic funeral you need pews with kneelers. We had to pay the money.

Nothing had changed. Christ was still hanging up front. Mary's baby-blue robe was still blue. And the solid gold chalice on the altar still glimmered with hope. But the center aisle was bigger than I remembered. The hand-carved cherry wood pews didn't shine as much and the ceiling holding the rich brilliant angels now looked drab and dull from dust.

Mom, Sean, and I could feel everyone's eyes on us, trying to taste our pain. It's funny but most people go to funerals only to watch the dead's family cry. Dad said God made woman to bleed and to cry. I'd never let all Dad's fake friends see me cry. I wouldn't even cry alone, never mind walking down St. Patrick's Church's center aisle. I'd tried. Last night, I shut the door to the bedroom and saw ghosts. Dad's face billowing out of the walls. But heroin heals much quicker than tears. Everybody should shoot a bag of heroin before a funeral. It completely annihilates any and all emotion in seconds.

Jimmy O'Donnell sat us in the front pew. Mrs. Kelly played

a soft "Danny Boy" on the pipe organ. She was my favorite organist. We used to say she looked like a walking broomstick with a gray mop head. And she was ancient when we were altar boys. But she never copped an attitude, or cared when we gave her the middle finger, or told the priest when we stole wine and host from the tabernacle right in front of her. She was blind and didn't care about nothin' but God. Maybe that's why she'd lived so long.

I squinted my eyes tight, but the darkness didn't change. Right through my eyelids I could see Father Muldoon entering from the back room. He wore purple and white long robes, and two little-squirt altar boys in black and white robes followed him. I couldn't pay much attention; just followed Mom and Sean as they sat, kneeled, or stood. In fact, when it was time for me to give the eulogy, Mom had to drag me out of my seat. I was scared. Could I lie? Or would I give up "House Business"?

Honest to God, I sometimes can't remember what is real. But right then, as I walked the center aisle, climbed three stairs, and followed the red carpet to the pulpit, I knew one thing. Dad was dead. All the eyes burning in the back of my head meant nothing. My job was to give the best performance of my life.

The pulpit rose from the altar floor as if it held all the forbidden secrets. Dad had said it was sacred ground. The place where Catholic priests revealed the true meaning of the Bible. The platform's magic seemed to reach over the crowd, and its height forced everybody to look up.

I was out of breath by the top step. My arms seemed to shrink as I clenched the rail and skimmed over the church. Heads, all kinds of heads: gremlins and trolls and giants. In the middle, I picked out the same bogeyman who hid under my bed when I was six. The smallest sounds became grenades. Kneelers talked in code. The hair on my head held a weird electronic tingle. I didn't hold my breath but I couldn't exhale. And a dozen ghosts of Dad's memory laughed.

Read. I saw Mom inhale. I heard her tell me I had to do it for Dad.

"When I was a young boy, my dad told me he loved me more than all the telephone poles in the whole wide world."

Somehow my mouth kept going as my memory cruised the church for a place to rest. I found Jimmy Foley sitting on the left behind the family. He was a teacher at Lowell High School with Dad. A tough Irish kid my dad took under his wing. He was built like a football player and wore a back brace from a severe car accident.

When I was eight, Dad and Jimmy united the teachers and led them on strike. I'll never forget it. My brother Sean and I had just stepped out the front door of the old YMCA with Richard Armstrong. Richard was a cross between a big brother, a good friend, and a babysitter. His mother was an alcoholic and his father up and left. He was one of my father's students from high school. Dad took him in.

The three of us were on our way home. It was Richard and Sean who heard the commotion in the middle of Merrimack Street. I was too busy eating my twenty-five-cent hamburger I'd bought a few minutes earlier from Paul's, a small luncheonette inside the YMCA.

"Look, it's Dad," Sean yelled.

And there he was; crew cut, waist-length, black leather coat, and steppin' out in full military style. Jimmy Foley jogged to keep up with him. It was Dad, my hero, leading hundreds of teachers, each carrying hand-painted signs.

Richard was short, a dirty blond with an athletic build.

He told me not to move, tried to make me stand still and watch with Sean. But it was much too tempting. Dad was marching the teachers toward City Hall and the Lowell School Committee members were blocking the steps. People ran and gathered to watch the collision. Man, I would have followed Dad any place that day.

One of the leaders from the school committee had a megaphone and warned of arrest if the teachers did not retreat. But my dad believed in justice back then. He was young, full of life; the threat didn't bother him.

"Sir, I'll ask you only once to step aside and let us into that meeting. It's a public meeting and we have a right to be there," I heard Dad say calmly.

True to form, Dad asked only once. Everything went daffy, and I was so small I only saw the rest of the teachers filing through the front door as they entered the building. Jimmy Foley and Dad had formed a human battering ram. Even the police didn't move in to stop them.

My dad made quite a name for himself that day. The teachers won. They received a new contract that year and brought a teacher's union to the City of Lowell. In an almost unanimous vote, Dad was elected to lead them as their new president. I'd give anything to go back to that moment. My dad was a hero. Everybody loved him.

"This church is brimming with people my dad's life has influenced. My dad was a champion, a true warrior for all he believed."

There were two of me. I remember ascending outside my skin. I watched my lips continue, but I couldn't hear. I spotted Paulina Lee in a pew down back. She never showed at Dad's wake. Maybe she figured I told Mom about the night I caught them together. The night Dad died.

Her eyes covered me like a mouse that'd been chased by a cat to a fatal corner. I zoomed in tight. Her jet-black hair and sensuous eyes screamed sex. Dad couldn't help it, I guess. One day she called; I answered the phone and being one sick bastard—I pretended to be him. People said Dad and me sounded identical on the telephone; not even Mom could tell us apart. I knew about their affair but didn't want to hurt my mom. I told Paulina I couldn't wait to touch her and run my tongue slowly over her nipples. I'm not sure if the phone conversation ever came up between them. Dad never scolded me for talking to her like that. Their secret was safe with me.

I saw a flash of fear in her eyes. I didn't mean to hurt her that night. But when I saw her bare ass on the floor, all I could think of was Mom in the hospital. I threw Paulina in the backyard like a shot put at a track and field event. I was engulfed in rage. She was actually airborne for seconds. I'm sure bouncing naked off the cement hurt.

"My dad was everything. He was a father, a husband, a friend, a lover, a fan, and most of all a teacher. The reason for anything I've ever done is now gone. I will never be able to replace him. And most of all, Notre Dame has lost its biggest fan."

Surprisingly, as I escorted Mom out of St. Patrick's Church— I felt good about lying. For a second, I actually wanted to believe it all. Dad was the star, the hero, playing himself in a Hollywood movie.

It was at the cemetery when it hit me what Dad really did to me.

"Rich, thanks!" Sean whispered as Father Muldoon read.

"Ya, sure, for what?"

"House Business."

I stripped off my coat and began to run. Most people thought I was crying. They were wrong. What my brother, Sean, said really hit home. I realized Dad didn't turn me into a football player because he loved me. Dad was ashamed that I was born with cerebral palsy. Nobody in my family would dare talk about my legs being crippled outside the house. Dad made me normal because of his pride. And that's why I have such a horrible time trying to hate my dad. If it weren't for him I'd be a cripple. He loved me. But I'll forever wish he would have loved Richie Farrell, not only that little boy he fought so hard to make normal.

It's 6 a.m. Despite the cramps and muscle aches in my lower back and legs, I must have fallen off to sleep for at least a couple of hours. Mrs. Kay wakes me up early. Louise has come to give me a message. She'd sworn never to visit me in one of these places. Said it made her too sad to think that after all of our schemes and dreams that I wound up in a hellhole, a place for broken people.

I don't have much time. Mrs. Kay is a stickler for the rules. Ten minutes, that's all the time we have for unscheduled visits. Nobody ever comes to visit me during regular visiting hours. I'm kinda glad; it would bum me out sitting there in the Day Room watching everybody getting kissy face with their kids and wives or girlfriend. A short nap is my psyche's way of self-protection.

My hair's a mess, squashed tight to the right. But what can I do, no time. I brush my teeth, just in case I get a little kiss, throw water against my open eyes, and straighten up my bathrobe and pajamas.

I take a deep breath, say a quick prayer, and head down the dull, greenish corridor. The chicken soup smell boils under my armpits, fear in the form of perspiration beading on my elbows. I have less than ten minutes to convince Louise I've changed, convince her that something inside my gut has become new.

Louise is sitting alone at the far end of the Day Room. I watch her for a moment before I fully immerse my body through the doorway. Time has been awful pleasant to her. In fact, her vibrancy forms a circle of energy that seems to swirl around her like a thousand fireflies.

She stands, slowly, timidly, her body moves toward me. Her jet-black hair bounces sensuously across the top of her shoulders as those chocolate-brown eyes turn to greet me.

My focus can't help but move down her midnight-blue top, past the green, plaid skirt slightly above her knees, stopping at her thin shapely legs. Those legs, so muscular, so defined, if only I hadn't fucked up so bad. Those legs were once all mine.

"Richard!"

I can do nothing but open my arms and attempt to swallow her. I squeeze, trying in vain to make us one. I inhale all the warmth of her breasts. And like the first day I met her, I love her much more than any one thing in my life.

"You'll have to sit down," Mrs. Kay commands.

That old battle-ax, witch, she needs to get laid once in a while. I swear she's a ghost. Somehow, without any warning, Mrs. Kay always appears. I don't care if it's six in the morning or twelve at night, Mrs. Kay jumps out of the walls to stop anything good.

"Let's go over here," I say, pointing. "She's been queen around here so long; got nothing better to do."

"She was nice to me when I signed in today," Louise says. "She told me all about how you were doing, the medical stuff, I mean."

After we sit, I can't help but feel the power of Louise's appearance. She actually cares. I can see it, her eyes; the tone in her voice is different for the first time in many months, I think. No, I'm positive. She actually doesn't see me as the scumbag junkie she's grown accustomed to calling me over the past several years. I want to kiss her, but figure her sparkle might instantly change to blind rage.

"Oh yeah, Mrs. Kay means well, but she gets hung up on rules."

Louise rolls her eyes wide and grins.

"The rules! You always played by your own rules," she says.

I smirk. I'd fallen head over heels into that one.

"No, no, I don't mean it like that. Stupid rules, I mean."

"Rich, I got it."

I clearly have marched right into a trap that had the potential to be lethal at any second. There's only one way out. Go for it. Tell Louise how I have changed.

"Richard, I need to show you something."

Louise opens her pocketbook and hands me a white envelope with the Internal Revenue's seal on the front. I focus on her as I open the unsealed back.

"What is it?"

"Read it."

"Come on, Louise, just tell me what it is."

I unfold the note and begin to read some legal mumbling that makes no sense.

"I had to catch the six a.m. bus this morning. They took your Mercedes-Benz on a flat-bed truck and left the envelope."

Everything in the room disappears—even the words coming out of Louise's mouth. The fact that I couldn't afford new boots but I drove a Benz is surreal. It was all image, what people saw on the outside. Sometimes I didn't have enough money to fill it with diesel. But I don't care about the car. It's a lease. My dad's been dead for over two years. I only picked it up because he had once told me the Germans built the best cars and even the Jews knew it.

"I don't have any means now to pick up food for the kids. Or even take them to the doctor's office," she says as her eyes began to fill with water.

"Louise!" I stop her cold.

There's a silence, the type of silence that is loud. Silence that leads me to believe that the whole Day Room has stopped talking to listen to what I am about to say. But we're alone.

"Louise?"

Her face skips from compassion to confusion.

"How are the kids?"

I can't do it, don't know where to begin. I mean how can I start a serious conversation when for the first time in years we weren't arguing?

"John talks about you every night when I tuck him in. I hear him actually telling little Ricky about you in the bathtub . . ."

Louise continues with a proud eye. She speaks as if I am a returning war hero and she is filling me in on all that I've missed. I can't pay attention. I want to cry. All I can see is John's face as he was born and the time he took his first steps across Dad's living room floor.

"Last night, after I read John his favorite book, *Beef Stew*, I told him I was coming to see you. I told him you were in a hospital. I told him you had been in an accident, but you were okay . . ."

I lower my head because I don't want Louise or anybody walking into the room to see me cry. Dad had always said crying was weakness, but I can't erase those words from my head.

"John said to tell you he loves you and misses you. Richard, he also made me promise to tell you something."

Louise squirms, obviously uncomfortable. I wipe my eyes discreetly and reach over to hold her hands.

"What?"

"He wanted me to tell you that he is going to be a football player just like you."

Louise can't look at me. Those words sting like rubbing alcohol poured on an open wound. If there is one thing that measures how much my lies have ruined my family—those words, "football player," are it. What can I say? The atmosphere is turning ugly. Louise's old look, that "this is too much for me to handle" look, is mounting on her face. It's now or never.

"Louise, something happened to me last week. Something wonderful."

Louise's face turns into a slab of pity.

"No, please listen, Louise. You know that guy, Beaver, the Christian guy? Something happened last week with him."

"You mean the guy that brought you over to the house, the last time you saw the boys?"

"Yes, he's the guy. You know he taught with my dad. He's the guy that's been after me for years with that Christian stuff."

"Okay, I remember," she says in a tone that confirms her suspicion.

"He brought me to church one day and something happened inside of me. I've changed."

"Well, what happened?"

"I'm not sure; I know that my actions since church don't prove anything. It probably sounds like a big lie after what I did. But I just know I want to change. Something in my gut tells me I'm different."

"Rich, you've kind of said this to me before. Why don't you just keep getting better? We'll talk about this later, at least you didn't die."

"That's it you see, Louise! I didn't die out there with Nicky and Joey. God spared our lives. It wasn't my time. God has something planned for my life!"

Louise begins to twist and turn in her seat. She looks at her watch and toward the exit. I stand up in desperation and that frightens her.

"Please, you gotta believe me this time. Something happened. I'm born again. I prayed this prayer and I felt this hot oil burning my stomach and I started speaking in this strange language. Beaver says I was touched by the Holy Spirit."

Louise stands up. Mrs. Kay, the ghost of Lowell Detox, has just announced, "Ten minutes is up" with a hint of pleasure. But I have to finish. I want her to believe me. I want more than anything right now to be different. The problem is I'm not sure I believe it myself. It may be too hard to turn my life around.

"Louise, I'm born again. I'll never be the same again. I know it sounds funny. I know you think it's another one of the lies I've told, but look at me. Look! I've changed."

"Richard, we'll talk later. Take care of yourself. Get strong. The boys need a father."

She's walking and I know I can't let her leave without her believing me. This is all or nothing. If not, my speech, my dumping my guts to her right now, will be nothing more than fodder for her laughter on the bus ride home.

"Louise, you gotta believe me. I can really be a father now. I've changed. The Holy Spirit touched me."

"Rich, I don't want to be rude, but why did you try to kill yourself after you were touched by the Holy Spirit?"

Finally, her disbelief is out in the open. Now I have a chance. She can't dismiss it.

"True, I did try after I saw you and the kids. I couldn't face how bad I'd messed up. But then, living, I know God saved me for a reason."

"Mrs. Farrell, I'm sorry but you'll have to leave now through the side door." Mrs. Kay has moved over close to our conversation.

I walk Louise to the doors and notice it's 6:43; Mrs. Kay has bent the rules for thirteen minutes. The nurses and orderlies are in the front office. It's only me and Louise, nothing else but fear and disbelief.

"Come on, I'll walk you down the stairs to the door," I say.

"Richard, can you? I thought you couldn't leave the floor."

I don't know how it happens but I'm through the swinging door and down two flights without much consideration for the rules. Louise doesn't protest too loudly.

We stand silently, together, awkwardly, like schoolyard lovers, by the door underneath the stairwell. I make the first move. But it's almost simultaneous. Inside her arms it's safe, like the warmth from an oven on a December morning.

The first touch of our lips, the first reach of my tongue into Louise's mouth, makes me rock hard. Louise's pelvic thrust nearly bends me in two, but the pain actually feels good.

Neither of us cares where we are. Neither of us cares if we get caught. The next thing I know Louise is on her knees totally engrossed.

Seconds into the warmth swallowing me, I need to fire. I can't hold it. I fight everything to keep it back. I think of my dad in his coffin. But Louise moves like a piston out of control. I bite down hard on my bottom lip. I want to scream but Mrs. Kay would hear me and I'd wind up in solitary. I count for ten seconds. The warmth surrounding me feels brand new; it moves up my loins and explodes into my brain. The explosion has detoured my reality. Louise isn't finished. I feel bad. I wish I could have lasted longer. Louise seems to need it worse than I do. She continues as if to say, "I'm not done."

"Louise," I blurt. "My aunt used to come into my room at night and give me blow jobs."

She stops. Her chocolate eyes seem to be puzzled. I can almost read those eyes attempting to recall what I said and at the same time fighting to make some sense of it all. It's almost as if the climax of our passion has been disrupted by a fire alarm screaming over our heads. But there is nothing but sheer quiet. I'm floored; I have no idea why those words jumped out of my mouth. Maybe it was guilt. Maybe it was because every blow job I received brings me back to my first. It was unforgettable.

"And I enjoyed it," I continue.

It's almost as if I'm possessed. Like the whole born again thing is forcing me to admit my darkest, sexual sin at that very instant. It makes no sense to me. Why am I telling her this now? My last words end everything immediately. Louise shoots to her feet.

"I was twelve and I liked it."

Louise doesn't react. I feel her arms resist when I hug her. But I can't blame her. I kiss her and we silently say our good-byes. She did manage a glimpse of hope to filter into my eyes. The door creaks shut and, through a rusted, steel, mesh-covered window, I watch her float across the parking lot. Maybe if I stand here all morning she'll come back. But in my reality, I know that isn't even remotely possible. It's only a matter of time. Mrs. Kay will materialize at any moment.

I have to get back to my life, to descend back into my nightmarish existence. I hear something or somebody above me as each foot methodically catches one stair after another. My mind dances backward at my attempt to convince Louise I'd changed. "I'm born again," I whisper. However, the physical climb forces me to think about what to do next. I can't help but wonder if I'll ever really change.

"Is that you, Richard? I thought I heard something down there." Dr. Levine breaks into my thoughts.

He's standing in the foyer directly in front of the hallway leading to the front desk. I want to ask him how long he's been there. But I don't have to. Levine knows. He's patient, kind; not disgusted by the sex part at all. He could have dropped a dime on me and called old Mrs. Kay. Maybe he didn't want to embarrass me.

"Hey, Doc, I was just walking my wife out."

He's caught me. I watch his eyes find the evidence on my pants. I can't hide it. The detox issue blue pants are as thick as tracing paper. I have to stand up straight. His eyes can't help but see the circular, liquid stain spreading, turning the faded blue color darker around my groin.

I move quickly to get past his gaze. My goal is to get

to the linen closet without being spotted by anybody else. Mrs. Kay and the day orderlies are reviewing patient charts at the front desk. Two new patients I haven't seen before are rolling cigarettes at the free tobacco table in the front foyer.

I hesitate bending over and looking down to see how bad the circle is growing. Better to pretend it's not there, but the draft from the corridor hits the wet spot and the entire area becomes cold. There is no way to hide what I've done.

Crazy Mary heads out of the dayroom. I try not to make eye contact, but it backfires. She calls me. Instinct tells me to keep walking, but she's relentless. She'll keep calling me and the repetition of my name with no reply will draw attention my way.

"Hey, Mary," I reply softly. "I'm tryin' to hit the shower before a newbie gets in there and uses up all the hot water."

She senses my anxiety and her eyes begin to scan my entire body. Bang, she hits the spot and gives me a "what have you been up to" smile. I shake my head and my eyes go wide. Most people understand and shut their face. But not Crazy Mary, if it has to do with sex, she's on it.

"Visitors. Oh, how I love to have visitors," she snaps sarcastically.

It is better if I don't respond, look at the floor, and keep moving. I figure if there's any eye contact with the staff at the front desk, I'm caught. It's not that I'll get in any real trouble. But who wants to be questioned about a blow job by Mrs. Kay? She'd probably just take my visitation time away or have the time supervised. Bottom line, it's embarrassing. You can see the tip of my pecker. Besides I didn't get away with it, I'm sure Levine will ask me about it later.

The linen closet is locked. Back in the room, I can't find replacement pants. At first, I lay on the edge of my bed. A soft drizzle hits the outside of my window. The raw, morning chill compounds the backaches coming on hard from the absence of heroin. I sit up and check out the stain. The leaking has stopped. My mind jumps to Louise. I wonder what the hell she is thinking right now.

I've gotta move, it feels like a German shepherd had a bite hold on my right calf muscle. Maybe coffee will help? Best thing I can do is wrap my bathrobe around me and tie the string very tight. I figure the spot will dry before my afternoon session with Levine.

Day Two: Afternoon

Levine doesn't skip a beat. I'm ten minutes early for our daily meeting. But he's ready. The window is open. A cool warm breeze pushes against the side of my face. Dr. Levine is smoking. Something new. No clues that he's a smoker. No ashtray on his desk. And most times I can smell smoke on people's clothes. The sides of his neck—from his ears to the tip of his shirt—are pink—flush.

"Do you masturbate every day, Richard?"

Shit. How does he know? Maybe I should lie.

"Wow, Doc, where did that come from?"

He seems to pause for more than just a deep suck of fresh white smoke. I hear a leaf blower from outside. An older man with an orange vest gets Levine's attention. The man is pushing leaves that winter has packed in the tree line. I focus on Levine. Smoke, lighter now, not as white, filters out his nose.

"Addicts are addicted to pleasure," he says. "Take a look at this."

He shows me a diagram of the brain from a text in the

144

bookcase behind him. Points out a section in the brain that is affected by both heroin and sex, and explains how it turns green in a Cat scan. He tells me again why the detox puts saltpeter in coffee so we don't get horny during our stay. I'm not sure but I guess Mrs. Kay has something to do with it. Levine says no and goes on about how the lack of a sex drive helps addicts focus on important things like how they got into detox in the first place. But saltpeter doesn't work for everybody, especially for people like Crazy Mary and me. I tell him I know all about that stuff, how the army put saltpeter in my dad's drink when he fought in Korea. Must be the same principle, the army wants to make sure their soldiers concentrate on staying alive. Levine lights another cigarette off the one that's already going. He wants to ask me about what happened under the stairwell this morning—I can sense it. But I'm not going to tell him and a cloud of silent, nervous tension invades the room.

"Okay, getting back to your masturbation question. What do you mean, Doc? Is the question do I masturbate once a day? Or are you asking do I masturbate daily? Because there are two completely different answers." I'm playing now, so no response from Levine is necessary.

"You see, many years ago, when I was a young boy, back in the woods at Camp Alexander." I stop abruptly and think twice about continuing.

The guy's not falling for it; I'm certain Levine knows I'm mimicking his whole line of questioning. And it doesn't seem to get him upset, almost as if he's expecting it. I guess if you deal with junkies all day you realize there is no such animal named truth.

"Forget it," I say. "The answer to both of your questions is yes."

My answer doesn't make much sense to him. He's trying to figure out what I mean by both. It's one of those moments when I'd begin to bullshit and suddenly cut it short because I'd start to wonder if the outcome would be what I expected. I was going to be an asshole and make something up about a game called "circle-jerk." I never played; this kid at summer camp told me about it when I was ten or eleven. It consists of a bunch of young kids sitting in a circle jerking off. The kid said you rest a saltine cracker on the bridge of your nose and the goal is to knock it off when you orgasm. The first one to accomplish it wins. But to be perfectly honest, I didn't want to risk the chance of losing Levine as an ally so early into my stay at Lowell Detox. The story had nothing whatsoever to do with his question.

"When did you start masturbating? How old were you?" Levine asked.

Smoke begins to stagnate around my shoulders. I have trouble breathing. Panic. It feels like somebody is choking me. Levine sees it and gets up quickly to open the window a sliver. You can almost hear a small sucking sound gulping the gray-white smoke through a half-inch opening.

"I was eleven. It was the *Sports Illustrated*, Swimsuit Edition."

Levine smiles as if to say "I did that."

"My dad caught me. Mom was there, too. It had to be the worst thing in the world to ever happen to me."

"And why was it the worst? The fact your mother and father walked in on you as you were masturbating?" he asked.

"Well, yeah, that too, but what my dad did was awful. He brought me to a Catholic priest for absolution, to cleanse my sins."

Levine lights another cigarette.

"He did what? Your father punished you by bringing you to a Catholic priest so that you could be forgiven. I don't get it. Would you mind explaining?"

At first, I suspect Levine might be playing with me now. But the look on his face is genuine. He's a Jew and has no understanding of the mysteries of the Irish Catholic beliefs.

I decide to tell Levine how it all started with the magazine cover. This girl in a yellow string bikini, brown skin, and green eyes looked right at me. I was embarrassed, my face became tight, and my neck got real hot. She sat on the edge of the sand, her legs spread, and I could see a line of white skin outlining the yellow V of her bikini bottom. A wave broke on her back, and miniature drops of water beaded and clung to her lips. Lips that were swollen, puckered, and opened just enough to see her tongue stroke the bottom of her upper bright, white front teeth. And that's when it happened. I instantly grew a third leg. And I only had one thought—get back to the couch, off the stairs, and do it before another second went by. Halfway there, my red Champion shorts caught around my knees, and one side of my jock strap was on its way down my thigh. I staggered around the Ping-Pong table, like two boys running a three-legged race. I tossed the magazine on the couch, sat down, ripped my shorts and jock.

I grabbed the sucker with one hand, held the magazine up to my face with the other, and let her have it. The second I finished it went limp in my hand. And when I dropped the book and looked up, Dad's eyes were on me, standing in the door. He immediately called for my mom.

I couldn't talk, think, or move. All I remember is the salty-sweat smell that filled the room, the hate in my dad's eyes, and the sound of my mother's feet scampering across the kitchen floor, heading my way. I yanked up my shorts and the elastic waistband smudged the sticky cream up into my belly button.

When Mom entered the room, she still had her gloves on, stained at the fingertips by rich brown soil. Her hair was pulled back, tied with a gold and blue scarf, and the gray reflected the light from the outside door. She couldn't figure out what was wrong.

Dad's eyes locked on mine and he lowered his head like a bull does before he makes his charge. The gray, white, and brown hair on one side of his head was flattened by his Notre Dame hat, and his green T-shirt said, GO IRISH. Mom saw the *Sports Illustrated* and understood immediately. She suggested we all go upstairs and talk about it at the kitchen table. But I knew that wasn't happening.

Dad didn't answer. And I was hoping he'd understand, take me upstairs, and give me the birds-and-the-bees talk. But my luck didn't seem to be going well.

Instead he screamed and hollered for my mom to call Father Dan so the whole neighborhood could hear him, spitting the words into the sunlight. I cried and begged him not to call Father Dan O'Connor, the parish priest, the good-looking one we called soft shoes because he always danced at the CYO dances. I didn't want him to know. One day, over pizza, Father Dan told me masturbating was something like abortion. He said all those sperm cells have a chance to become little babies. And if we shoot them out of our body for sheer pleasure it is the equivalent of aborting.

Mom was on my side and joined in with the attempt to sway Dad away from Father Dan coming over to our house for her youngest son masturbating to a girl on a magazine cover. But of course, Mom was no hero. Fear is no match for Irish Catholic rage. She backed down and dialed the number of the church rectory where Father Dan lived.

I thought my luck was about to turn; Father Dan was on call at St. John's Hospital and couldn't leave until after supper. But he could speak to me in the hospital's chapel. Mom stayed home; I think she went back to her gardening. Dad drove the car like a soldier on a mission. He didn't talk, shout, or even look my way. But his lips moved quickly, touching, like small nibble kisses. And every once in a while, his tongue would dart out between them. I asked him several times to think about it, but he stuck to the belief he had to get this right with God.

He stepped out heel and toe, down the corridor. And I followed without asking another question, up two flights on the elevator, and across the hall to the chapel. And there he was—Father Dan sitting in the first pew.

There was no "how do you do"; Dad demanded me to tell Father Dan what I did. The priest lowered his understanding brown eyes to mine. He knew, and I remember my forehead began to sweat. Little drops trickled down to my eyelashes, beaded up, dripped on my lips, and tasted salty and warm.

By now things were moving too fast. The chapel was very small with only eight pews, four on each side of the narrow middle aisle. Everything around me felt heavy—my father, the priest, Stations of the Cross, the gold chalice on the altar, even the air.

Suddenly, my stomach muscles tighten, anxiety seems to swallow me whole, and I feel the need to end the conversation immediately. But I know Levine wants to hear more. He's completely fascinated by the concept of a priest being in charge of administering penance for the act of masturbation as a teen.

But no how, no way, am I not going to tell Levine or anybody what happened next in the confessional. I was young and maybe it was just my imagination. It was too weird, the black, wire-mesh screen that turned Father Dan's face into silhouette, covered too much. I couldn't see clear enough. But the fact his voice became increasingly forced and shallow on each question—freaked me out. I bolted out of that confessional, past my dad, and down several flights of stairs into the street before anybody knew what happened. Some stories I'm going to die with.

Levine shuffles papers. He's preoccupied and doesn't notice my silence. There's something I notice in Levine's mannerisms. His lips are pursed into a perfect pucker, and I think he knows something went on inside that confessional.

"Richard, were you sexually molested as a child?"

Something bad begins to brew inside of me. My face becomes instantly hot; anger washes over me like I've been hit by a giant wave at the beach. Levine is no longer Levine. I trusted this motherfucker and now he's going too far. If I want to talk about my aunt, it's up to me to bring it up. He was listening on the stairwell this morning. He heard me tell Louise. My heartbeat becomes a third person in the office.

"Doc, if we're gonna sit here talking like this for a week, I want you to be perfectly clear on one thing. Okay?"

He sits back immediately. I refuse to say another syllable until he acknowledges me either verbally or nonverbally. Levine is visibly shaken. Frightened by my abrupt transformation. He nods.

"My name is Richie. People call me Richie Farrell. That Richard bullshit is something my father would say before he gave me a beating. You got it, Doc?"

But I don't care if he gets it or not. I'm sick of where this is going. I'm dope-sick; I need a bag of heroin; I don't need to talk about what a fuckin' Catholic priest said to me almost twenty years ago. Why should I have to give details about sick shit like sexual abuse? I liked having my aunt come into my room every night and suck my cock. I liked jerking off to the girl in the swimsuit. I question these guys who want to know the details. I wonder if Levine gets off on this stuff, like the priest did.

"And furthermore, what's going on with these fucking questions today? Huh? You aren't light in your loafers are you, Doc? Because I don't go for that homo shit."

Silence. The room is so tight it seems like thick molasses separates the two of us. Dr. Levine is totally aware of all the possibilities. He thinks about reaching for another smoke, but his hands fail him.

"Richard." Levine pauses. "Richie, I'm asking these questions to help you. Statistics warn us about sexually molested children, especially sexually molested boys. The numbers suggest those children run a fairly high chance of becoming a sex addict."

I jump to my feet and slam my left fist on the open file in front of Levine. *Whack!* His eyes flinch and he rockets back in his chair. The back of his head makes a hollow thud on the top of the bookcase behind him.

"There is nothin' I can do or say to erase what happened to me. So, Doc, as far as you're concerned, why I'm here at Lowell Detox, I tried to kill myself. That is it. Got nothing to do with jerking off or being sexually abused as a child.

I like jerking off. Jerking off is the only thing left I got. I'm out!"

My lips freeze. I almost blurted out how much I loved Aunt Phyllis coming to my room. But I didn't have to; Levine knew what I was going to say. I'm convinced he heard me tell my wife this morning under those stairs about what my aunt Phyllis did to me when I was a teenager. Poor Louise, she'll probably never talk to me again. And rightly so, I guess. Right now, I cannot even imagine what Levine would think if I talk about all the sick shit I have done sexually. He'd never talk to me again, either.

Levine wants to say something, but discretion tells him he probably should hold it for another day. I control the room. He understands anything he says will only send me deeper into my tirade. But I shouldn't leave his office without explaining my reasons. The last thing I need from him is to be frightened of me.

"I apologize for punching the desk, Doc. A lot of times I act like an asshole to those people who really don't deserve it. I'm such a sick bastard when it comes to sexual stuff and I'm embarrassed."

"I understand," he says very cautiously.

Now I feel rotten. The guy is trying to help me with explanations from medical books and I made him slam his head and almost piss himself. I contemplate telling him a few things only. If not, he'll probably just yes me to death the rest of the week. I take a moment. Levine waits for my next move. He thinks about standing, but I'm standing. He decides it may be a bad move. I turn slowly to look at the chair; he may not look so intimidated if I sit. Instead, I stay right where I am.

"What would you think of me if I told you I found pictures of my parents posing naked and doing sex acts?"

Levine hesitates.

"You wouldn't be the first kid in the world it happened
to."

I should tell him how it happened. Levine should know
I wasn't snooping around my parents' personal belongings. I
didn't wake up one morning bored and say, "Hey, let me go
find pictures of my parents fucking and sucking." I was in
my dad's walk-in closet looking to steal a cigarette. And it
happened; my arm knocked Dad's strongbox off the shelf
and pictures popped out. I had to look. It's only human nature. But explaining is pointless; I have no explanation for
what I did with the pictures.

"What if I told you I saved one of the pictures to look
at while I jerked off? You'd think that was normal maybe,
right? It was a close-up spread shot of a pussy. You still think
pretty normal? What would you think of me right now if I
told you it was my mother's? What about now, you still think
I'm not the only kid in the world to do something like this?"

Bells sound loudly inside my head. Levine looks painted
into his chair, painted into his bookcase. I stop and turn very
slowly. One foot moves, then another. If I don't get out
now something bad could happen. My earlobes tingle. I cannot believe those words actually have come out of my mouth.
For the first time in my life, I've told another human being
my darkest secret, the sickest, most disgusting thing anybody
could ever do.

It takes me several minutes to cool down on the front
steps. The neatly landscaped quad that separates me from the
main hospital appears much smaller than the day I arrived

with the police officer. Suddenly, I realize I'd failed to ask permission to leave the detox. In fact, I'm not quite sure how my body transferred itself from Levine's office to sitting high up on the cold concrete steps.

Reality hits me hard. The dope-sickness carries anxiety and confusion. Thoughts race around inside my skull like eggs in a blender. I can't understand what's happening to me. It's the second time today that I've blurted out past crazy shit I've done sexually. Maybe I am born again? Maybe this is how it happens? But first I have to purge myself of all the shit before I can get better?

I feel the muscles in my rear end going numb. I hear my dad's voice telling me I'll get hemorrhoids if I sit on cold cement too long. I figure that is the least of my problems. Right now, I'd exchange a half dozen bleeding hemorrhoids for being in this joint. Fear grips me. I wonder what else I'll tell Levine and how he'll use it against me.

Across the courtyard lawn, the main hospital building rises six floors. Nothing but new red bricks and glass completely block the view of the Merrimack River. I see a pretty blond nurse in a third-floor window. She's in a deep conversation. She stops, spots me, and quickly pulls down the shade.

A hundred yards away several normal folks enter the main lobby to visit their loved ones. Some cling to flowers; a new father awkwardly holding an infant's car seat bounces with pride; others carry sadness like sandbags on their shoulders. As if they know the end is near. Not one of them finds me sitting there, watching, wondering if I'll ever be normal, if anybody will come to watch me die.

The Shedd Building is fifty yards to my left. Several wooden benches, painted kelly green, sit in the grass outside the front door. Built around the same time as the detox, much of the building is in full decay. It, too, serves as temporary housing for misfits and degenerates. But worse, the patients there are out of their fucking minds. The rooms are padded. Sometimes, late at night, you can hear chilling screams.

An ambulance pulls in without sirens blaring. Two EMTs help a good-sized guy to his feet. I can't tell his age from where I am, but he doesn't look healthy. As they get closer, I can see he's young, over six feet, and a solid 230 pounds. He cannot walk on his own; his legs drag across the cement sidewalk. Twice he's dropped by the EMTs; no way this guy wants to be where they are taking him. I guess the destination is Shedd, but I'm wrong. This kid is on his way to detox, a young alcoholic.

I know him. It's Roland Brown. I met him here a year ago. I named him "Downtown Rolly Brown." I'm not sure why now, probably something to do with the rhyming thing. I liked him. He didn't make stuff up. Actually, he lied only to himself. Together, we'd convinced Mrs. Kay to let one of the weekend orderlies take us to 10 a.m. Sunday Mass at St. Patrick's. The ushers removed us right in the middle of Father Conroy's sermon. Never forgot it; together we split our guts laughing. Old Conroy was deep into some Holy Spirit talk and this newborn baby decides he or she is hungry. Little shit goes off with this high-pitch wailing. It grows so loud, Billy Burns, one of the detox patients who came along for the ride, wakes up from his nap in the pew.

Finally, Father Conroy has had enough. He yells, "Why are we here?" Immediately all sound in the church is muted, except for the scuffle of the baby's mother fleeing with the infant through the side door. Then, out of left field, Billy Burns, an old friend of mine from the old Acre, who now has "wet-brain" due to alcohol abuse, stands up and almost chants, "Because we are not all here."

I smile at Brown, remembering the moment as they file him up the stairs past me. He glances over but is far too sick to acknowledge me. Last time, they told him his liver was shot. Mrs. Kay said he'd die if he kept drinking. I'm positive he's younger than me.

Right now, he's green, a sure sign of Antabuse poisoning. They give this drug to alcoholics who want to stop drinking. You have to take it every morning. But it doesn't stop the urge to drink. It's meant to act as a deterrent because you get violently sick if you drink any alcohol while Antabuse is still in your system. Pretty foolish, I think, taking a drug that doesn't get you high.

Downtown Rolly Brown is like the rest of us in here. Each and every one of us is being stalked and hunted by ghosts. It doesn't matter whether we were carried in, brought in chains, or called Mrs. Kay for a bed. Something bad is after us. Some kind of pure, fucking evil brought us all together, a power that is much stronger than reason or logic. I guess his time isn't up, either. He made it back to detox for one more chance.

Chapter 9 ....

Day Three: Morning

I feel a suffocating malaise. Mrs. Kay takes my vitals and alleges I am clinically depressed. It's normal for someone in my shoes, she reassures me. But at the same time she decides my daily dose of Librium will be decreased to one pill every eight hours. I object by ripping off the blood pressure cuff.

Orderly John suddenly appears in the room like he's fuckin' Super Man here to save the day. But John's heroism hits a brick wall when he reads the desperation in my eyes. He backs up quickly to the edge of the doorway.

"You can't take me off the Librium," I demand. "I need it to cut this anxiety."

Mrs. Kay doesn't have time for what she thinks is nonsense. Matter-of-factly, she explains my vitals are close to normal. The heroin is leaving my body. "You can see inside my body, huh?" She looks at John but tells me she has to gradually reduce my dependency on other drugs. I don't go for it and head for the front desk to forcefully take my medication out of the tray. John steps in my way. I stop inches from his nose. It's tense. I must have something in the tank. John flinches. He is afraid; he backs away and lets me walk.

I really don't have any options. Neither John nor Mrs. Kay follows me out of the room. The drugs are under lock and key. They're used to dealing with drug-addict low-lifes like me. I pass the front desk without even a glance and turn sharply into the lounge. Several people are making their way into seats with their morning coffee. I wanna tell them the shit has saltpeter in it and they won't be able to jerk off to go to sleep. But I hear Mrs. Kay calling Levine on the phone. She tries to whisper, but I know they're talking about me. I consider making a scene. Crazy Mary spots me and drags me off. I try to become dead weight in the corridor. She has my arm and pulls me as if she is trying to save me from something I'm unaware of.

"Come on," she insists, "don't be afraid. We're just going to my room, outta sight, so you can get ya head right and not do anything moronic."

"I'm not afraid, Mary. I want my fuckin' Librium! They have no right to take them away from me now. They're fucking with me. I don't have to take this shit."

Unfortunately, in reality, I do. I surrender some of my resistance and accept Crazy Mary's pull the rest of the way down the corridor. Inside her single bedroom, she pushes me onto her bed and stands watch at the door. It's against the rules to be inside a member of the opposite sex's bedroom with the door shut. Crazy Mary tells me to chill as she peeks around the corner to find the footsteps she hears approaching.

"Don't be such a brave ass all the time, Richie. In here you have to plan your moments," she reminds me.

Funny thing, I tell her, how hilarious it would be if people ever find out what a fuckin' coward I really am. I have this reputation as a badass. It's nothing but legend—none of it is true.

I tell her about the time I was at a local watering hole in downtown Lowell. The Press Club had a horseshoe bar and was usually filled with local businessmen and lawyers from district court. The owner was a Cracker Jack. He liked his cocaine. I brought him an eight ball every week and made fifty dollars. Just enough cash for a couple of bags of heroin and two White Russians before I left the bar.

This particular day, directly across from me sat this kid, big, blond, dumb, and maybe twenty-six-ish. He was drunk and telling stories. All of a sudden, I hear, "Richie Farrell." It was some good listening. Supposedly, one night around midnight, Richie Farrell was trying to get into a house party behind Left's restaurant on Rodgers Street. The kid said nobody would open the door. "So what does Richie do? He puts his shoulder down and takes the door right off the hinges. And he then proceeds to knock out about fifteen guys."

I yelled across the bar, "Hey, you know this Richie Farrell?" He told me they were good friends. I didn't have the balls to tell him who I was. It sounded so good being a hero like that. Who the hell was I to get in the way of that story being repeated over and over again?

"You want to know what really happened behind Left's that night?" I ask Crazy Mary.

As if she really cares, she slides down the wall and collapses onto the floor. One foot is a tad into the corridor

and the other she places a few feet up onto the doorjamb.
I watch her bathrobe slide down exposing her inner thigh.
The material all crumbles together and rests right over her
private. She's aware of my interest and forces her foot a little higher. I take a deep breath and tell her what really happened that night. I was drunk. Actually, I could barely stand
straight. I saw a bunch of cars I recognized. Stopped. Knocked.
The music cut out. Nobody would open. I got nutty. Went
to run through the door. But somebody inside the apartment was watching me from the peephole. He opened the
door at the same time I went to lower the boom. I projected
into the room and knocked down about a dozen people.
Got up, hit one kid, and fell square on my face. Everybody
panicked and ran out of the back room. Two kids who lived
in the apartment picked me up and threw my ass out the
back into the mud.

"Doesn't the legend sound better, Mary?"

She reminds me that my story has nothing to do with
being afraid. How I cannot be responsible for what other
people say about me. Says she has mastered not caring about
what people think of her. How she likes to suck cock and
that doesn't make her a bad person.

"However, Richie, you never fooled me once. I've known
you weren't a tough guy from day one. That bravado shit
is just a game you play."

I feel tightness in my chest and my ears begin to burn.
Anxiety kills me. If only I had a bag of heroin. One quick
shot in my vein and the anxiety would go to sleep for hours.
But right now I'll have to deal. I immediately focus on Crazy
Mary sitting against the wall with her legs open. I want to
fuck her. Sex kills the anxiety almost as completely as heroin.
In fact, the worst panic attack I ever had was wiped from my

body with nothing but sex. Did it with my wife in the morning, went to an AA meeting at noon and got a blow job in the parking lot outside, visited an old girlfriend in the afternoon for multiple orgasms, and played with my wife again at night.

Crazy Mary stands and offers to shut the door. She says nobody will ever catch us. A quickie she calls it; be over in a few seconds. Offers to bend over and let me put it inside of her. I'm a little amazed she wants to do more than a blow job. The door shuts and I leap to my feet. I cannot breathe. Small sips of air suck sharply through my mouth. Doom. It grabs my testicles. Sweat begins to drip down my right nostril. I feel a warm vice, squeezing. It hurts. Something is going to happen or I might explode.

I tell Crazy Mary I want her so bad. But for the first time in my life I can't. My entire body begins to tremble. I beg her to open the door and let me out. Her face instantly clouds with confusion and disappointment. Immediately, I let her know it isn't her. She senses the panic in my pleading and quickly opens the door. Her hands reach for me and guide me into a chair next to her bed. Water begins to bead on my temples and the feel of hiding from the orderlies in Mary's room becomes familiar. I flashback to Dad trying to bust down the door to my room with his shoulder.

Mary sits on the edge of her bed and listens as I tell her the story. How Sean came home drunk and my father went after him. He was eighteen; I was seventeen. How I'd been sleeping already about two hours when my room exploded into chaos. I jumped to my feet. Naked. Sean and my mother were attempting to hold off my father. The hollow wood door was bulging inward. My father had run amok. They had barricaded themselves behind the door of my bedroom. Screams, begging, crying, and sweat filled the darkness of my room. My mom and Sean would always run to me for help with Dad's outbursts. Nobody cared if I was naked. I was big. I was strong. But most of all, I was a soldier in the same war. I had to do something to stop him. So, instead of putting my hands over my ears and wishing it all went away, I let out a bloodcurdling scream, "Get the fuck out of here or I'll kill you!"

Stillness. Complete motionless, tranquility. Dad stopped pushing on the door, creating an instant peace as if somebody had turned off a flashlight in a tunnel. Ten minutes later, nobody had spoken. The hush of the house made us anxious. Twenty minutes later, without warning, Mom let out a shriek when the table in the kitchen tipped on its side. We could hear the sounds of my father smashing things on the floor, the flower vase, the sugar bowl, the milk bottles, and then calmness.

Serenity again. We waited, holding our spots on the door in case he made a spontaneous charge. I offered Mom my bed. Her silhouette stunk of fear. Sean slept on the floor at the foot of my bed—close enough to spring into action. I slumped to the floor, my back wedged in the middle of my door. An hour later, a few smashed windows trumpeted the end. The next day, everything was normal. My mom acted as if nothing had happened. Dad went to Mass, the gym, and home for his afternoon nap like any other day.

"Sometimes, Mary, I wonder what really did happen? Do you think people just make up their lives? Is it possible my mom didn't see what I saw that night? Because to this day, I freak out whenever somebody shuts a door on me and stands in the way."

"Maybe your mother just doesn't want to remember, Richie?"

Suddenly, my stomach starts to growl and breaks apart the conversation. It is amazing how talking about stuff, letting people you trust know what happened, actually weakens the panic that the event causes. Crazy Mary puts her hand on my inner thigh and licks her lips. I go immediately hard.

"If you don't get breakfast," Mary reminds me, "you'll have to sit through Short Arms' therapy session and listen to your belly dance."

She follows me to the cafeteria. The boiled eggs are green-yellow and my plastic white spoon sticks straight up in my bowl of oatmeal. We're alone. She sits next to me and asks question after question about dying from AIDS. Now she needs me. She doesn't want to die. She asks me how I think it will feel? Will she have giant oozing sores on her face? What will it be like not being able to suck cock? "I'll miss that the most."

I'm unresponsive. My eggs reek. They chew like chalk. But it's the best I've got. Crazy Mary will not shut up. I don't know the answers. But that doesn't matter to her. She doesn't want answers. She only wants to ask questions. And she was there for me, so the least I can do is sit with her.

I glance over at her lips forming words I cannot hear. Just watching them move as her tongue dances methodically from top to bottom. I like Mary. She's been through hell. In fact, Crazy Mary never had a chance in life.

"Mary?"

She stops as if to say, "Hey, you were just supposed to listen."

"Can you get AIDS from a blow job?"

A beat. Everything—from noise, to time—seems to be right there in that beat. We hold each other without arms—warriors, survivors, two people who never asked for what we got. I love her.

"No!"

Crazy Mary stands without emotion and takes my hand. I don't speak. I don't throw away my tray of half-eaten food. Somehow my body instinctually follows her to the bathroom. It's vacant. *Click.* She secures the door so nobody will enter. I look up at the same pipe Doc tried to hang himself on.

Twenty minutes later, I turn off the shower. Crazy Mary slips out without a word. The warmth of the water helps me deal with the loss of my medication. I wasn't prepared to take a shower, so I use my bathrobe to blot myself dry. My head becomes fuzzy and small specks of darkness dance in my vision. I lower the toilet seat to sit on and gather my thoughts. The backs of my upper thighs hurt as they meet the cold plastic. The muscles are tight balls, hollering for me to get them some heroin. I move my ass onto the edge of the toilet seat to remove pressure and the discomfort.

I can't help but drift back and recall how I first learned to sit in a chair to take away pain. My eyes close and I flinch as the skin on my back meets the cold ceramic tile. Suddenly, it is as if I'm watching a movie of myself on my eyelids. I can see Billy Burns and me cutting through St. Patrick's School parking lot.

We were on our way home from a YMCA dance in downtown Lowell. I was sixteen. It was blistering hot. Jim Higgins sat outside the green utility doors trying to stay cool. He'd been the janitor at St. Patrick's for almost thirty years. A brain injury left him nearly retarded, but the Sisters of Notre

Dame felt badly for him. He told me how he remembered my dad and uncles when they attended St. Patrick's.

Billy had to piss and Jim allowed us upstairs to use the first-floor bathrooms. We were alone. The corridor lights were off. Billy led the way to the men's room. We were inside now and the moonlight slithering through the windows changed everything grayish-white. I couldn't piss even as I heard Billy's stream hitting the urinal. I'm not sure why he did it, but after Billy finished he jammed one of the white, round urinal pucks into the toilet and flushed. And without a word between us, we walked back outside. Jim's chair was empty and he was nowhere in sight. Together we continued our journey home across the North Common.

Outside my house, Billy just disappeared. Everybody inside was asleep. I lay down on my bed and watched the moon glow illuminate my Notre Dame poster on the far wall. Then I heard a car stop outside in front of my house. Men talking, confusion, something is wrong. I hit the floor and crawled to the bottom of the window. It was the Lowell Police. At the front door, I tried hard to convince the officers they had the wrong house. But the commotion woke up my parents, and soon after the cops followed them into the kitchen. My dad placed me in the walk-in closet under the stairs. Solid darkness. I squeezed my eyes tight trying to convince myself that it was my decision to look at the blackness.

My ears focused. I heard the fat, older cop telling my dad that somebody broke into St. Patrick's School, kicked in the pipes, and water flooded the entire basement. The voice of the other policeman says the damage is in the thousands and Billy Burns has admitted I was there. My ass started to tingle with the anticipation of Dad's leather belt. It was a special belt. The buckle had been removed and stitched together neatly at the end. The belt had been given to him by his father and crossed the Atlantic from Ireland. Dad called the belt God's punishment. Said I had to take it like a man. Five lashes; he called them "zebra stripes." But Dad was smart. He never hit me on the fleshy part of my ass. Instead, the lashes cut their red stripes on the back of my legs, right below my ass. Dad said that would make it possible to still be able to sit on the edge of my seat in school without the teachers wondering or finding out about his "zebra stripes." Dad reasoned that by sitting on the edge and naturally leaning forward, they would only think I was anxious to learn.

I heard Mom crying when the fat, ugly cop suggested I be taken to a juvenile detention center. He said either I learn a lesson now or learn it when it's too late and I go to what he calls "the big school." I guess he meant prison. There was a lot of whispering, and I followed the steps of several people from the kitchen, past the closet door I'm in, more whispers, and the front door closing sharply.

I was completely focused on the darkness. I tightened my eyelids in a last-ditch effort to save my ass. But I clearly understood that the wrath of God himself was upon me. The door creaked open as light stole away the darkness. I could only peek. The way Dad curled his lips into a tiny circle, I understood he was looking for revenge. Then I'm out of the closet and heading for the stairs. Mom has vanished.

I walked slowly up the stairs. Twelve of them, a picture of Christ at the sixth, His heart glowing red with fire. I wonder how He felt walking up Calgary. Dad stood by my bed, belt in hand, waiting, fuming.

"No, Dad, please. Let's talk about it."

"Bend over; take it like a man."

"Please, Dad. I didn't mean it."

"Over!" he screamed.

"Daddy, one more chance. I promise I'll be a good boy."

I bent over slowly, stammering and whimpering, hoping he would stop and remember I'm sixteen, or remember I'm his son. But he didn't. My eyes focused on the star of my red Converse sneaker sticking out from under my bed. The ones Dad bought me for my last birthday. At the same time I tightened every muscle in my body, waiting. The shadow of his thick arm rose over me. I closed my eyes and the first thing I heard was a mad rush of air. My ears tingled and burned red at the tips. And then a mighty clap engulfed the room a split second before the rip and sting of my flesh hurt all the way to my ankles. I didn't dare fall over or my face and back might get it, too. One, two, three; Dad dug in. He swung harder each time, and then harder still. Each and every time, more than five, I stopped counting; Dad nailed the target, the back of my thighs. It pierced like hot razors slashing my skin. The louder I cried and pleaded, the harder he swung.

"Dad, please!" I jumped up and down wailing and thrashing. "Daddy, please stop, I promise. Please, one more chance."

Every time the leather made contact with my flesh a loud clap signaled that another was shortly behind. Each connection seemed to flush out the years of anger and frustration hidden in Dad's bones. He kept on flailing with his whip until I fell over onto my face howling for mercy. "Daddy, Daddy, Daddy."

I thought, Why won't Mom stop him? Why won't she scream, "You're killing him!" Foam oozed from the left corner of Dad's mouth. His eyes bugged out, and his neck was pink and pulsing. Behind Dad, on my wall, is a poster he'd given me after our football team won the city championship last season. NOTRE DAME OR BUST. He noticed me looking, spun around, read it, and that was the only thing that saved me. Not Mom, not the police, but Notre Dame.

"Now get the fuck out of here!" he yelled. "You're scum."

"Yes, Dad." I answered only because I had to.

"Look what you've done to my reputation, to the Farrell name."

Somebody abruptly attempts to turn the doorknob and push the bathroom door open at the same time. Dazed, I stand but don't respond. Whoever it is figures it's occupied and walks away mumbling something under their breath.

Back inside my room, Crazy Mary is waiting for me on my bed. She's reading a magazine about Notre Dame football my brother, Sean, sent me. At first, I worry about her feeling attached but quickly realize life in here is limited to eight days; nothing lasts beyond that. She doesn't even look up as I drop my bathrobe and head to my footlocker naked.

Downtown Rolly Brown snores deeply in the cot tucked neatly between two footlockers in the rear of the ward. The blanket over his head hides him from Crazy Mary. She doesn't like him but refuses to tell me why. Probably has something to do with high school. Rolly told me once he met her there. Supposedly, she was a star athlete, a tomboy, and was voted the most attractive in her class. She starts to ask me questions about Notre Dame football and what it was like to play there. I don't want to talk about it because I never did and I'm tired of lying. Rolly rips a monster fart and begins to giggle. Crazy

Mary laughs until she figures out it's Rolly. Her anger saves me from more lies; she whips the magazine at his head, gives me a "how dare you" glance, and storms out of the room.

Rolly sits up, focuses, and rips another fart. His complexion has improved. The greenness is now yellow-gray. The dimples shine on his face after he confirms who I am.

I jump up on my bed and pivot my hips so my pecker swings in a circle. Rolly looks away and shakes his head as if to say, same old Richie Farrell.

"Downtown Rolly Brown"; I raise my head to the ceiling and let the words roll off my tongue. "Mary Hart cannot wait to hear what you been doin'."

Chapter 10 ....

Day Three: Afternoon

It's Crazy Mary who sets me straight. "Push-ups!" she says. "Play the game if you want anything in here," she reminds me. She's right. I take her advice. About forty-five minutes before dinner, Mrs. Kay will take our vitals again. My goal is to earn another chance to increase my dose of Librium. If I can do enough push-ups to get my heart rate through the roof I'll get three pills. It won't do me like heroin, but right now I'll do anything to switch off this shrieking, inaudible pulsating in my forehead.

It's time. Mrs. Kay will start taking blood pressure and pulse and reassess the medication. Everybody is in the lounge waiting to be called in numerical order. I'm in bed 8. The trick is to time it right. Mary sits next to me and gives me a slap on the knee. I head for the cover of the pool table as soon as I hear orderly John call number 7. I drop to my knees and frantically start to do push-ups. Crazy Mary is my lookout. My arms tremble but I push on. Years ago I could bang out a hundred and loved the pump I'd feel in my chest and triceps. Today my shoulders hurt and my fingers begin to cramp. I use my football training to go on. Dad told me never to concentrate on the pain. He said pain was only fear leaving the body. I keep my eyes on the prize: Libriums. Crazy Mary coughs but I'm too focused; I never consider it a signal or warning.

Soft laughter slows me down. I lift my head and refocus on everybody watching. But some are looking past me, directly at the back door out of the lounge. Heat begins to rise in my neck. This isn't good. I look to Mary but she won't even meet my eyes. In a flash, I catapult to my feet and spin around. It's too late. Orderly John has walked in the back door from the kitchen. I don't know how long he's been watching. The bastard never stopped me. He's been there long enough to send for Mrs. Kay. Her presence overtakes the audience. John looks pleased. Murph smiles, as if to say, "You tried, man."

"John, bring Mr. Farrell to the isolation room," Mrs. Kay orders.

"No, no, you cannot take me off everything! I'll lose it! I'll die!"

John moves toward me and slowly reaches out to secure my left arm. I resist. The isolation room directly across from the front desk is used for only two things: for patients so physically sick they need constant medical attention, or as a place they send troublemakers. Patients who are ordered to go cold-turkey have no medication to soften the physical effects of kicking alcohol or drug addiction. Zero. Nothing. Mrs. Kay said that is the reason for the large observation window. Since there are no heart monitors or adequate medical staff, the orderly stationed at the front desk will be able to react in time if a patient in the isolation room goes into cardiac arrest or has a seizure.

"Shake it out," she explains. "Every decision you make in here brings a consequence."

"I'm not fucking going!"

Murph steps in and leads me a few feet away from John and Mrs. Kay. He tries to reassure me it won't be that bad in isolation. Tells me that I'm in a fix and the rules of engagement are simple—you always accept the least amount of grief possible when your shit is against the wall. Explains to me I'm not gonna get any better than isolation out of this infraction. I got caught with my pants down and I just gotta suck it up. "Be a man," he says.

Reluctantly, John leads me by the front desk and past the observation window. Mrs. Kay lets Murph tag along in order to diffuse any violent reaction on my part. Inside feels like a fish tank. My first thought—no jerking off in here, everybody at the front desk could watch. The bed is high and centered. I sit on the edge of the bed and slide. Plastic sheets. Murph takes a seat on a small wooden chair beneath the window. John tells me to hang in there. I think he's beginning to like me. "It's for your own good," he says, leaving with Murph. I squish back into the plastic sheets and relax. Might as well, I'm here.

For my own good? Whenever my father said that to me, it usually meant the opposite. I still have this reoccurring nightmare about the day me and Artie Fossett were at the old YMCA lifting weights. The day Tommy Parks pranced into the room, grabbed a forty-pound weight, threw it against the wall, and announced to everybody that he was gonna kill me for taking Patty Kelly away from him.

Tommy was a crazy mother with quick hands and maniac strength. But I wasn't scared of nothing back then. And besides, I wasn't about to give up my French-kissing sessions with Patty every night at the Shed Park Field House.

Tommy's quick blue eyes were wide and violent. And for an instant, I almost blurted out a lie. I liked to lie back then. I wanted to tell Tommy that me and Patty had done all the bases and we were rounding third for home. But you know, somehow, no matter how much I wanted to say it, something told me to shut up.

"Meet me at Shed Park in an hour," Tommy challenged. "I'm gonna teach you a lesson about touching people's property."

"I'll be there, pimple nose," I said, real brave like.

What could I say? It was a matter of pride. Everybody would have called me a coward. What would Patty have said if I hadn't defended her honor and stood up to her ex-boyfriend? Besides, Tommy was such a fake.

Okay, well I spent the next half hour finishing my workout. No way was I gonna let anybody know I was scared, never mind even thinking about it. So I kept my best poker face until Artie spoke up and my stomach started with the somersaults.

"Nervous, Richie?"

"Nah!"

"Well, we better finish up if we're gonna make Shed Park! You know—we don't have to go."

"What you talkin' about?"

Artie was my best friend. He wasn't a fake at all. He lived right next door, a short little squirt with a dimple in the middle of his chin. All the girls loved him. But you know how best friends are—they always say what you're thinking.

"Well, you know, Tommy is one tough kid! I've seen

him kick ass. Mean it. These two kids from Tewksbury gave him a rash of bull one night at the drive-in. God; he booted the crap outta both of them. They were a hell of a lot bigger than him, too, Richie!"

Now, why did Artie have to tell me that?

"Yeah, well, we'll see," I said. "I'll kill him."

I remember looking at the clock in the YMCA lobby; I had fifteen minutes to get there, no car, and nobody to bum a ride from. We'd never make it by foot. And that's when Artie suggested we thumb.

This hippie kid gave us a ride almost all the way. I tried to talk him into going one more mile. Told him I had to be there early. Told him how important it was to have time to psych myself up. But he was high on some ragweed and only laughed.

We couldn't run the distance, because I'd be out of gas. Tommy would surely have killed me then. So, what did I do but stick out my thumb one more time. And you know, if I weren't so desperate, I would have seen Dad coming. I always watched for him.

"Jesus H. Christ!" Dad's voice appeared out of thin air.

Artie ran. Before I even opened the door handle, his back was nothing more than a blur.

"Dad, let's talk about it."

"Sure, we'll talk about it. Get in. Right now!"

Somehow, I knew the moment my ass hit the seat that most of the talking would be from his mouth, not mine.

Whack! Whack! Whack! Open hands bounced off the side of my face. My eyes filled from a quick shot to the bridge of the nose. Dad's speed and the sting of the slaps hurt, but if I covered up I knew his open hand would close.

"Dad, I was just going to the park. Right there." I pointed as we drove by the Field House.

Blood inside my mouth made everything warm. I saw Tommy standing there with ten or so of his friends. He was shadowboxing and I wished I could have gone just one round with him. I would have killed him. Knocked his head off. I was tough back then. But it had nothing to do with me. Dad taught me how to be tough. You see, if you could take Dad's punches, you could take anybody's.

Back at the house, things really went south. Dad told Mom to get out of the house; told her to take the car and not come back for an hour. You know, when Dad's eyes were berserk, you did what he said. No sense in asking why, 'cause the wrecking ball would take you down, too. Back then, it was like being in a war zone. Survival was your only thought; it was the only constant; it propelled you. I don't ever fault Mom for leaving that day; she was a victim and there ain't nothin' fake about being a victim.

Dad pulled the kitchen chair into the middle of the floor and ordered me to sit. I did. And even when he left for what seemed like fifteen minutes, I never thought about bolting. But I should have.

Finally, Dad came back up the stairs. In one hand, he had gray duct tape and his face wore an "I got you now" grin. And you know I was much more scared of Dad than I was of a dozen Tommy Parks.

"Lesson time. Put your hands down on the arm rest," he ordered.

Dad proceeded to tape my wrists tight as possible to each of the armrests. Then my ankles. Then my mouth and nose. I struggled to breathe. If he'd clamped or squeezed the tape down so it completely covered my nostrils I'm sure I'd have suffocated. He loved it. I'll never forget the sick, insane look in his eyes. Demonic almost, his eyes seemed to glow red in the very center.

"Now, let me show you what happens when the 'bogey-man' picks you up thumbing, Richie boy!"

I knew the crap was on the wall when Dad opened the second drawer below the sink. I knew my youth was over when he slowly pulled out Mom's new, double-blade, electric carving knife. I watched him, petrified, setting it up—lining up the two jagged edges, pushing the red button, and inserting the blades. My thoughts boiled when I saw him plug the cord in over the toaster. But I never flinched until I heard the sound of the blades humming in perfect formation. I squeezed my eyes tight, but the humming only penetrated deeper. The darker it got on the back of my eyelids, the faster the blades seemed to run.

It was the humming that I'll always remember.

I opened my eyes and saw Jesus watching from His cross on the kitchen wall. I can never recall any physical pain. It was the mental thing that's forever real for me. Dad standing there with his lips moving to a silent Hail Mary verse. He was saying the Rosary—his eyes, holding that knife, staring into the back of my brain. I just prayed for this lesson to end.

"Okay, Rich, now it's time for the jugular vein."

And that's when I started to cry. Dad saw my tears and turned the volume up on the Hail Marys. The Rosary turned into a chant. The louder I sobbed, the louder I heard—"Thy will be done."

When Dad put down the knife I thought Christ had saved me. But then Dad took the duct tape and completely covered my eyes. Nothing but gray.

I remember hearing the knife click on. But I didn't panic. I actually felt peaceful all over; kinda like the way I always did after a good cry. The sound got louder. I sensed the dead space between the knife and my neck getting smaller. I started laughing and crying hysterically, right through the tape forcing my mouth closed. A warm tingle raced down my legs as piss pooled in my sneakers. The cold steel touched my neck right below my Adam's apple. It was a trick. Dad had touched my throat with the dull side of the blade.

I collapsed into a glob of jelly in the chair. Dad tore the duct tape off my ankles and wrists, eyes, and nose as if he was trying not to rip away my skin. He picked me up and cradled me like a baby. I felt his rock-hard biceps cut into my sides. He said I was safe. Asked me to breathe; it was all over. He said, "You're too young to understand. But I did this for your own good. This will protect you. Believe me. If a bad guy had picked you up he'd cut you in two pieces. Someday you'll understand—it's for your own good."

He went on and on about how much he loved me. He said he'd cut off his right arm for my bother Sean and me. I cried when he told me that it takes the highest form of love to administer torture to a loved one like he had just done to me.

My mom's arms wrapped around me as she appeared out of nowhere and dropped to her knees, her head pressed sobbing into my chest. Over and over she whispered, "I'm sorry." She'd stayed in the house trying to muster the courage to stop him. I found the bat she was going to hit him with leaning against the walk-in closet door at the bottom of the stairs. After Dad left to work out at the YMCA, Mom made me promise never to tell the story to anybody. She begged me. At first, I didn't answer her. Something changed inside of me that day and it certainly wasn't for my own good. But I loved her, she was my mom, so I promised. I guess some truths can never be told.

By nightfall in isolation, I've lost two pounds in sweat. I'm having chest pains, an anxiety attack. Impending doom. Cold sweat. Shortness of breath. The door is locked. I have to knock on the window to use the bathroom.

I'm shaky. My legs are Jell-O. John allows Murph to help me out of isolation and down the corridor. Crazy Mary blows me a kiss from the dayroom. She is sad and mouths the word "sorry." I know it is not her fault. Her plan would have worked if I hadn't been caught doing push-ups. Murph hooks his right arm under my left shoulder and supports my lower back as I step one foot after the other. It's all I can do to squeeze my butt cheeks tight. If I even fart—my insides will pour out. Murph talks to me about tough times and how they make tough people. I half listen to a story about his company being pinned down for days by the Viet Cong in the Quang Ngai Province, how some kids panicked and died and how others became men. After, he sits me on the edge of my bed and tells he'll be back to get me for morning group therapy session.

I manage to ask him to let me be if I'm sleeping when he comes to get me. He says Mary Hart will never allow me to sleep through her groups. She has principles. But I'm not sure if Mrs. Kay will allow me to leave. If my vitals are poor, maybe she'll give me a few Libriums.

Chapter 11

Day Four: Morning Therapy

Mary Hart wants us to talk about something good in our lives. Hope, she calls it. But she ain't got a clue. There are twenty-two of us today. And that is the one thing we all have in common—hopelessness. We're all fucked. Each and every one of us is living proof that the world doesn't even know we exist.

Murph talks about his granddaughter. It is the one thing he regrets most in his life. How Vietnam took away his children. His voice cracks when he describes the second chance he has now with his daughter's daughter. But he can't seem to control the booze. He loves the kid. "But the eyes still chase me," he says. Hart jumps in to ask him to explain. Murph doesn't miss a beat. Fuck Hart. What does she know about eyes chasing you all day long? "I see the faces of every kid I ever killed. I watch them die over and over," Murph tells the group. Something in his face changes. The lines of his body, once relaxed, now are tight and rigid. He tells the group his time at the detox is running out. How he'd rather stay because it is safe here.

"I belong here," he says, "but out there things don't feel right. I'm so afraid I'll fuck up my granddaughter like I fucked up my own daughter."

Murph lowers his head and leans forward in his chair. Funny thing about detox, we all feel safe inside these walls. It is like being granted a stay of execution, but only for eight days. Inside here we have this phenomenon. Patients begin to get antsy around day five or six. And then on either day seven or right before they leave some type of drama goes down. Several patients get depressed and have a meltdown, but most seem to randomly divulge information—to the group, to Mrs. Kay, to the orderlies—they've wanted to abandon for months or even years.

Crazy Mary hops into the mix. She senses Murph needs help and begins to tell Hart about her first hit of crack the day she takes the streets back. I notice Crazy Mary's eyes are void of all matter. Nobody is home. Her soul is gone. I love her now even more. She's picked a sore under her right ear the size of a quarter. It oozes watery blood. But she's still beautiful. Occasionally, as she preaches on, she wipes it clean with a wad of balled up tissues in her left palm.

Other patients I don't know ramble on about nothing. This new kid with a ponytail and long horse face rambles on about how he played drums for the Boston-based rock band, the Cars. Most in the circle are mesmerized as he plays the air drums and at the same time talks about why the lead guitarist didn't like him. Says he slept with the guy's wife. Tells us the band members were all jealous because he was the one who always snagged the pussy. He's fuckin' lying.

When I was eighteen, I dated a girl who was best friends with the lead singer of the Cars. Every time they played at the Rats Keller in Boston we went and partied with them. I personally knew every member of the band. I think about calling him out. But I don't have the energy. Besides, not one person in this fucking hell hole speaks the truth. Junkies and alcoholics are so used to lying on command. They make up things even when they do not have to.

Without a doubt, that is the number one reason I don't want to know everybody. I don't give a flying fuck about the others. They are weak. They wouldn't know a hard time if it shit on their head. Like the girl with the hair braid who talks about her cat dying of leukemia. I contemplate screaming out, "It's a fuckin' cat, asshole; buy a dildo and get over it." Or the big French kid with the monster hair crying about his wife deciding she is gay and leaving him for another girl. Fuckin' grow up, asshole. Tough shit, your wife went from the pole to the hole. There's another bus coming in ten minutes and another one ten minutes after that. In other words, find another woman. The majority of them don't chow on pussy. But mostly I don't wanna know them because the past they speak of is irrelevant to me. And nobody—Hart or any of the other patients—disputes anything.

"This is bullshit!" I yell out. "It's all lies."

"Mr. Farrell, this group is not about truth or fact, but rather about getting people talking." Hart corrects me harshly.

"These people wouldn't know the truth if it was a twenty-pound bag of wet shit and it hit them right under the nose. I refuse to talk bullshit."

Hart says she'll come back to me—it is mandatory. That's her mantra: "It's mandatory." She recited it to me ten times this morning after I refused to get out of bed for Murph. Mrs. Kay told her my vitals weren't high enough for Libriums and the more I sat up the better off I'd be.

I'm dope-sick. Straight liquid diarrhea. Maybe I should shit myself and show all these assholes the truth. Knots in my leg muscles. I crave heroin. Hopeless. I wanna ask Murph: "If war is hell, then what is this?" The mouth of my black smiley-face, orange, foam, one-size-fits-all slippers suddenly starts speaking to me. My father appears, laughing at me. "I told you so," he says. "Loser. Good for nothing. Cripple."

A new patient arrives. The kid's Italian, maybe twenty-four, square jaw, with a stocky, confined body. He dominates. Hart lets him. Fuckin' A, now Mrs. Hart might forget about me. Murph shoots me a glance, rolls his eyes: bullshit has a way of finding its way to the surface. I watch the Italian kid's mouth. He enunciates each word. The lip movement is not in sync with his audio. I immediately nickname him Asshole Mouth.

You give everybody names in here, except Murph; every detox has a guy without a nickname. Asshole Mouth removes his smiley-face slippers and exposes a tattoo with a number on the heel of his left foot. Tells the group he hopes for his own death. Sold his body to Harvard Medical School for $10,000. Blew the money on a girl he loved. Took her to Las Vegas. She dumped him for a dealer. Caught them fucking in the room he spent $300 a night on. There were mirrors on the ceiling over the bed. He says he cannot look into mirrors now. Sees his love sucking some guy's cock every time he does.

Mary wants to know if the ceiling mirrors are the reason why the room was so expensive. Asshole Mouth freezes.

Murph and I tense up. If he says anything to Mary we're on him. But instead he goes on. Tried to kill himself, drank two bottles of Southern Comfort in under five minutes. I don't believe him. He'd be dead. Another example of a fuckin' hero sounding off, truly a legend in his own mind. Murph begins to fidget. Hart interrupts and says it's my turn.

I refuse again.

I'll talk to Levine but not to these people. It's so boring making up stuff. It's never gonna change a lick of anything in my life. Done is done, man. You gotta suck it up and go on from here. My father always said talk is cheap. Action is the only thing that matters in this life.

But Hart makes a stand. It is a showdown. Murph feels bad for me and tries to take my place and go again. No go. Asshole Mouth laughs; tells me it will help me get sober— to be honest. I put my head as deep as I can into my lap. If only I could suck myself off. I'm angry and frustrated. If I look over at Asshole Mouth, for an instant I consider getting up and shutting him down with a forearm to the side of his temple.

"Say something," Mrs. Hart demands. "Anything."

The silence is thick. She pitches the reason for group therapy to all but only looks at me. I cannot hear; the audio has gone off inside my brain. Her lips move and I miss a long block of nothingness. She comes back on and says the others will learn. She cuts to the chase and ask me if I have anything to teach "my friends."

Out of nowhere a mosquito lands on my forearm. *Whack.* I've got it. I'll share the "Skeeter Song" I learned at Camp Alexander in Pelham, New Hampshire, as a teenager.

Hart realizes something is up. She shifts. The plastic chair cushion squeals as her ass slides awkwardly back and forth. Murph's face sparkles. He's been here before. Lucy sits up straight and winks.

"Okay, I'm gonna teach everybody a song."

"This better not equal mockery, Mr. Farrell," Hart chimes in.

"It's legit as hell. I was taught it by a camp counselor at camp when I was a young kid."

"Sing it," Asshole Mouth demands.

I sigh deeply. I wanna go over and slam his forehead into the armrest, snap his neck, and take a crap down his throat. But I stop when it becomes apparent my song is far more important than shitting up Asshole Mouth's neck.

"It's easy. Just three words. I mean what you guys sing, the chorus is just three words. And it won't work unless everybody sings."

"Why don't you stand up and lead us, Mr. Farrell," Mrs. Hart says sarcastically.

She thinks I'm embarrassed. She thinks standing will kill my will. She thinks if she puts me in the spotlight I'll fold because I refused to speak. For some reason, she thinks I'm afraid. But she fuckin' loses big time.

I leap to my feet and clear my throat in one steady motion. Without hesitation, I take a position in the middle of the dayroom, surrounded by a sea of pin-striped bathrobes. The two front doors are closed, but thick-paned windows in the tops allow me a clear view of the front desk. I glance over at the pool table and the rear door into the kitchen. Both are secure. Sometimes an orderly will sit on the pool table if the drama inside the circle of patients becomes too intense.

"Ready, comrades? The chorus is "Whack it off" and it gotta be loud. When I signal, you guys jump in. Got it?!"

Muph and Crazy Mary have got it. Murph nods up and down. Crazy Mary winks. And even Mrs. Hart knows she's about to be fucked.

"Ready?"

"Yeah," several patients scream out.

I fuckin' love this—total control of a bunch of misfits, losers, liars, and criminals. It just doesn't get any better.

"There is a skeeter on my peter, whack it off."

I flash the signal!

"Whack it off!" several yell.

"There is a skeeter on my peter, whack it off."

"Whack it off!"

Everybody is in. The place begins to rock.

"There is a skeeter on my peter, whack it off."

"Whack it off!"

Mrs. Hart stands up and yells something but nobody can hear her. Her eyes look like tiny slits in a blanket.

"There is a dozen on my cousin, I can hear the bastards buzzin'. There is a skeeter on my peter, whack it off!"

"Whack it off!"

Rock on, man, rock on. This is the best I've felt in years. Right now, the whole world can go fuck themselves. I'm busy getting even.

"One more time!"

Mrs. Hart bolts for the front desk. When she leaves the room, Murph follows her and starts barricading the front doors with an old couch and coffee tables pushed aside at the beginning of group in order to form a therapy circle. Murph, Crazy Mary, and I slide the pool table against the back door. Lowell Detox has been commandeered.

There is a skeeter on my peter. Whack it off!

Whack it off!

There is a dozen on my cousin; I can hear the bastards buzzin'. Whack it off!

Whack it off!

Ten minutes later, we are fully in charge. Most of the patients are standing now, in the dead center of the dayroom. Several are standing on their chairs. Downtown Rolly Brown has gone off by himself, pulled up a chair directly under the TV mounted on the far wall, and blazes the volume. The drummer boy stands on top of the pool table and plays whip-out into the air. And all Mrs. Kay, John, and Mrs. Hart can do is stare through the glass. Then Levine arrives and asks to speak with me. The two doors are hinged on the sides. There is a half-inch gap in the middle where we can talk. Most everybody trusts him. He convinces us Mrs. Kay will call the police if we don't open the door. Murph whispers in my ear, "Let the cops come."

But Levine is right. We win if we end it now. If the cops come everything we accomplished gets written off. I make a concession to Levine. Murph smiles and goes along. I almost catch Levine smirking. One more time we feel the power.

"There is a skeeter on my peter. Whack it off!"

"Whack it off!"

"There is a dozen on my cousin; I can hear the bastards buzzin'. Whack it off!"

"Whack it off!"

I'm shown the way back to the isolation room and the others are all sent to their beds. No Librium for anybody. Teach us a lesson. About an hour later, John brings me lunch. The instant he opens the door, a verse of the skeeter song follows him in. Murph is still at it from the ward.

My father would be damn proud if he could witness this.

He always said I was better when the odds were stacked against me. Probably he'd make some lame comment associating my rebellion to the Acre. Or even more asinine, equate it to my Irish heritage. I sit comfortably into my chair and flash back to the last time I ever saw my dad. All these movies rush in my head; I see him dead. But not dead on the floor, I mean dead dead at O'Donnell's Funeral Home. The memory of seeing him naked and helpless on that cold metal gurney fucks with my mind a minimum of once a day.

I had to meet Dad's sister Teresa at O'Donnell's Funeral Home at 9 a.m. to make the arrangements. The morning was fiery in a glorious way. The old mill buildings in the city looked like paper silhouettes being sucked up into the sun.

O'Donnell's is a short walk from the place Dad and I went for our daily "heel and toe" walk in the North Common.

We'd walk the cement path cut through the middle of the common. I hated it and tried to walk on the edge of the grass. My gait was so awkward it forced my shoes to make sharp slapping sounds against the concrete. Pain burned a line up the back of my right calf. My muscles twisted and stretched like twisted elastic about to let go. The old-timers Dad and I passed sitting on the benches never looked up at my face. And the laughter from the older boys playing basketball always cut into and penetrated Dad's cadence. Dad was blind to it. All he envisioned was me normal.

"Heel and toe! Step out, Richard! Heel and toe!"

"I can't, Daddy!"

"Are you a Farrell or a little whiny baby?"

"I'll try, Daddy."

"Pay attention. Heel first, roll to your toe. Don't drag your foot. Pick it up. Stretch those muscles or they'll die."

I didn't want them to die and I was too embarrassed to cry in front of all the old gawking Irish. I couldn't wait to get home, close the door to my room, and pretend I was a hero running-back for the Green Bay Packers.

"Let's rest a minute, Daddy."

"You have to push on. Discipline. You have to make those muscles work. We're almost there."

"But it burns, Daddy. If I stop for a second I can make it to that big white house up there."

O'Donnell's was at the top of the cement pathway. It marked the end of the slapping claps announcing to everybody that I was different. I couldn't wait to see the structure grow larger and take up all of my eye space. It was the end of being a cripple for the day.

The gray, slate roof overlapped the grounds and white angels concealed themselves safely at all four corners. Dad told me those angels escorted you right to God's throne. At night, their silent wings hidden under the roof looked like white puffs and organ music appeared as if it were emanating from the angels. When the moon was just right, O'Donnell's resembled a giant bald eagle standing guard—ready to pounce on any foe of the Acre's Irish.

That day, the walk seemed much shorter. I had to shoot a bag before I met up with my aunt Teresa at O'Donnell's Funeral Home. She was my favorite aunt, but I couldn't be straight and speak about Dad yet. I was early and Jimmy O'Donnell's son Jim greeted me at the side door and does the phony "I'm so sorry" routine. I'd gone to school with him for a year at Pike in Andover. He had a big head like his father.

"I know you're sorry, Jim. But where's the bathroom?"
I could never figure out why, but in a strange way, I always
liked the bastard. He was six feet four inches with this little white pencil-neck—you figure it out.

Inside the bathroom, the search for a good vein was easy.
Funny, it had only been three days since McGinn shot a bag
into my shoulder. Today, all my fear about stickin' myself was
gone. The first rush gave me a hard-on. I had to wait a few
minutes for it to go down. I didn't want Jim to get any
wrong ideas.

Teresa was waiting for me in the office. She looked sim-
ilar to all the Farrell women—thick boned, weathered jaw,
and brilliant ivory-pink skin. But she had a spirit that always
calmed everybody. Dad said she was once a nun. She left
the convent to take care of her dying mother. But I knew
deep down, she left because it was all fake. She couldn't pretend anymore, all that Catholic stuff.

How the hell did God expect healthy humans not to
have an orgasm? Dad called masturbation "beating the bishop."
I know it had to be the Catholics that invented the rule
about no orgasms for nuns, priests, and unwed kids. Because
God doesn't torture people like that.

"Richard, your father would want you to pick his coffin," Teresa whispered.

"You can pick your friends. You can pick your nose. But
you can't pick your father's nose."

The heroin jumped my humor right over her head.

"I have to tell you about the night I found him, Teresa."

Suddenly, the space between Teresa and Jim O'Donnell
began to close. Teresa stole a glance at Jim and shook her
head once. And right then, I saw Dad's genes in the brilliant
slide of her jaw.

My heart was in my head. Dad was here.

"This is bullshit. I wanna see my dad now."

"Let's pray, Richard," Teresa said.

"Jim, one second, Teresa, bring me Dad's body."

Teresa's neck turned as red as her scarf. She squeezed my hand slightly. Jim wanted to say no but didn't have the balls.

"Bring me his body!" I repeated with more vigor.

Jim squirted out of the room and Teresa guided me to a small office with yellow floral wallpaper. The walls were loaded with instructions for insurance payments. Deposits were required. A sign gave notification of procedures to follow—a video presentation, a tour of the coffin showcase, and setting dates for the last time we spoke of Dad in public places.

"Can I say a prayer?" Teresa asked.

Teresa was faithful. The Acre had taught her well. Pray. God can get you through anything. My dad fed that crap to me with a snow shovel. But there was a difference—she believed it. Dad was just doin' it in case it was the truth. 'Cause for Dad there were no truths other than the truths he invented.

One of the wheels squealed and Teresa prayed louder. Dad was coming. It didn't sound like fingernails against a blackboard. Right now it was only noise that sounded more like my mother's old sewing machine's foot pedals.

It was the perfect trumpet for Dad's arrival. But the peculiar thing was, even though he had no power over me anymore, I felt the same way I did when Sean and I were kids playing Ping-Pong and we'd hear the hum of the electric garage door opener warning us of Dad's presence. Everything would change right there and then. Sean would stop kidding and I would stay alert to all the possibilities.

The wheels skidded on the red-carpeted hallway. Dad was here. Jim O'Donnell was in white and I couldn't see Teresa's eyelids. She held her rosary beads and her lips danced with Hail Marys.

"Daddy!"

I stood and went to him. I'll never forget that lifelessness. A white sheet covered everything but his head. The guy who'd beat and loved me more than anybody ever could— was nothing. I wasn't scared of him anymore. For the first time in my life, I had power over him. It may sound odd, but I was reveling in his dead body. He couldn't hurt me lying there. I had life and he was nowhere to be found, big tough bastard gone at fifty-three. I wanted Dad to get up and stop faking, but it was over. It was all over.

There wasn't a hint of color. The sheet, his hair, and his face were as white as fresh fallen snow. His lips were clear, transparent as the glue that kept them closed. And Dad's earlobes were shapeless.

Jim stepped away as I bent low to kiss him.

"Fuck with me now, asshole!" I whispered in his ear so Teresa couldn't hear. "Beat Mom now, you prick! Come on, get up off that gurney and let's see who's tough now!"

I watched Jim O'Donnell wheel him out of sight. Teresa stood next to me, supporting herself with my forearm. The slant of the morning sun angled down off the paneled walls. The remnants of cigarette smoke painted yellowish-brown streaks on the Madonna painting hanging over the front exit. The parlor filled with hazy light from the big picture window.

Everything in the room turned into a brilliant, fake fog brought on by the heroin. The people who entered here gave up their bodies. But in the mirrors across the room you could almost see the demons through the fog. Souls who had wronged one another were brought together in this room. This was the place devastated children discovered their mothers and fathers. Dad was free and his demons were mine.

"Sir? Miss? I have to show you this short video required by the State of Massachusetts," said a young female voice.

I never looked at her. Just sat down and watched her sleek fingers play with the tape and buttons on the television. It must have been the heroin; unlike a lot of people it made me hard. I started to think about sex and the length of her fingers. I wanted to orgasm. I wanted all this pain to explode outside of me. Teresa watched as a middle-aged man in a gray polyester suit spoke of encasements. I heard him say for three hundred dollars we could buy reinforced cement guaranteed for life. I watched Teresa say the Rosary as I listened to the sales pitch.

"Is God real?" I asked her.

"More real than you and I," she never hesitated.

"You mean I'm fake and He's real?"

"Richard, one day my father sat all seven of us kids down on the couch. He told us all to remember one thing. He said there are only two things in life that are real. The first is God and the second is the Acre."

"But what about Dad? He believed. He went to Mass and Communion every day. Why did he come home and beat me and Mom?"

"One thing I know. God will bring you through anything."

"Was God helping Dad in his life?" I asked her.

She nodded.

"Well, screw Him. 'Cause if God helped Dad, then God helped Dad beat me and Mom."

I'd hurt her. She lowered her head. Some things with God you never spoke of.

It was time to purchase Dad's coffin. The young girl with the long fingers escorted me toward the stairway. Teresa wanted to stay. Her hip was bothering her. But I wanted to talk more about this God she and Dad believed in. I wanted to tell her how unfairly God had treated Job. Test, my ass. That was more like torture. The Viet Cong were nicer to our prisoners of war in Vietnam.

"Take your time. If you have any questions, I'll be sitting at the end," said the young girl.

"Do you think God's a fake?" I asked her.

"Pardon me?"

"Forget it."

I wanted to tell her how the Bible had to be fake. How it contradicted itself. How God played favorites and wasn't fair. But she was a fake like the rest of them. Besides, clueless people don't get it no matter how you explain. Heroin was beginning to win. The coffins all merged into one big blur. The music lost its bass and the walls began to beat. The young girl's face was sleek like her fingers. Her lips were black. An oversized top hat swallowed her head. Each coffin had its own story. Most were lined with colorful velour. Some were padded thicker than others. One had nice cherry wood that gleamed like freshly polished chrome.

"Dad. Dad. I love you!"

She heard me. And I didn't care. I could see him underground. The lid sealed tightly, his eyes open and staring into the dead darkness. I saw him standing beside me. He was cradling a football against his stomach. I could see his scapular hanging outside his black sweatshirt. It held the heart of Christ and was the same one that protected him as he lay dying, wounded in Korea. I saw his flattop hair move as he smiled and called my name.

"You're the best," he said. "I love you, Richard. I'd cut my right arm off for you."

"Are you all right?" Teresa asked.

"I'll take the best one, this one right here, the cherry model. See how it shines, Teresa?"

The sign on the wall spoke of payment. But expense never entered into any part of my decision on what type of casket to purchase. It was Dad's money paying for it, and I couldn't focus. Teresa merged into the young girl and the top hat she'd been wearing seemed to grow.

"How would you like to pay? Mr. O'Donnell said we can wait for the insurance policy if you'd like."

"You either pay getting on, or you pay getting off. That's what my dad always preached."

The young lady's confused face suddenly came into focus. Her nose and chin protruded sharply out over her thin shoelace lips. Teresa nodded. She took my hand and led me upstairs. The young lady froze, wondering what option of payment she'd tell Jimmy O'Donnell we chose.

"Dad is gonna pay getting off."

"What do you mean, Richard?"

"Everybody pays, Teresa. Everybody."

Mom and I knew the secret. For as long as I can remember, Dad pulled his father's wake pictures out of the closet on the anniversary of my grandfather's death. I'd never met him. He died of a heart attack while my dad was in the army fighting in Korea. A Catholic priest found Dad in a foxhole and asked him if he was a man. The priest told him his father had died. Said they buried him six weeks earlier. The family took pictures so Dad could have some type of closure. But my dad hated to hold the last memory of the man he loved in a box, with a flag and no life. He'd cry and demand Mom never to allow his casket to be opened. Dad's last will and testament specified details of a closed casket. Dad was so fake; I think he didn't want people seeing him for what he really was. He'd seen death. He knew how he'd look in that box. But tomorrow, at the wake, the casket would be opened. Mom and I had hidden his will.

Now, getting revenge on a dead body in a casket might not sound like a significant form of retribution, but for me and Mom, the glimmer of hope that Dad's spirit might be looking down on us, watching, gave us enormous satisfaction. Nobody knew but us.

Like I told Teresa, Dad's gonna pay getting off.

Crazy Mary startles me with a soft continuous knock on the observation window. She blows me a kiss as her eyes hunt for Mrs. Kay. She fails to see the orderly watching her from inside at the front desk. I can't make out which orderly it is. He's standing deep within the rear of the office. I signal "no" by moving my eyes; she gets it immediately and moves out of my vision in a heartbeat.

Day Five: High Noon

I refuse lunch in my room. Mrs. Kay instructs the orderly John Hardy to force me to eat. She tells him to make sure I understand food is my quickest road to recovery. I sit up as if I'm going to cooperate, pretend I'm attempting to feebly slide the tray closer to me for easier consumption, eye the circular barrel near my nightstand, and in one motion dump the entire contents inside the barrel. Hardy is paralyzed with disbelief and scampers out of the room. I smile because he surely won't tell Mrs. Kay. She'll blame him for not doing his job, paying closer attention to me.

I like to be alone. The fish tank feel of the isolation room has worn off. It no longer bothers me that the observation window allows my entire world to be on display for everybody in the vicinity of the front desk. Other than not being able to jerk myself off to sleep, the solitude is helping me remember the stuff I choose to forget.

Mrs. Kay fights to keep me in isolation. Dr. Levine pulls rank. He informs her nicely about his responsibility to evaluate my mental stability. She's old school; thinks being alone will be good punishment for what she calls my act of civil disobedience. She's so far off the mark. It completely eluded her as to why I did what I did. I wasn't being disobedient; I was lashing out because no-one tells the truth in here and not a single soul calls anybody on it. And, boy, did she have the isolation bit fuckin' wrong. People kill themselves when they're alone. And I bet it stems directly from all the shame and guilt from the past.

Two orderlies I've never seen attempt to escort me to Levine's office. New guys to the job, young kids who look petrified of the unknown. They explain how I'll have to wait until he is finished with an intake on a female inmate. I fuck with them, refuse to walk without getting a pair of new slippers. Both my big toes are popping through the foam. They drag me, backward, each hooking an arm under my arms.

The orderly with a broken front tooth opens Levine's door and together they guide me inside without stepping in themselves. I throw my hands in the air and say, "Welcome to my nightmare." The other orderly with the long black ponytail tries to shut the door quickly. I stick my foot out to block it from closing and startle both of them. They hesitate. "Don't you guys listen to Alice Cooper," I ask. They nod in confirmation but close the door without a word.

I'm alone again, sitting, waiting. I can't stop the fucking runaway train. My brain aches; it actually feels as if a bowling ball is spinning around and around inside my skull. Nothing makes sense. There is no logic. I can't concentrate on one individual thought. Visions and memories skip through my mind like a violently propelled flat rock on a perfectly serene lake top. I wonder if my brain will ever find peace. Will it ever be able to escape from the memories of all the mistakes and bad things I've done?

There is no way I can make any sense to Levine today. In twenty minutes I'll have to try to explain to him why I fucked up again. Dad said I'd always make bad decisions. He constantly told me to think about the consequences. He said I never took into consideration the feelings of others. Told Mom I was selfish and had no remorse for what he called my sins. Today I feel tremendous guilt about things I made Louise do. I hurt her real bad. My dad was right. One bad decision I made fucked up a whole bunch of lives.

As I sit here waiting for Levine, I can't help but think that maybe I am a selfish bastard. The one thing that haunts me the most in life is what I did to Louise. It wasn't the fact that she found out about Melissa. It was how she found out. Those two morons up in Pelham, New Hampshire. I'm not making excuses for how bad I hurt Louise. I was the guy who cheated on her. I was the guy who betrayed our love. But if I could have gotten away with it, I would have put one in each of their brains.

Now, let me tell you, up until my affair, things were great—financially I mean. Louise and I had just purchased our dream home in Pelham, New Hampshire, right on the Massachusetts line. The ad I answered to check out the property read, "Perfect for the Gentleman Farmer!"

The farmhouse was beautiful, everything we ever wanted, twelve rooms, two fireplaces. And three bathrooms. But it needed a ton of repair—plumbing, electric, and roof. In fact, we had buckets strategically placed all over the house to catch the leaks. Ricky would be constantly tipping them over to watch the water spill and then run like hell.

Outside it was paradise for Louise—being from the reservation and all—a little shy of twenty acres, two trout ponds, and the far hill lined with apple trees. We could have been so happy there. But then I met Melissa and the cost to keep her a secret spiraled out of control. The money I should have used to pay the mortgage on the farmhouse was now being squandered on hotels, fancy restaurants, and first-class trips to Florida. I've made many mistakes, significant ones, but losing that place, in the big picture, was perhaps the worst of all.

Everybody knew I burned the place down. But you know, who cares what they believe—it's gone. And like my life, it's nothing but rubble.

Louise found out about my affair the day after the fire. I should have taken the phone off the hook at my mother's house because of all the calls coming in. All night, it rang with a steady flow of nice people offering support and aid. The kids' pediatrician called and told me his services would be free. People I didn't even know asked where they could send me money.

It's ironic. I burned the farmhouse down to the ground. It was my plan. There was no surprise. But no way, no how, could I have prepared myself for the devastating loss of everything I ever owned. Everything Louise ever had. It was like our entire past and future had been wiped clean in one day. And every picture and memory from the past now lay in a heap of ashes.

I remember letting the phone ring; it was early, maybe a little after 8 a.m. Something told me to walk away. Then, my mother called my name and anxiously whispered that Chief Rollins from the Pelham Police Department wanted to speak to me. I acted confused but agreed to meet him at the police station in Pelham around 11 in the morning.

When I put the phone down, the kitchen began to move. Both my mother and Louise knew what was happening. John sipped from a glass of chocolate milk and Richard smudged buttery toast all over his lips. I remember getting energy from them. I had to be strong. The boys didn't know what was going on.

In the shower, I psyched myself for Rollins's questions. I called upon the same principles I'd used to get me through life to this point. The same principles my dad had taught me in the backyard when I was twelve—concentrate on your objectives, execute, and win at any cost.

I stopped on Adam Street in Lowell to buy a bag of heroin before I faced my inquest. Some Cambodian junkie with a tattoo necklace let me use his bathroom to cook it. Great stuff, packed with confidence. Lady Heroin made the ride so smooth, nothing could stop me. The butterflies only started fluttering when I pulled into the police station parking lot.

My first sense of something wrong came as I walked to the front door. The instant I read Chief Rollins's name at the foot of his empty parking space—I knew. The cocksucker had set me up.

The cop at the front desk made it official. Rollins was at a meeting in Lowell with the state fire marshal. He watched me sitting in my car. He saw me crying, but I didn't care. You see, I wasn't crying for me. I was crying for Louise. I loved her and she'd never heal from this one.

They told me what happened, Mom and Louise. Fucking shame. Son of a bitches. Walked right up to Mom's door, Chief Rollins and Steve Fraust, the State of New Hampshire's fire marshal. The first question they asked Louise killed us more than any fire, or any amount of drugs.

"Did you know your husband was having an affair with Melissa O'Brien?" Chief Rollins asked.

Mom never let me forget the squeal of pain Louise let go of. I can hear it right now, even though I wasn't there. And they went on and on, as Louise cried and cried. One question after another; they had no mercy.

Mom couldn't remember which one of them asked what when I pressed her for answers. But she did remember the look in my son's eyes as he clung to Louise. And then the motherfucker Fraust topped it off when he pulled the ten-year medallion out of his pocket after offering Louise a Kleenex.

"We're sorry about this, Mrs. Farrell, but it's our job," he said. "Do you see this medallion? It's from Alcoholic's Anonymous. I've been clean and sober for ten years. Perhaps Richard could use some help?"

It's their fuckin' job? What kinds of animals actually sit down and plot a scheme like that? The fucking scumbags knew they had no evidence to arrest me for arson. So the sick pricks got their revenge by taking down my wife and children.

I didn't go home that day, never even called. Stayed fucked up and hid out in Melissa's house on Little Island Pond. Louise never got over it. Nothing I could ever do could ever take back that level of betrayal. We split up over it. I killed our whole world because I liked sticking it places the little head brought me. But I did do something for her she doesn't know about. I got revenge on the state fire marshal, Fraust. The little prick. Yes, I did.

It took me four months, but I did it. I found the AA

meetings he attended in Concord, New Hampshire, and waited for the perfect moment.

Fraust had just finished giving his drunk-a-log. He was shaking people's hands, kissing young girls, and hugging old ladies. Thought he was real cool. I watched him walk to the coffee pot, pick up a cup, pour, and walk toward the rest rooms.

When I reached the men's room door, I felt vindicated. Almost like a Higher Power had sent me on this mission. I scanned the stalls and there were no feet visible. Nobody at the sink and mirror, only Fraust looking down as he pissed into the urinal. I pulled my stocking cap over my eyes as his piss bounced off the drain. He never heard me coming. I remember wanting to say, "Hi, my name is Richie Farrell." But I knew better.

His forehead and nose cracked off the cinder block wall with a pop, sounding like a baseball leaving a fiercely swung bat. From behind, an explosion of blue-red blood splashed off the puke-green paint. It was a perfect forearm shiver. The exact same shiver my dad taught me up against the old oak tree. Fraust slumped to the floor unconscious like he'd gone to sleep on his feet. I made sure he was still breathing, walked nonchalantly out of the bathroom, poured a cup of coffee, and exited the building. It took about ten minutes, waiting for lights and passing through school zones, before I was back on Interstate 93 and relaxed enough to turn on the radio. For a good twenty miles, I kept one eye in the rearview mirror. But nobody ever came after me.

Chief Rollins, he got his, too. No, not from me. Not like I didn't think about fucking him up, but being a law officer and all would have changed the rules of confrontation.

No, Rollins got his from God. Rollins's wife accused him of molesting his four-year-old daughter. The State investigated and a doctor found probable cause.

I can't understand that shit—touching your own kid. But I guess, as you get older, evil gets easier.

Chapter 13 . . . .

Day Five: Afternoon Therapy

"Is something wrong, Richie?"

I never heard or saw Levine enter the office. I guess the guilt of cheating on Louise swallowed me. He seems motivated, engaged, almost thrilled to see me. I don't feel the need to answer. Not because I want to fuck with him or not cooperate; I don't have the mental ability to pay attention. Maybe, if I had a few Libriums, I'd be okay.

"I guess you know you're not on Mrs. Kay's favorite list?"

"Truth is, I don't care. Right now I'm not in any mood to talk."

Dr. Levine senses I'm someplace else. I focus my eyes on my toes, the rip in my slippers, and the thinness of my feet. Some things are more important. I'm not on anybody's favorite people list. And haven't been for years.

Levine asks me to take a written test. I refuse. He informs me I have a disease eating away at the portion of my brain that stores memory. PTSD he calls it, "post-traumatic

stress disorder." He thinks the test will diagnose me with
PTSD.

"Will it cure me?" I ask.

He doesn't answer. I feel bad, like I've let him down.
He fiddles with picture cards on his desk. Levine sheepishly
explains the cards are another diagnostic test. Flash cards,
spots of ink that shape images on the dark side of your brain.
I can't imagine how this will help me.

"How it works is quite simple," Levine explains. "I'll
place a card from the deck with an image in front of you,
and I'd like you to respond to that image with the first thing
that enters your mind."

I agree to the test only because I cannot even explain
to him why I should refuse. Levine is reluctant also. Something isn't right. He reaches for the tape recorder and pushes
RECORD. It's dead quiet. I hear the tape moving slowly. I'm
not comfortable. PTSD?

"T.A.T card number one," he says.

The silence is coming on hard.

"T.A.T. card number two," Levine moves on.

I shake off several of the first cards he flashes. I'm not
trying to be a wise guy; my brain is mush. I see my dad
yelling from the sidelines, my mom crying on her bed, Sean's
face covered in hives, and Levine's lips moving in slow motion. Everything morphs together. Finally, I respond to T.A.T.
card number eight.

"Here is what looks like a skeleton of a person, with two
coyotes at it, one on each side. The skeleton is trying to
hold off the coyotes."

"T.A.T. card number nine."

"Three people on a farm. The young girl sees different

things. She wants other things in her life. Her father and mother work hard from sunup to sundown. She loves her parents. I even see the spirit of my own father in her parents. My dad chose for me as they are doing for her. But she wants something else, something other than working a farm. She doesn't want to hurt her parents. However, she feels that a strong mother and a strong father is the only way out. She has a different destiny written in her face."

"T.A.T card number ten."

"Wait a minute. Hold on. How can a disorder eat your brain?" I ask.

Dr. Levine takes a full twenty seconds; he's struggling on how he should proceed. First, he pulls back the card in front of me. His eyes shoot a glance at the tiny green light on the tape recorder.

"Well, it's the consequences of PTSD that takes away the things in life you should have. Essentials you're entitled to." Levine stops because he knows a more thorough explanation will only kick me harder in the face. He can tell I'm struggling to comprehend.

The fact I don't understand is irrelevant. What matters to me right now more than anything is that I don't want to understand. I avoid his answer by getting him to speak about himself. Levine obliges. Two kids, boy and girl, teenagers, drive him nuts, a beautiful wife. I see her picture on his desk. She isn't really beautiful; but she is to him. He went to Yale but dropped out after his father died. Had to finish at a state school working full-time.

I lie and tell him I went to school at Notre Dame. Played football. He played baseball in high school. His father taught him. Mine, too, I say. I ask if he ever played Pepper as a kid.

No, he answers. I tell him Pepper was my dad's favorite game. Levine seems genuinely interested and asks me to describe the game to him. I tell him the object of the game is to build your reflexes, make you quick, get your eye and your timing down. Dad said Pepper was designed to increase your hand-to-eye coordination. Swore it would improve my response time, increase how fast I reacted to a hard ball ricocheting off the wood of a baseball bat.

I hesitate, wondering if I should cut to the chase and give the technical definition of Pepper or go into the story about how I came to play the game. I quickly decide to go on and see what happens, telling Levine how we had recently moved to Belvidere, the best section of Lowell. A place with a bad reputation for snobs, stuck-up types, and in general, people who thought they were better because "they came from Belvidere."

The only good thing about the neighborhood was the kids. There were a lot of them, all normal, too young to have acquired the "Belvidere syndrome." On my street, Star Avenue, I had four best friends the first week: Artie Fossett, Ed Obie, Mike Duns, and "Skunk" Harmon. And my brother, Sean, of course.

Artie had red-orange hair and stumpy legs. Ed was fair, tall, and thin with enormous feet like a clown. Mike had a barrel chest and buck teeth. "Skunk" was a midget with a stomach disorder, and Sean was the brother whose only reason for existence was to make my life miserable.

That spring all of us guys went to Little League tryouts together. It was on a Saturday morning at 8 a.m., and Shedd Park was bursting with fathers, sons, baseball bats, and Bazooka bubble gum. The park itself was built fifteen or twenty feet below the street level. There was a football field, a quarter-mile track, cement tennis courts, two basketball courts with lights, and a Little League field.

The Little League field looked terrifying, like a giant glove forcing its fingers wide. The tangy smell of the fresh, lime-painted white lines and the soft April breeze made my nose run onto my top lip. And what I couldn't snort back in, I wiped away with my shirtsleeve. A big fat guy with no neck, holding a bullhorn, stood on the top bleacher and shouted out instructions. We got in lines according to our ages. My brother, Sean, was a year older; he was forced to stand in line with the kids he didn't know. I don't know why I felt sorry.

"Sean," I whispered, "come stand with us."

"Tell them you're twelve," Artie said.

"Nobody will know," Skunk yelled.

"No," Sean said. "If Dad finds out, I'll get killed!"

There were six teams. The coaches sat inside each of the chain-linked dugouts, writing on clipboards, yelling out instructions, and asking for names. The test was easy: batting and fielding, five ground balls at shortstop, and five fastballs behind the plate.

As the line grew smaller and I moved closer to the front, my mouth got dry and I had to piss. But I couldn't leave; the line behind me was twice as big as when I'd come. Artie went first. When the fat guy called my name, a little urine leaked out below my zipper.

When it was over, I was the only kid in the neighborhood who didn't make a team. I was a cripple again—different from everybody else in my neighborhood. Mom cried and even Sean looked a little sad. I heard Dad screaming at somebody on the phone about me being a handicapped and how I had more courage that anybody on the field.

For a split second, I mentally come back to the office and tell Levine I'm not sure how or when I came up with the idea to steal Dad's razor-sharp, silver letter opener from the desk downstairs. But I remember wrapping it in a piece of paper, forcing the front of my sweatpants open, and carefully placing the letter opener inside my underwear.

That night, I held the cold metal in my hands and waited for the lights to go off. I could hear Sean snoring. But I needed another half hour to guarantee everybody was asleep. Soon, I would get even with God and his kid for making me a cripple. Dad told me God was in charge of everything and had a reason for why things happened the way they did. He said Jesus could perform miracles, let blind see, the deaf and dumb speak, and the cripples walk. I prayed for years to be a miracle. So now it's payback time for deciding I remain a cripple.

The hallway was a patchwork of gray from the moon's dim light. Dad's door was locked. And there they were, hanging there on the wall, all self-righteous, like they didn't do nothin'. I started with the statue of Jesus. He was the biggest fake. I remember how the crimson red heart almost glowed on His chest. Quietly, like a convict digging a tunnel, I stabbed the shit out of His heart. Each stab brought a feel-good whisper, "Cripple."

The Blessed Virgin Mary was next. How could she let her son be so fuckin' mean. She had to take some of the blame. She was a fake, too. Like she didn't spread those legs to get pregnant, right? The next morning, Jesus' heart and Mary's face lightly covered the light-brown baseboard as tiny, white, plaster specs.

I thought for sure I'd be dead before breakfast. But in Dad's haste to make Mass and Communion, along with help from the early-morning darkness—he never saw it. Or if he did, he let it go because he knew firsthand how broken my heart was over being different. Mom vacuumed it up while Sean was in the shower. She never spoke of it.

When Dad arrived home after church he called a family meeting. He told us he'd got an answer from God that morning after Holy Communion. It was the birth of the Shedd Park Minor League. He told Mom it would take him a month to raise the money in order to start a minor league organization. Every kid played; every kid made the team. That was the policy.

The next morning he called Lowell attorney Dick Donahue. He was our neighbor; lived in a twenty-five room mansion on the hill behind our new house in Belvidere. I think he had almost a dozen kids. His wife was beautiful, so I can see how that happens. I didn't know it then, but Dick Donahue had been an adviser to President Kennedy in the White House. The details are unclear, but I know Mr. Donahue wrote Dad a check enough for him to get a good start.

From there my Dad found Whitworth's Sporting Goods in Lawrence, Massachusetts. I was with Dad when he convinced or almost begged the owner into taking partial payment for supplying bats, balls, and catcher's equipment for eight minor league teams. The guy wouldn't go for fronting any money for full uniforms. However, Dad wouldn't take no for an answer. He promised full payment from fund-raisers, tag days, and raffles. Mr. Whitworth compromised with shirts for eight teams.

For three weeks, almost every night, Dad called anybody and everybody. He needed coaches, umpires, volunteers to sell refreshments, park time from the City of Lowell, insurance, and more money. Almost exactly four weeks from the morning Dad came home from church, give or take a day or two, my dad held the very first sign-up day for the Shedd Park Minor League.

Only one problem: Dad envisioned me as a great athlete. He certainly didn't want to be embarrassed by my ability in front of all those people he'd begged for help and money. So, any free moment he had away from building the league, he spent with me, in the backyard, working on my game.

Dad said the answer to my problem was Pepper. Said he and his friends played it on the North Common as kids. I stood, glove in hand, with my back to the wood picket fence. The one he had just dug and put up because he hated Mrs. Pete, our neighbor. He stood fifteen feet away with a baseball bat and a hard ball. I pitched; he was supposed to bunt, and I was supposed to react. A line drive was an out. Same rules as baseball, three outs and it was my turn at bat. The intent was to improve my ability to see the ball to the bat and react to the ball off the bat. But it didn't work that way. He took half swings, line fuckin' drives, bullets. He played it with a vengeance. Almost pissed, because he had to listen to God.

The ones I didn't catch either put welts and stitching marks in my flesh, or got by me and busted pickets in the fence.

After a while, the crack of the ball exploding off the bat became my friend. Fear taught me how to judge speed and angle. But that's fuckin' nothing compared to the Saturday morning he decided there were fence posts that had to be fixed. It was just after he'd finished his coffee, ten minutes or so after he came home from his daily Mass and Communion at the Immaculate Conception Church. I was ordered to get together the severed fence posts; he got the Elmer's glue, and we met in the garage by the vice.

I'm not sure what it was—whether it was because I couldn't hold the broken pieces steady enough, the glue wouldn't hold, or the vice wasn't big enough, maybe all three. But he beat me with a broken fence post, across the face and arms and head. He screamed for me to hold on. I remember the evil shape of his mouth. I begged and begged for mercy. But he didn't give me any.

I guess Pepper worked. The next season, I was a much better baseball player.

My mind focuses back to real time. I'm standing by Levine's window. He's writing. A dozen pencils are on the floor. All are snapped in two. I'm not sure if I've broken them. I tell him I have to piss. He informs me we're done for the day and thanks me. I'm surprised, confused; it doesn't feel right to reply cordially with a "you're welcome." It's awkward. But I should say something to him before I leave.

"I never really liked baseball," I say. "But wasn't my dad nice to start an entire league so I could play? In fact, the league is still there. There is a monument down at the field. A tribute to my dad."

Chapter 14

Day Six: Midnight

It's the last day of March. A hard rain keeps me from sleeping. I'm slop. Memories bounce across my mind. A light from the corridor filters into the ward. Everything's gray. Murph crawls over slowly to my bunk. I can smell the sweet aroma of dried sweat. Murph doesn't shower unless Mrs. Kay threatens him. I sit up startled. He covers my mouth quickly. Quiet. His head signals me to follow him. I can feel the excitement in his eyes.

"Where we goin'?" I whisper, pressing my knees and hands slowly to the ground behind him.

"We're on a mission from God," he mimics.

"I saw that movie. Belushi is dead."

But Murph is the type of guy I'd follow anywhere. He's been in the shit a hundred times. I don't give a rat's ass what people say—experience matters. Fear has a way of exiting when you've been up against it a dozen times. I don't know where I'm going, but it doesn't matter. Murph wouldn't have come to get me unless he needed me. You gotta be loyal in this place. We're all we've got left.

Two night orderlies man the front desk and double as security. Easy duty. One sleeps, the other watches late-night television on a black-and-white TV that Mrs. Kay has brought in for special news events. She hated television. "Read," she would always say. If she were boss of Lowell Detox there wouldn't be a television or radio allowed on the premises. Funny thing about her, she always played the consequence card. She had this internal dialogue where she always had to be the winner. Even if she lost, there would be a consequence. As if she said, "Okay, you guys want television and the big shots won't back me. I'll give you television. Black and white."

Crazy Mary's given me the scoop on night security. She never sleeps. Says her mind won't shut off. Almost as if a radio transmission's bounced from station to station, never staying long enough to enjoy the entire song. She'd have to walk. It was the only thing besides sex that quieted the sharp frequency change from the radio transmitter screeching inside her skull.

One night, in an attempt to combine her night walks with sex, she had tried to take both the orderlies on at the same time. Told me most guys go for that stuff. Dressed up in a teddy, a silk black lace lingerie that buttoned at her crotch. The guys were watching the rerun of a Yankees and Red Sox doubleheader from the previous baseball season. They weren't happy. It was a September series, the year the Yankees beat them five straight at Fenway Park. Knocked them right out of the playoffs.

Crazy Mary had heard them yelling and went around

the front desk. She let her hospital-issue bathrobe open and stood right between their seats. She offered them a little ski pole action; jerk them both off at once. Told them the release would help them with their troubles. But they laughed at her.

Stuff like that never happened to Crazy Mary. She could always suck a cock or get somebody off. She was crushed. Since that dreadful evening, she'd plotted intricate plans for payback. One night, she actually heisted the younger orderly's toothbrush while both of them left the desk area to handle a situation. Mary ran down to the toilet, scrubbed inside the bowl with the orderly's toothbrush, and got it back into the exact position before anybody knew a thing. Crazy Mary was Murph's eyes. She said most nights the orderlies on guard dozed off right after midnight.

Murph goes vertical in the hallway. If anybody had seen us on our hands and knees they would have suspected something was about to take place. A foot before the opening at the front desk, Murph quietly drops back to the floor in the hallway. I follow.

Murph doesn't even consider taking Crazy Mary. He likes her, but I have a hunch he knew she was bad for a mission like this. For some unexplained reason she makes this snorting noise from the back of her throat whenever it's time to be quiet. It reminds me of my mother-in-law in church or in the backseat of the car. People that snort do it subconsciously. I'd ask my mother-in-law if she needed a tissue and she'd ask me for what.

We sneak past the orderlies. The toughest part is opening the doors to the stairwell on your knees. The blackness holds different shades of shadows. Murph told me the new guys in Vietnam would flip out. They'd see things, Gooks moving slowly in the tree line. Some would open fire and blow their cover. Murph said the toughest thing was teaching a young kid to control fear. "Gooks are Gooks and shadows are shadows," he'd tell them. "One will kill ya and the other will hide ya if you let it become your friend."

We make it down the stairs. The outside door says ALARMED, but we know the system broke years ago. Moonlight illuminates an almost empty parking lot. Trees line the far end, and a cool, steady breeze ruffles the spring leaves. The leaves sing quietly and cover our footsteps on the blacktop. Across the parking lot, an old Volkswagen van waits. Pitch-dark inside. We jump in.

Two women, Murph's friends, both in their forties, black: one has beautiful features, mulatto maybe; the other is fat with enormous breasts. They crack cans of Busch beer and pass it over. I pass on it and ask if they have a bag of heroin and a needle. The pretty one rolls a joint, which I don't refuse. Murph spends most of the time with the fat one. He tries to get her to go to the backseat. She wants to talk.

The pretty one asks me if I'm prejudiced.

I say, "No! I think everybody should own at least two slaves."

I'm high. Complete silence, except the rain has started again. Murph searches me for answers and starts to laugh. He tells them I played football for Notre Dame. Said I was a superstar. Tore up my knees and took up pain medication.

The pretty one relaxes. I never ask their names. I tell them my dad hated black people, except in football. I tell them a racial joke my father used to tell me. It's not funny but the pretty one gets it. However, Big Boobs is still leery. I can see she wonders if I really believe everybody should "own at least two of them."

I interrupt Murph's explanations as to why weed in Vietnam was far better. "Okay," I said. "I'm sorry; I don't believe everybody should own at least two of you." Silence. Murph looks more confused. Big Boobs relaxes but not for long. "Just one," I say. The pretty one and Murph laugh hysterically.

Murph says we have only an hour. The orderlies do a bed check at 3 a.m. The pretty one moves close to me. She wants to know about football. She puts her hand on my inner thigh. I get rock hard.

Deep down I don't want to lie anymore. I've been telling the same fuckin' bullshit story for so long it bores me. Every small detail is etched on my brain as if it really happened. I'd done the research in order to cover my tracks. My brother, Sean, went to Notre Dame; I visited the campus in South Bend, Indiana, partied in the dorms, watched a game on the sidelines while the stadium was fifty thousand people strong, actually stood inside the locker room prior to a game against Miami, and had really been a football star in high school. If anybody listening to my story had ever been to Notre Dame, they would not have caught on to the fairy tale I was spinning.

Right now, the pretty one's succulent, plump lips are more important than Notre Dame. The very last thing on earth I want to do again is repeat a fictitious story about how I played a fuckin' game there. But no, here I am again sacrificing something real, like getting laid, in order to go on living within a lie. I glance down at her hand, my hard-on, and shake my head. Her eyes become clouded with confusion. She thinks I don't want to go on talking about football. She has no idea I cannot believe how sad this situation really is to me right now.

All of a sudden, the truth slams against my chin with the impact of a baseball bat. It's not Murph's fault I'm telling this story again. In reality, I'm too far gone. I've invested such a large chunk of my life to the story. This is my identity. If I wanted to stop telling it, I would. And that's the only thing that's real right now; I'm not sure I can.

Her hand begins to wiggle closer to my groin. Her head rests on my chest and she wants to know what I'm waiting for. I'd like to tell her the truth, but I'm not sure how Murph will accept it. I give in and start telling her how my brother, Sean, and I were brought up on God, Country, and Notre Dame. Dad told me from the time I was twelve years old that I'd play football at Notre Dame. He played semi-pro in Massachusetts, but his career ended with grenade shrapnel in Korea. Sean hated football, so Dad spent all his spare time working me in the yard. He'd make me run full speed at a giant oak tree and cut sharply at the last minute. The object was to get as close as I could to the tree without hitting it. One day I didn't cut in time and lost my two front permanent teeth. Dad drove me to the dentist cursing, calling me everything from a sissy to a coward. After that incident, he drove me to steep hills and made me run up and down until the muscles in the backs of my legs burned like hot coals.

I skip through much of my usual Notre Dame bullshit and add a little truth about how I fell in love my sophomore year. Uda Levenson was mulatto, with black eyes, and long, black, straightened hair down below her waist. I tell her I met Uda on the Notre Dame campus. But in reality she was an airline stewardess I'd met on a plane to Florida.

The pretty one kisses the side of my face. Not quite sure if the kiss is because she is feeling sorry for me, or if it is a silent gesture beckoning me to stick my tongue down her throat I take a deep breath, spin around to see Murph, and weigh my options. All eyes are on me. I can't stop now. But I'm horny. Murph's impatient. He wants me to get to football. Not because he gives a rat's ass about Notre Dame football; he's anxious for me to finish so his fat girl with the big boobs will pay attention to him.

I jump back quickly to game day. Explain how Saturday came too fast, and there was never enough time to mentally prepare for getting rocked by some three-hundred-pound gorilla who's been visualizing knocking my head off with his forearm.

Murph's pissed now. I can almost feel the daggers from his eyes stabbing the back of my neck. I wrap it up and bring my charade to one hour before kickoff. Suddenly, the sound of a sudden hard slap brings me back to real time. Startled, I immediately lose a piece of my high. Murph's fat girl with the big boobs whispers, "Wait, let him finish." Most likely he went for her boobs and she let him have it. Murph has waited long enough. He has to realize we're almost out of time and figures one way or another he's going for it.

"I'm done. That's it. We're almost out of darkness," I project with a little bit of attitude.

For forty-five minutes, I've enthralled this beautiful girl with luscious lips—who should have been using them to suck me off—with tales of football glory at Notre Dame.

She's mesmerized. For a second, I wonder if she'd still have her hand on my pecker if I weren't a football star at Notre Dame.

The moaning and grunting from the backseat signals the pretty one to reach into my bathrobe. I stop her and her face goes blank as she moves away from me. "We don't have enough time," I tell her. But I'm lying. The truth is ever since my aunt Phyllis gave me blow jobs, I cannot get it up if anybody else is in the room. The fact is I can't even jerk off if a dog or cat is present.

I pull her back close to me and begin French kissing her passionately. She giggles as I bite her top lip tenderly. I shut my eyes, really getting into what I'm doing, and my mind drifts back. I see myself almost asleep on the top bunk, one cousin sleeping below me and another on a single bed directly across from him. I've just become a teenager. My aunt Phyllis enters the room. Her lips meet mine, I open my mouth, and her tongue darts in and out. I feel her hand moving down my chest until it wraps around my hard-on. Slowly her lips move down my stomach; I open my legs to greet her tongue. It's warm and I cannot last long. Her hand grabs hold of my shaft and the tip of her tongue finds the hole in my penis. Carefully, she removes any traces of cum and exits the room without a word.

It's time to go. The outside sky is threatening to become our enemy. The extreme darkness is dissipating gradually. Murph isn't happy. The fat chick wouldn't have sex with him; all he got was a quick feel and some heavy petting. I wondered if he was mad at me. But he's the one who brought it up—me being a football star.

I kiss the pretty one good-bye. It dawns on me; I don't

even know her name. I don't think it's the right thing to ask her now. I'll probably never see her again and I want her to remember me as a football hero.

Murph and I make it safely back into the building. He is still not in a good mood. Tells me he has blue balls. His girl wouldn't have sex because I was in the van talkin' nonsense. I tell him I'd rather have had sex with the pretty one than tell her about Notre Dame. I wanted to be truthful, but I couldn't tell Murph.

All hell breaks loose as we enter the doors leading to the corridor. The sounds of a commotion in the ward echo in the corridor, and we halt. The young night orderly, his back to us, stands frozen in the middle of the corridor. There is no sense getting on the floor. Crazy Mary enters the corridor from the dayroom, spots us, immediately understands we're about to get caught, and provides cover.

"I think he's fucking dead in there, guy," she screams at the orderly pointing toward the ward.

Murph and I are dead still. Neither of us has a clue what is happening. Panic and gut-wrenching gurgling noises make the short hairs on the back of my neck stiff.

The orderly takes off to assist.

"It's Brown," Crazy Mary says. "He downed two large bottles of Listerine in less than a minute."

"What should I do, Murph? They know I'm not in my bunk."

"Just go back," he says. "Tell them you couldn't sleep. They won't believe you, but they'll never be able to prove anything. Don't tell 'em nothin'. I gotta get back to my room."

"I'll tell them you were in my room, Richie," Crazy Mary offers. "With the door open. It's completely at the opposite end. They never went down there. Never left the front desk."

Murph's a ghost and decides to move into the action in order to be seen. I kiss Crazy Mary as I walk past her. Inside the ward, both orderlies work on Downtown Rolly Brown. It's dark, but the ammonia smell of puke hits my eyes and they begin to tear. One of the orderlies holds Rolly's face sideways against his bunk so he won't choke on the shit coming out of him. You can hear his stomach muscles convulsing, dry heaves. He's gagging on oxygen attempting to enter his lungs past the bile from his stomach. A doctor and nurse from the emergency room next door arrive and begin to pump his stomach. One of the night orderlies gives me a sharp stare of suspicion but never asks me where I've been.

I should have paid more attention. I remember seeing one of Rolly's girlfriends bring him in a large bag of snacks and toiletries earlier in the evening. She must have slipped in a few bottles of mouthwash at the very bottom. Downtown Rolly Brown was smart, a real pro. He knew the front desk would only move around the items on the top of the bag during inspection. Most of the time the night orderlies only squeezed the bottom of bags quickly in search of glass. Mouthwash was rarely confiscated prior to evening visits. But only a fool or a rookie would attempt to sneak it in during the day when Mrs. Kay conducted the visitors' bag checks. She caught it every time. It's an old trick alcoholics use when they are desperate. Listerine and Scope have a 10 percent alcohol content. More than beer and wine, but you have to be in pretty bad shape to manage two large bottles in your stomach. I knew a guy on the street who drank it all the time; burned his esophagus so bad, blood filled up his belly and he almost died. It might get you a buzz, but the sickness it brings is close to being dope-sick.

I should have checked the bag when he offered me snacks earlier. Rolly's my friend. If I hadn't gone to the van, Murph would have gotten laid and I would have stopped Downtown Rolly Brown from nearly killing himself.

Brown's gone. They've taken him over to the emergency room. The doc decided Rolly needed adequate observation and he wouldn't get it here. I'm alone in a ward full of empty beds. The other patients can't take the smell and move to soft chairs in the dayroom. I could never sleep in a chair. I can't help but dream of the pretty black girl's lips. I sit up and walk over to the window. The dawn's shadows of light begin to creep over the main hospital. I shake my head in disbelief. Not at the fact that Downtown Rolly Brown drank two bottles of Listerine, but rather, the fact that Notre Dame and my aunt Phyllis robbed another potential unbelievable moment out of my memory bank. The pretty one wanted me. I wanted her. It shouldn't have mattered that Murph was in the backseat or whether I was really a Notre Dame football star. I guess telling the truth, admitting I never played football at Notre Dame, would have been far too great of a threat. In the end, even though my dad was dead, pleasing him took preference.

Chapter 15

Day Seven: Morning

My eyes open, and I realize that today is my last full day at Lowell Detox. Tomorrow morning I'll be discharged.

I lie still, listening to morning sounds echoing off the walls in the corridor. Shower heads spitting water slowly over a new guy's back, the wheels of out-of-date linen carts slithering like snakes over time-grooved linoleum, and chatter congealing to mar the morning solitude. All the sounds line up in the corridor and enter the ward as a cloud of smoke reminding me again it's almost time to go. I'm afraid to leave the safety here. I may be physically stronger than the day I arrived here, but I can't leave this place tomorrow.

The game plan is to wait until breakfast is almost complete. If I go into the cafeteria ten minutes before the kitchen workers come to break down and clean up, most everybody will be in the dayroom watching television. I hate the ego of some of these people. They all lie. Everybody in here lies.

But things don't play out this morning. I'm not alone. Breakfast with Crazy Mary and Asshole Mouth isn't all bad. I can just eat and watch. Asshole Mouth tries to preach to Mary, says she's passing HIV to unsuspecting customers.

"Don't you care about anybody?" he asks. "What about your customers' wives? They didn't ask for a bug that is going to eat them from the inside out."

Mary disagrees. Gets right in Asshole Mouth's face. He laughs but it's only to cover his fear. Her eyes are bananas, bulging red, and wide as the sockets allow.

"If they want to drive an hour to get their cock sucked, who am I to play God and refuse?"

"So you don't care about anything, right? If they have kids, if they're going to go bang their wife later in the evening, nothing matters to you but getting your money for another hit of cocaine. Right?"

"Listen asshole, that's how much you know, you cannot get AIDS from giving a blow job. It's not fuckin' airborne, moron. If you knew anything you'd know ya gotta work at getting an HIV infection."

It's funny to watch. I'm rooting for Crazy Mary. Any minute, any second now, she's planning to haul off and stick a plastic butter knife in Asshole Mouth's ear. Most people think they only use plastic utensils because of HIV contamination, but that isn't all of it. Plastic forks and knives have saved numerous people in here. I've seen it a dozen times. You can pretty much call it. And right now, it's not *if* it's going down, but *when*.

"Ya know what you are, Mary?" he asks with a smirk.

"What, moron?"

You can see this isn't going to be pretty. Flip the coin,

heads or tails, Asshole Mouth loses this one. He's so arrogant and repulsive. On the streets we would have fucked him up bad. Probably conduct the magical urinal ride. Take him for a drink at one of the local watering holes where everybody but him would know what was coming.

Of course, the goal was to convince him you'd be his friend. Old Asshole Mouth would get up to piss after a few drafts, the bartender would signal, and the bathroom would be off limits. Ten seconds after he entered you'd sneak in without a sound. He'd be holding his prick, staring straight at the local sports-page clipping hung on the wall about six inches from his nose.

One violently quick blast to the back of his head and he'd bounce off the clippings. Most guys that took the magical urinal ride crumbled into bones on the floor. It was customary to kneel them and arrange their chin so it hooked on the bottom of the urinal. Funny as shit to see, out cold, looked like they were praying, their prick hanging in the breeze.

Crazy Mary has the knife loosely clutched in her left hand. I pull back. Should I break it up? Nah, why get involved? I'm closer. She doesn't have to reach; I'll become the target. Asshole Mouth is a first timer here. In fact, he's probably a cherry to a street addict like Crazy Mary.

"You're Satan's repugnant daughter," he taunts.

Crazy Mary doesn't react. For sure Asshole Mouth will lose his right eye. But it's obvious she doesn't know what repugnant means and throws the remains of her hot coffee at him. Chocolate-brown liquid hits Asshole Mouth's right ear and cheek as he tries to dodge the incoming dark cloud. He howls like a guy who's been stabbed in the eye with a plastic butter knife.

"What's the matter?" she asks. "You got nothin' more to say to me now? Do ya?"

Crazy Mary catapults over the table. Her legs scissor Asshole Mouth's waist. I push away, far enough to be out of the scuffle when the orderlies arrive. It's the number one rule here, and in prison. Never, ever get blood on your clothes. The guy who gets even the slightest droplet of blood on his clothes is the guy who gets blamed.

With both hands, Crazy Mary is ripping away hair from Asshole Mouth's temple. The howls turn to blackboard-scraping, chilling, help-me screams. Asshole Mouth is paralyzed, helpless. This place is insane. We're all lunatics. It's never peaceful here. No, it's one fucking chunk of sheer madness after another. Everybody in here is damaged goods, even the fucking orderlies.

Crazy Mary is up in his face. She earns her name and goes for the kill. Opens her mouth wide and bites down hard on Asshole Mouth's forehead. I can't see any blood. Her bite's too wide; she doesn't get enough leverage to break skin. Fuck this; I ain't getting involved in this one. I hop to my feet and try to run. Shit. I can't leave my tray. I'll be asked what I saw. I didn't see a thing if I'm not caught in the room.

John the orderly appears, looks, and—*whack!*—hits a wall of vertical terror. His mouth opens to the size of a golf ball. He focuses on me. I'm standing, trying to place my tray in the rack. Asshole Mouth is crying like a baby escaping the birth canal. Crazy Mary has released his forehead and is now head-butting the bridge of his nose. Small taps, nothing to cause major damage. Asshole Mouth has enough sense left to cover his face with both forearms.

"What are you doing?" John asks me.

"What am I doin'? Are you for real? I'm getting ready to pack my bags, you fuckin' gutless wonder."

Another orderly slashes by John and tackles Crazy Mary from behind. The blow is enough to separate her legs from Asshole Mouth and knock her to the floor. But she bounces to her knees like a super ball. Now she goes for the plastic knife. I have to laugh. John is floored by my reaction—anything to pull him away from jumping and stopping Crazy Mary. Nothing's changed for me; I've got a long history of laughing at the wrong situation. But Asshole Mouth is right about one thing: Crazy Mary surely looks like she could be related to Satan.

Another orderly enters quickly and they corner Crazy Mary against the rear wall. John shouts out instructions from a safe distance. Crazy Mary swings the knife aimlessly, completely missing her target. Her hand hits the cinder block wall and the plastic knife shatters. Mary stops. A wave of sanity washes over her. In a heartbeat, she's totally back to normal. I can't believe I let this crazy bitch suck my cock. What the fuck was I thinking?

John commands the orderlies to put her in restraints anyway. She objects; cannot understand why. Two of them drag her to the observation room. Mrs. Kay will have to deal with her. If they don't call the cops or if Asshole Mouth doesn't file a complaint, she'll be back in population before I leave.

Once Crazy Mary is no longer a threat, Asshole Mouth sits up and begins to whistle. There are small teeth marks engraved in the middle of his forehead. But no real remnants of blood; there is no blood supply in his forehead, nothing but bone beneath a few layers of skin. Asshole Mouth smirks like he's just won a contest.

"Pretty brave now, huh?"

"She's nuts. What would you have done?" he asks.

"In what situation? If I was her or if I was you?"

"What happened?" John jumps in.

"I didn't see anything," I reply, moving toward the sink to empty my coffee cup.

John knows from my tray I was there eating. He also understands I'll never tell him what I saw. Asshole Mouth listens for my response while he begins to check the damage. For some reason he thinks I'll side with him and give up Crazy Mary. But he gives up quickly on that hope and reaches up with both hands to feel the side of his head, inspecting for missing parts.

"She shouldn't be in here, John. She should be in the psycho ward at Shedd next door," Asshole Mouth whines.

"Did she start it?" John asks.

"No!" I quickly inject.

Asshole Mouth leaves without comment. John tucks his fear between his legs and follows. I sit alone. One more day and I'll be on the streets. I plot my first high, which house would be safest, which dealer I should rob. I can taste the heroin.

"I don't want to get high," I blurt out to eradicate my sudden lust for heroin. My stomach knots. I gag in anticipation, a reflex that happens when you pour the bag of heroin into the cooker. I am afraid again. I don't want to leave tomorrow. How will I survive one minute on the streets without heroin leading me?

Dr. Levine enters and sits down slowly across from me. He's pensive, but I'm not sure why. Does he want to ask me something about Notre Dame? He has never before talked to me about important things outside his office. Maybe Mrs. Kay sent him in to get the details on Crazy Mary.

"Asshole Mouth set off Mary," I say.

"How are you feeling?"

"She was just sitting here with me and Asshole Mouth got a hard-on for her. Started preaching about morals."

"Do you know Asshole Mouth's first name?" he asks.

"No. I don't wanna know."

Levine likes me. He is genuinely looking after my best interests. You can tell these things when you've been on the streets as long as I have. It is almost instantaneous; some people want to hurt you out here and some people want to help. After you've crashed and burned a few times it's not hard to pick up the fakers. Funny thing, I don't care if he knows the truth about me. I bet he probably doesn't. I'm just so fucking paranoid; it happens whenever I'm straight. The heroin makes me an actor. I can play the role. It helps me believe the role.

Levine looks older today. The smile lines in his cheeks appear more like wrinkles from aging. All this stress must be playing with his mind. Think about it, I'm only one person he's listening to describe his personal, living, walking, breathing hell. I wonder if he brings the shit home and talks about us to his wife at the supper table. I wouldn't. I wanna give him a pep talk. Direct him away from the madness of this place. Let him know he's not one of us so he shouldn't have to become one of us.

It's the one thing that's always bothered me about these social worker types. Most of them want to get down to our level. But they don't understand; it's impossible to go where I've gone. Sure Levine can listen, but he'll never be able to truly comprehend. It's like trying to tell somebody what shit tastes like; you just gotta taste it for yourself.

"I just had a long talk with your mom."

Complete silence.

"She dropped in early this morning."

Levine watches my reaction. But I'm a poker player. He'll never see my true feelings. I'm sure my mom meant well, telling him whatever she felt she had to. But it's her side of the story, and her version isn't necessarily the truth.

"It wasn't a planned meeting, Richie."

"I don't want to go home tomorrow, Doc."

"She wants to come in and talk to you about something."

The silence suddenly lasts longer than either of us feel is comfortable. He's tense. He knows something about me. But he knows nothin' actually. None of the dark stuff, the crap Dad knew—and he's dead. So it's just me holding on to what really happened.

"There's an issue, and she feels it is very important for her to express it before tomorrow."

"Can I stay another week or at least two or three more days? I don't think I'm strong enough, Doc."

Levine remorsefully shakes his head and stares at the tabletop. He tells me I cannot stay another week. He explains how limited the area is for free beds for alcoholics and drug addicts. He tells me there are many, many, like me, waiting for beds.

"Unfortunately, Richie, there's no alternative for us. Seven days is all we have in this place."

"Us? You can go home to your wife, family, and friends." I angrily raise my voice. "What am I going home to? My father's dead. My family's all gone; there is nothin' left at my home, Doc."

Levine stands. He has other things to do. I know he's

not listening. I know he's not taking anything I say to heart. But I want him to understand I'm not ready to leave here.

"So what the fuck you talking about *us*, Doc!" I yell as he disappears through the archway into the corridor.

I cannot move. My entire body is slop in the chair. My feet and arms are stuck in a tub of molasses. I'm all alone again. I can actually sense the holes in my arms from the prior needles—every puncture and vein I ever hit or missed. There is no way I can leave this place. I'll wind up in jail or dead again. I'll have to beg Mrs. Kay before she goes home for the day.

My mother enters the small kitchen in slow motion, black and white. The hum in my ears removes the rest of the color from the room. Her face is so surreal to me. She's aged since the last time I've seen her straight. It's been some time I guess. The last time she sat with me I couldn't keep my eyes open. Two bags of black heroin will do that to you. That's if it doesn't stop your heart. It's crazy how you don't notice certain things about a face when you're just lookin' to shake them down for money to buy heroin. I was glad to see her. I'd missed my mother. She was the one lady who'd always loved me.

Nobody ever visits in the kitchen. She's the last person I'd expect to visit me here at Lowell Detox. Shocked, I don't greet her. She sits gingerly across from me. I think she's afraid. She's seen me high. Horror has a way of replicating itself.

"Mom? What are you doing here? Levine said you were by this morning? How long you been waiting?"

"You can't come home," she says.

"What do you mean? I haven't been home in years. Where the fuck is home?"

She cries and says she went to get help, talked to a shrink. Several. She talks about her search for a different answer, but none came. She tells me about "tough love," how each psychiatrist came up with the same advice. She says my children need me.

"I don't wanna come home. I'm going to stay for another week."

"Don't call me again," she whispers.

I'm waiting for her to finish the sentence like I expect her to, waiting for her to say, "Until I have a good foothold in sobriety." But she doesn't. I'm crushed. I love my mother; she's all I have. I begin to cry. My mother, the last and only person who loves you forever, has thrown me to the wolves, the streets, and heroin. I need her today because I understand how hard it will be to not get high tomorrow. Without her, I have nobody but heroin. She tells me I need a priest.

"A fucking priest?!" I scream.

"A priest could absolve your sins, set you free of heroin addiction."

"I don't believe in priests!" I'm hysterical now.

"Calm down, Richard."

She reaches her hand across the table and places it on the top of my left hand. It's hot and wet from fear. There is something extremely soothing in a mother's touch. It's almost funny how mothers have an innate way of making all the badness drift away.

"You'll have to start taking control over your emotions," she continues.

I focus on her wrinkled hands covering my scarred hands. My mind flashes back almost twenty years. The night my dad beat me to a pulp. I was seven. Dad and I were in his bed watching *The FBI* on a Sunday night. Mom and Sean were in the kitchen making cookies. It was during a commercial. Dad loved to tickle. The covers suddenly ripped off my little body and Dad's fingers began to dance on my stomach. His legs wrapped around my legs in a scissors hold. I was pinned, insane with laughter. I was going to die. In the struggle for my life, my elbow smashed against his nose. First, it was blood everywhere. Within seconds, violent slaps echoed to the kitchen. Mom ran in. My eye sockets were bleeding. I couldn't hear Mom screaming. The monstrous blows to my ears had touched off bells inside my head.

I look up at Mom's face and wonder if she remembers how she saved me that night. I want to know if she remembers how we drove around Lowell until 3 a.m. I'm curious to test her memory. Does she remember how she promised she'd never let it happen to me again?

"Richard, a Catholic priest is the answer."

"Fuck the Catholic priest!" I blast.

Mom's shocked. It immediately reminds me of how she'd cower when Dad went off in a tirade. There is a slight tinge of guilt. I don't want to bring her back to that level or remind her of the instant rush of fear. But a fucking Catholic priest? I cannot let her get away with it.

"Do you remember the time Dad walked in on me masturbating over the cover of *Sports Illustrated,* Swimsuit Edition? Do you remember how humiliated I was when he brought me to Father Dan?"

She remembers. But there is so much more to the story. I want her to hear it all. I'd promised myself that the story would die with me, but Mom needs to know the truth about what happened when Dad brought me to Father Dan at the

Church of the Immaculate Conception. I don't care if it's more dwelling in the past, like she always throws in my face. I'm going to tell her every last detail.

"Mom, the first thing Dad said to Father Dan was, 'Look, Father. He's proud.'"

And you know for a minute, I just might have been. But I had to lie.

"No, I'm not, Father Dan. Just scared," I blurted.

The priest put his hand on my shoulder and squeezed, like the Brady Bunch father would do before he sent one of the kids to their room.

"Richard," said the priest. "Would you like to go to confession?"

"By all means, Father, take him into the confessional," Dad said.

The confessional was up front near the altar. Three of them, side by side, like coffins standing up straight with hinges and doorknobs.

I walked quickly next to the priest, never once turning to check on Dad's whereabouts. Father Dan opened the middle door, stepped in, and vanished. Then the light over both confessionals started to flicker from red to green, red to green. And I picked the door to my left, opened it slowly, and stepped into a pitch-black, padded, frightening place.

At first, I couldn't find the kneeler and closed my eyelids tight, groping around like a blind man searching for the toilet bowl. Finally, I found it and it was a seat, and the seat folded down off the sidewall, like the ones in the old Lowell cabs. But I couldn't find any place to rest my hands.

I heard the sound of wood sliding on swollen tracks, and saw a weak gray light cut a square in the wall about eye level.

There was a thin black screen and the silhouette of a man with tiny gentle features. The priest pressed his ear close to the screen and waited.

"Bless me, Father, for I have sinned," I said.

"Do you wish to confess?"

"Yes, Father."

"Don't be nervous," he said. "Get it off your chest. Your dad can't hear."

I remember thinking, Why do I have to tell the priest? Why couldn't I just tell God and ask Him to forgive me?

Eliminate the middleman.

"Richard, I'll ask you a few questions, give you some penance, and this will all be behind you, okay?"

"Okay, Father Dan," I mumbled.

"Do you do this often?" the priest asked. "Without honesty, you will not be forgiven."

"Yes."

"How often?"

There was another long pause.

"Once in a while," I said. And he knew I was lying.

"How did you get caught?"

"I was reading the Swimsuit Edition of *Sports Illustrated*, and things just happened," I said.

"Did you orgasm?" he asked, and his voice cracked.

"Yes," I said very weakly.

"Do you do this alone?"

"Most of the time, Father."

"Do you ever do it with other boys?" he asked.

I remember wondering why he was asking me these things. I thought he was going to give penance and forgive my sins. But I felt a little tinge down there; my pants got tight and I knew it was growing. And I didn't want it to. I felt like the kid with his thumb in the dam. I wanted to run, but Dad was lurking right outside.

"Richard?"

"Once or twice, Father."

My face grew hot and I started to sweat behind my ears. Each pause between questions seemed longer than the last.

"Did you look to see who had the biggest penis?" said the priest.

I remember thinking about pulling it out right there. I knew it was wrong—there was no *Sports Illustrated*. But talking about masturbating and penises in the dark, Dad outside and the priest's face behind the screen, made me hot. And suddenly, a bell went off in my head, and I fumbled opening the door. In a flash, I was running, didn't care about the zebra stripes I was going to get. Dad was sitting in one of the first rows holding his rosary beads and I didn't find it necessary to stop and talk.

I fade back to real time and Mom's not even paying attention. I wonder if the memory just played in my head? Maybe time froze, like a Hollywood movie where the main character relives an entire incident and suddenly flashes back to reality where it never happened.

"Forget about it," she tells me. "Go to another priest. Boy, you've always had a wonderful imagination."

"You were listening to me. But you think I made it up?"

"Why didn't you tell Dad?"

This conversation is over. My dad would have given me a double beating. It was a fucking sacrilege to say anything about a man of the cloth. She knows that. But that's my mom's way of surviving. Everything goes away. "Object Permanence": if it is not physically in the room, then it simply doesn't exist.

I don't answer her. I have to leave the cafeteria now. "A fucking Catholic priest." It just won't stop ringing inside my head. Mom sits clutching her purse to her stomach as if I might make a run for the door with it. I think, Am I that low of a motherfucker to rip my own mother's pocketbook off?

Pressure mounts in my temples. I don't like feeling this way. I hurt people when I'm frightened. It's my dad's temper. For me, fear doubles with extreme injustice. I picture Dad's face; every lash he ever administered to the back of my legs with his belt strap begins to throb. Zebra stripes. Five. Welts so thick with rage I couldn't sit right for two days.

"Bend over," he'd scream! "Grab your ankle with one hand and cup your balls with the other!"

I lose it and grab the ketchup bottle in the middle of her table. Mom twitches and attempts to bury her chin. Without warning, I squeeze thick, fire-engine red ketchup all over my head, my face, and my chest.

"I'm ketchup! I'm fucking ketchup!" I holler as I rub the redness onto my skin.

Mom is aghast as I pick up the mustard bottle and squeeze yellow mustard over the red ketchup.

"I'm not mustard! I am fuuuckkkkinggggggggggggg ketchup!"

Mom's eyes fill with tears but there is no turning back now for me. I hesitate and she slowly stands. I've seen the identical look in her eyes a million times growing up with Dad. We were soldiers in the same war. But today she's on her own.

She tries to run. I catch both arms and pin her to the wall. The purse becomes tangled and bounces off the floor. Her rosary beads spill out onto my hospital slippers. A well of tears rush up my spine; I'm hysterical.

"Dad always wanted me to be a Notre Dame football player. He wanted me to be a *fucking Catholic priest!* Notre Dame! Catholic priest! Notre Dame! Catholic priest! I'm a fuckin' cripple, Ma; I'm a fuckin' cripple!"

"Let go of her, Richard!" Mrs. Kay yells from the doorway.

"Why can't she see it, Mrs. Kay? Can't you see it?" I turn just my head, directly toward Mrs. Kay. She looks extremely hesitant about coming into the kitchen. "My dad wants me to be something I ain't, Mrs. Kay. I'm not mustard! I'm ketchup! I'm a cripple, Mrs. Kay. I'm nothing but a fucking cripple!"

Suddenly, all the air pressure exits my head. Mom's arms have purple indents, finger marks from my frustration. I feel like I've been slapped hard across the face. I always preferred being punched—something about a slap in the face is pure humiliation. Dad always slapped me. He didn't have the balls to punch me. I step back and watch Mom as she bends to retrieve her purse and rosary beads.

"Don't call me. Don't come home. You need help. I cannot help you, Richard. I don't want to see you until you get help," Mom cries, moving quickly past Mrs. Kay.

Mrs. Kay tends to my mom and leaves me there crying. After a while, Levine comes in and sits next to me. Mrs. Kay has called him. The ketchup and mustard have congealed. Some of the mustard has clogged my right nostril. Levine's quiet, just there to keep me company. The silence in the room gives me a feeling of safety. My stomach muscles ache from crying, but the tears have washed away years of pent-up, make-believe bullshit I fed myself trying to live somebody else's dream. Acceptance washes over me. For the first time in my life, I acknowledge the words, "I'm a cripple."

Chapter 16

Day Seven: Afternoon– Levine's Office

Fear. Anxiety. Depression. My head feels like a fifty-pound dumbbell. My heart is threatening to implode. My lips are tight, tight—and purple. Sweat on my forehead turns to ice. I sit alone in Levine's office, waiting.

The late-afternoon light filters through the window and onto the floor at my feet. The sound of a car's engine soothes the silence holding the room hostage. I sit in the familiar cherry-wood rickety chair, moving the back just enough so it creaks like floorboards on an old porch.

Random thoughts create vivid images, moving snapshots of my childhood. Suddenly, tears cut a path down my cheeks, drip off the edge of my chin, disappear, and form small dark dots on my bathrobe.

I can't believe it's almost over. I'll miss Dr. Levine. Not that I really got to know him. He rarely ever spoke. Just sat there and looked at me for hours. But I guess his presence, his position, and this detox forced me to talk about things I thought I'd forgotten. I must have cried two or three times after leaving Levine's session. I wish I'd had enough balls to tell him everything, the truth about the night my father died.

Mrs. Kay knocks and enters with questions about another patient. She doesn't look up, assumes Levine is sitting behind his desk. She smirks nervously after nobody answers. It was a first for me; I'd never seen the old lady embarrassed.

"Can I stay one more day?"

"Seven days is seven days—no exceptions," she explains.

"You made the exception for Doc Adams."

"He hung himself," she reminds me.

"So that will do it? A failed suicide attempt?"

Mrs. Kay does not find me even a little amusing. She struggles to turn her upper body and legs in unison. Respect is not something I give easily these days, but as I watch Mrs. Kay struggle I am overcome with admiration. She's given her entire life to losers like me. She had to be tough, set rules, and demand certain expectations.

"Tomorrow, immediately upon discharge, go sign in at the Shedd Building next door—the psych ward. Tell them you're going to kill yourself. They'll pink-slip you. Keep you for forty-eight hours while they evaluate your threat level," Mrs. Kay says as the door closes and she slips out of sight.

I love her. The old battle-ax has just given her rendition of keeping me off the streets for forty-eight hours. It hits me deep down in my belly—she isn't being sarcastic. No, just the opposite: she's handed me a game plan if I ever have to use it. And it's illegal, a lie; she'd get fired if they ever found out I was faking suicide at her suggestion.

Levine enters. I sense an uncomfortable manner, something about his gait. His eyes are fixated, distant, and full of questions. He places the file he's carrying quickly onto his desktop, removes his glasses, and reaches for the longest, half-smoked cigarette butt in the ashtray.

"You tryin' to quit, Doc?"

"You been waiting long, Richie?"

"What's up? Rough day?"

It's the first time he's ever sat on the edge of the desk hovering over my chair. He forces himself to reopen the file at his side. I try to move forward and sneak a peek. But then I get scared. Is it something medical? Do I have AIDS? My mind jumps like a car radio scanning for a favorite song. This has to be bad. Levine lights the cigarette butt between his teeth.

"Doc, come on, what's the matter? Is there something wrong?"

"Richard, did you play football at Notre Dame?"

"What?" I say, forcing a nervous grin. "Oh! God."

It was worse. Those words, "Notre Dame," send my heart pounding; my lips and throat feel like sandpaper. My Adam's apple feels as if it's choking me. My right shoulder throbs with a deep, shooting pain. My fingers go numb and I can feel my heart beating in my temples.

"What? What did you say?"

"Richard. Come on, you understand what I asked. Did you really play football at Notre Dame?"

I can't believe he's asked me again. Something is up. He has never questioned my status as a football star. Pressure inside my brain becomes pins and needles dancing madly. My face turns hot and tight; my whole existence is in jeopardy. My gut tells me to spit it out, tell Levine it was nothin' but bull-shit. But suddenly, I realize there is no need to. He's seen me walk. He knows I'm a cripple. I think of my dad and how I should proceed. Should I continue to lie out of love for my dad?

I remembered Friday nights when I was a young child, the times Dad would carry me up two flights of stairs to pick up pizza at George's on Broadway. I couldn't climb the stairs because of the braces on my right leg. But Dad knew how much I loved that pizza. He always chose me over my brother to ride with him. God, how good it felt, Dad's mus-cles ripping tight against my crippled legs.

I was safe with my dad. Nobody got in his way, the heel-and-toe walk, the chest expanded, the flattop, nobody dared. I remember how people turned to look at Dad as he en-tered rooms. He was a runaway steamroller with the charm of a prince.

Levine begins reading the pages inside the file; he real-izes I've drifted away. I'm not sure where to go. I like this guy. Confusion swirls my thoughts into mush.

"Richard, do you know what it means to be a patho-logical liar?"

I know but hesitate to tell him. I don't want to be wrong. I'm sure he already hates me. I'm convinced; he's lost all respect for me.

"Well, a pathological liar invents his or her own reality. Usually, something—either a traumatic event or an illness—takes control of the person's ability to see the truth. People who are pathological actually believe the fantasy worlds they've created by lying."

"Come on? You're kidding me," I said weakly.

"No, Richard, it is a very common human condition. I think all of us, if we were honest, lie to some degree."

"Really?"

"Yes; however, some people take that degree too far and it hurts them. Do you understand, Richard?"

"Kinda, Doc!"

I know and he knows, but neither of us knows how much the other knows.

"Your mother told me you never played football at Notre Dame. She explained how you invented a fantasy world in order to be accepted by your father."

"My mother hates me. She told me today she never wanted to see me again. She disowned me, Doc."

Suddenly, I see compassion on Levine's face. He likes me again. I guess the shock of finding out, thinking I was somebody else, has worn off. Funny how people always held me in high esteem because they thought I played football at Notre Dame; I was a superstar. Most people want to be around somebody who is great at something.

"Richard, it's all right to be who you are!"

Suddenly, a ton of pain inside the middle of my gut swells up like a fifty-pound rock. I feel dizzy. The tears won't stop. I can't face Levine. I can't deny it or confirm it. My thoughts skip to Dad, working out with me in the gym, pushing me, loving me, holding me. All I ever cared about was pleasing my dad.

"Richie, the trauma in your life is real. It all happened. It's documented over and over by countless people. You were a great football player. But your brain was damaged at birth. The doctor had to rip you out with forceps. Your mother almost died. The violence and the urgency of your delivery left your right leg crippled."

I manage to stop crying, and for the first time in my life I sense the true feeling of being a cripple. It all comes rushing back to me. All the feelings as a young child, when I really was a cripple. All the stares, all the laughs, God—I hated being a cripple.

"I'm not sure if I should tell you this, Doc. But I didn't lie about everything. I'm embarrassed. You can't leave here thinkin' I'm one of those paper-ass pansies that makes up everything."

"You don't have to explain anything to me, Richard. I understand," he says, moving around his desk to sit.

"No, no"—I interrupt him—"you gotta hear me out."

Levine understands. He reaches for the ashtray; his fingers fish frantically for another already smoked butt.

"There was only one thing I ever truly wanted in my life. I wanted my dad to be proud of me. And I would have done anything to accomplish it."

Right now, I need Levine to understand where it all started. How every Saturday morning when I was a child, at 10 a.m., Notre Dame football highlights would be rerun on one of the local stations. Dad, Sean, and I were religious: it was bacon and eggs, Notre Dame, and church—in that order.

"Dad wanted me to play football for Notre Dame. I had no choice," I explain to Levine while he settles back in his chair and relaxes. No doubt, he recognizes my urgency to clarify how the Notre Dame myth evolved.

I begin by asking him if he remembers when there was no cable television, no seventy-two channels. Back then, three local VHF channels gave great reception. And you had a half dozen or so UHF channels that came into focus depending on the weather.

Tell him some days that the picture was so bad it was more like listening to a radio. Other days, the sound reminded me of a ham-radio operator from China. But we didn't complain or even acknowledge a problem—it was Notre Dame football.

"But I don't want you to think I just watched Notre Dame football on Saturday mornings and invented myself."

Levine wants to know how I became a high school football star. I smirk and begin the story. My dad taught at Lowell High, so attendance there was not even in question. My next stop was at Austin Preparatory High School in Reading, Massachusetts. The thing I learned the most from Austin Prep was how to get high. Every morning, me and Rocky Boisvert drove down I-93, smokin' a fat joint of blond pot and sipping on vodka and orange juice. The first class, our homeroom, was the old Pewter Pot Restaurant in Reading, Massachusetts.

In fact, if it weren't for Sandy Ruggles, our backfield coach and science teacher, I probably wouldn't have had a football career. The rules were you had to be in school on Friday before the game or you couldn't play on Saturday. But of course, I was always down yonder at the Pewter Pot.

You see, each homeroom teacher took attendance and put the slip in a small box outside the classroom. And every morning, especially Fridays, someone would come around and collect them en route to the office. Sandy knew the exact time and always found a way to have my name scratched off the sheet. I'm not saying he did it, but it was done.

For me, football was only a place to enforce my violent behavior, a place to exercise my rage and get noticed for it. The girls liked me and the guys were scared of me. Shit, how can you beat that?

In fact, it was at Austin Prep that I acquired the reputation of being dangerous. My coach benched me for my performance in the Tewksbury game. I was hung over and ate too many "Black Beauties." God did I get sucked in on a quarterback draw. The kid ran for a good forty yards before I ran him down. But I fixed Klimas in practice that week. I jumped over on the third defense and cracked the shit out of our first team offense.

I'll never forget it. At first, when Klimas saw me over on defense, he tried to hurt me. He called a trap block, a cheap shot. Terry Burke, a 230-pound tackle, came down the line and blindsided me. It killed. I wanted to cry, but instead, I jumped to my feet. Everybody thought I'd never get up. "Same play!" Klimas yelled. And on the snap, I turned and flung everything I had into Burke coming down the line. *Crash!* I can still feel the impact.

Guess what? I jumped up, nodded my head at a truly disarrayed Klimas, and screamed, "One more time!" Burke didn't want any part of me. Klimas had to start me, and my teammates knew I was crazy.

I'll never forget the letter I received from Joe Yonto, the Notre Dame recruiter. It had the little gold helmet up in the corner and I kept it in my pocket forever.

Hey, my quest to make Dad proud became my reality, a reality I'd never want to change. Because right now, if I heard the "Notre Dame Victory March," I'd cry. I'd never give that up!

"Let me explain a few facts that may help you." Levine's words bring me back to real time. "It is very common for people who suffer from PTSD, post-traumatic stress disorder, to invent or create a safe environment to live in. You've done nothing wrong, Richard!"

"You mean I'm not some sort of sicko?" I ask.

Levine smiles. I smile. He understands, I think.

"Your mother talked about the pain and beatings you suffered. She called them zebra stripes. She explained how even after each terrible beating, you held no grudges. In fact, the next day, you would idolize your father even more."

Levine has my full attention. All the truth, all the demons, everything is about to explode. I feel sick. I am going to puke. But nothing comes. Dry heave after dry heave, nothing but thoughts and scenes of how much I tried to please my dad. I can't speak, but I want to.

"Richard, you must let Notre Dame go. You will be better off. Everything around you will look better. It was not your fault. None of it was your doing. Let the lie go."

"I just hope this don't change the way you look at me."

He smiles, pushes the file closed, leans back in his chair, and lights a whole cigarette from a full pack he'd been hiding in his top drawer. After a deep, almost righteous inward pull of smoke, he moves forward and offers me one. I refuse.

"Richard, you're the same today you were yesterday. At first, I felt a little cheated. But I realize the aura of your football career should in no way diminish or heighten the significance of trauma you experienced as a child."

It's time to go. I stand, and something inside me feels clean or new.

"Besides, growing up, I hated Notre Dame football," he says with a smirk.

"Thanks, Doc, I appreciate the fact you allowed me to

go on and on about my glory days in high school. I know it's not the same as being a football star from Notre Dame. But it's more than some kids ever did," I reluctantly, almost meekly say as I begin to leave his office for the day.

As I turn to walk back to my room, I'm embarrassed, pregnant with shame. I'll never again be able to stand behind the shield of being a Notre Dame football player. Dad's light suddenly reaches out and holds me. I let him down. Now, I stand naked. The whole world is laughing at me. They can all see my flaws.

I decide to find Crazy Mary. She'll understand. I'll practice telling her the truth. If it goes well, I'll tell Murph. Mary's sitting alone in the dayroom, silent, staring up at a blank television screen. She tells me Murph left without saying good-bye. She's sad. Tells me she's leaving with me tomorrow. I bend over, kiss her forehead, and decide to let it go. It's not the time to tell her my secret.

Chapter 17

April 1, 1987–Discharge Day: Morning

Today, breakfast is not an option. I've tried. The boiled eggs wouldn't chew. No amount of butter moistened the toast enough to swallow. My mind is pure mocus, not one thought would stick.

I am alone, dressed in my new stonewashed dungarees and a blue-and-green polo shirt that my mother dropped off at the front desk late last night.

My room is dead quiet; everybody is at late-morning meds. I pack the hospital-issued green garbage bag with my old Notre Dame football jacket, three clean, hospital pin-striped robes for souvenirs, and the letters I've written and never sent. God, it's hard dealing with the full use of my senses. I can hear the dull hum of the kitchen dishwasher for the first time since I'd been here.

Time to go. Levine is waiting in his office.

The final walk down the green-tiled, poorly lit corridor

is slowed by orderlies, nurses, and new patients who wish me well. They seem invisible. My handshake is almost mechanical. Crazy Mary sits on the floor outside of Levine's office. She springs to her feet and embraces me with a death grip. Through the smoked glass, I can make out Levine's shadow moving around the office. Neither one of us wants to be the first to release, but I wait to feel her grip relax.

"I love you," Crazy Mary whispers before turning her back and stepping out.

Those words are like a sword piercing through my side. It wasn't that we were lovers in the true sense of the word. Certainly we had sexual relations, but our love was far more important than having an orgasm. What Crazy Mary and I shared was ironically the most contaminated and unpolluted human bond between a man and a woman. We were forever linked by intimacy derived from shamefaced, emotional pain and the unbearable struggle for survival. I'll miss her and wonder if I'll ever see her again.

There he is, Dr. Samuel Levine, just as I suspected, rocking in slow motion on the other side of his cluttered desk. His squinting, brown eyes look helpless, sad, like a pitcher who's given up a home run and is solely responsible for losing the big game.

"Richie, what are you going to do from here?"

I hear his question, but it's like I'm not in the room. Instead, I focus on the lilac tree on the other side of the window. I thought about spring, how four months could change a barren tree into a vivid, red and purple display of blossoms or flowers.

Levine turns his back, stands sharply, and walks to the window. He lights a cigarette, drags deeply, and opens the window wide. A rush of smoke escapes like a ghost seeping into a brick wall. The smell of fresh, brisk air replaces the stink of stale nicotine, and tiny particles of dust swirl around in the sunlight.

I sneeze.

"God bless you!"

"No, I don't think he did, Doc."

I don't know where those words come from. But suddenly, I'm back to reality, back to being scared, back to wondering about my next move.

"What?" Levine asked.

I reach for the Kleenex on top of the steel-gray desk and blow my nose. Levine glances at his watch, aware time is running out.

"Richie," he asks again, "what are you going to do? You must have some kind of plan or you'll fail."

Now, the fear grows so large, I can't control myself. We stand together, side by side, focused on the dew lifting off the tips of the dark green grass.

"I know, I know, I don't think I'll ever get over my father's death."

Levine is so different from all those doctors I'd scammed for pain pills. Should I tell him how I killed my father? He seems to still like me even after the Notre Dame bullshit. Maybe I should hug him, walk away, and die with the truth.

"Richie, we're all going to die. Your father died, you'll die someday, but that must not stop you from living."

"Shit, I don't care about dying, Doc. I've been dead so many times it ain't funny. I'm scared about living out there," I say, pointing a quick finger toward the window.

"Well," he says, chuckling, "you don't hold any patents on that fear. Life isn't easy. But it can be a wonderful experience once you take control."

"Doc, I'm just sick and tired of living inside this fucked-up self. I don't want to be a loser and junkie forever. I'm running out of chances."

"Well, let's get back to a plan!"

"I don't think I'm going to make it, Doc."

"Why?" Levine lights another cigarette and opens the flap to offer me one. "Want one?" he asks.

I slide one out, stick it between my teeth, and move closer to Levine for a light. Silence holds the room until I put out my cigarette.

"I'll never get past the dream I have every night and sometimes during the day. It's not picky about time. Funny, it has a mind of its own. I cannot even will it away."

"Is it a nightmare or a specific psychotic episode that haunts you?"

Psychotic episode? My ass finds the chair quickly. I don't know what that means. But Levine's eyes beam like headlights on a dark country road. Invisible rays of gold seem to tie me to the chair. I can see he hasn't a clue. But that moment I trust him.

"It's my father's death," I say. "I don't know if I can handle stuff that really happened the night I found him."

I can feel myself beginning to crumble. No matter how big or strong I thought I was, my weakness is the dream— the night I found him."

"Have you ever talked about it before?"

"No."

Levine is paralyzed.

"Do you feel comfortable talking to me about your father's death?"

My body tenses. I mumble. Dr. Levine doesn't move.

"What did you say, Richie?"

"Doc, I'm comfortable. The question is, if I tell you—will you be comfortable?"

Maybe it's a foolish thing to say, but I have to warn him. He's a good guy, and he's about to be stuck with information he hasn't bargained for.

Levine is now sitting in his chair. It's surreal. I can't remember him moving away from the window. He stretches his neck toward the ceiling and nervously fumbles, trying to light another cigarette. He doesn't offer me one.

"Well, what do you mean? Will I be comfortable?"

"Doc, tell me about client/doctor confidentiality."

"You are losing me, Richie," Levine says. "What are you trying to tell me?"

"Okay, I'll tell you my dream, but it's between me and you. Remember, I'm not telling you it's real!"

"I hate to keep going back to this, but is it a dream in the true sense of the word? Do you know the definition of a psychotic episode?"

"That's just it, Doc. I'm not sure about anything. I'm not sure if it's part of my memory or something I've imagined. All I know is these giant puke-green frogs chase me all the time. The frogs force me into this one room. They don't let me leave. I have to watch my father die over and over."

"But your father was already dead when you found him, Richie?"

"Well, Doc, that's what I'm not sure of. I mean, that's what I tell people. And it's kind of like the Notre Dame story; I've told it so many times, I guess it might be real."

Levine's right hand rushes for his pen and notepad on the desk. He stands up, closes the window, and pulls his chair around to my side of the desk.

"Tell me about the dream."

"It's always the same. I wake up in my bed to the sound of the phone ringing and ringing on the kitchen wall. When I jump out of bed to answer the phone, I see the frog. He's outside my window, watching me. I swear he's gotta be ten feet tall and four feet wide. His eyelids are always shut, but they're transparent and he stares at me. I run to the phone. It's my mom. She's calling from the hospital. She just had a hysterectomy that morning and was still quite medicated. Her speech is slurred. I turn and the frog is still there—watching."

Levine relaxes in his chair and reaches back for his cigarettes. This time he offers me one but I refuse.

"Mom tells me Dad won't answer the phone at their home and she's worried. I glance at the frog and tell Mom I'll go right over to check on him. The second I put the phone down, something feels wrong. The frog is gone. I have the same feeling I used to get before Dad gave me zebra stripes.

"It's about four thirty, and in the winter it gets dark early. When I pull up in the driveway, the outside lights aren't on. Dad was a light freak; he hated the dark. The lights were always on. We grew up in a split-level with a two-car garage underneath. I open my mom's side because Dad has an electric door on his. The door from the garage into the house is locked, but I know where the key is hidden. So I open the door and go in."

My heart begins to race and sweat drips under my arms. I can smell the rancid stench of my own sweat. Levine is chain-smoking and the cloud starts to make the room stuffy and hot.

"Are you all right?" he asks. He sounds more frightened than curious.

My skin begins to get cold and tight. But I want to finish.

"I go up the first flight of stairs and turn. The night light is over the sink. And I see him. From where I'm standing, I'm eye level to the kitchen floor. Dad's feet are the first thing I see. He's face down, not moving, lifeless, and I know he's dead. I scream his name and bolt toward him up the remaining stairs. His red velour bathrobe glitters as I draw closer. He looks so small there, lying there, so insignificant. But he's my dad and I have to help him."

I stop because my lips are quivering. I stand up and sit down, desperately trying to keep control. I can't cry. Dad told me never to cry at important events or crucial moments. I can still hear his voice speaking to me.

Levine looks at his watch. Almost noon, discharge time. We both know in fifteen minutes it will be over. Mrs. Kay will be knocking at the door because another loser like me needs the bed. Sometimes I ramble. I have to talk faster.

"I roll him over and still can't fucking believe what I'm seeing. Shit, Doc, he's green, black, yellow, and blue. His eyes are wide open; the whites are red with blood. His skin is frozen. His lips are crimson-purple, like the color of that lilac tree when it blossoms in spring."

I stand up, walk past Levine, and open the window. The smoke is choking me. My eyes are burning and Levine might think I'm crying.

Outside there's a young maintenance man pulling an orange rake back and forth near some shrubs. The kid must be in his early twenties; he has a baseball cap and headphones in both ears. I watch him for a few seconds. Not a worry in the world, his head and shoulders dancing to the beat of the music. Levine has both hands cupped against the top of his forehead. His elbows rest on the edge of his knees. He watches me through the tunnel his fingers have created.

"I pound on his chest and his fucking sternum snaps. I shut my eyes, pinch his nose, and my lips open wide to cover his mouth. I blow air and his chest rises; I open my eyes and nothing happens. Nothing. But the frog is back, his brown eyes bugging against the kitchen window. I feel like I'm under water fighting to get to the top so I can breathe. The phone rings and I just scream to get the ambulance. I don't know who it was, but when I hear the ambulance, I stop, kneel before him, pick up his head, and press it tight to my chest."

I can't sit down. The anger and rage inside me begin to swell. All I can do is pound my fist on the windowsill. I want the maintenance worker to look up and see my pain. But he doesn't. I'm going to cry.

"Dad's silver-gray hair is still alive in my hands!" I scream.

Levine stands and starts toward me.

"Let it go, Richard!"

"Why, Dad? Why, Dad? Why did you do it?" I can't control my sobbing. "I had to Daddy, you wouldn't stop. The pain, I had to. You left me no choice."

"You had to what? What did you have to do?"

"I . . . I . . . I. . . ."

"You what?"

Something is grabbing my throat; I can only whisper. But then like the light in a convict's tunnel, the words pierce the room. "I murdered the motherfucker."

It's the first time I've heard myself audibly say the words.

Levine isn't shocked. In fact, I think I see him smile. I fall to the ground and crack my head on the lime-green cinder block wall.

A fast, sharp knock on the glass in the door interrupts the tension in the room. Through the thick, tinted glass in the middle of the door, the shadow of someone's shoulder-length hair is visible. "Is everything all right in there?" asks one of the orderlies.

"Everything is okay." Levine hesitates.

It's exactly noon. The orderly's silhouette disappears. Levine removes his white coat and covers my shoulders. I guess he thinks I'm shaking from the cold air entering through the opened window. He sits in my chair, lights a cigarette, and waits. I cringe and sob in a fetal position.

"Richie, do you want to sit up?"

"No."

Time is up. I'll have to leave any minute. "What happened that night?" Levine asks.

"I fuckin' killed him, Doc. I've done everything I could trying to forget, but I can't, Doc. I just can't."

"What do you mean you killed him? He died of a heart attack, didn't he?"

"I took his nitroglycerin pills away and watched him die. He cried. One tear rolled down his face and cut a dry white line down his cheek. He begged me to help."

Suddenly, I sit up. I feel alive. Levine's plaid tie is undone and his shirtsleeves are rolled up, exposing the thick dark hair on his forearms.

There's another knock on the door. I help myself to a cigarette on the desk. Levine stands.

"Yes," he says.

"Dr. Levine, Mrs. Farrell is here for Richard," replies Mrs. Kay.

The thought of my mother's voice and face make me feel warm all over. She said she never wanted to see me again. She disowned me.

"Make her comfortable in the lobby, Mrs. Kay. We'll be only ten minutes."

I wonder if Mom will wait ten minutes.

"Do you want to tell me what really happened that night?"

I can see the compassion, the true friendship in Doctor Levine's smile.

"I'm going to trust you, Doc. And I hope I'm not doing the wrong thing."

"It will stay with me, I promise."

I knock the head off my cigarette and begin to pace the five-by-ten office.

"My Mom had been operated on at nine a.m. I took Dad to see her around noon, but she was out of it. After we spoke to the doctor and found out everything was okay with her, I drove him home. My dad had a bad heart but he wouldn't let anybody stay with him."

"Hold it, Richard. I don't mean to push you, but your mother is out there and Mrs. Kay will be back any minute."

"Sure, sure. Well, when I came home from shopping at the mall, I felt sad and decided to take a ride up the street and check on Dad. There was a brown, late-model Monte Carlo parked in the driveway. I knew who it was. My mom's friend, an Asian lady my mother had tutored in English."

I stop to catch my breath.

"The garage door was unlocked. I walked right up the

front stairs and there they were, the two of them, Dad on top of her, pounding her bare ass up and down. They were so busy they never heard the garage door. Both her feet were pointing straight up, lace underpants dangling from one ankle, moaning and groaning in some kind of gook talk."

I stop by the window and watch the young maintenance worker. I'll be thirty-one years old in December. The young maintenance worker reminds me of how much of my life I've squandered. I hate his youth.

"Did you leave?"

"No way. I walked right up to them. He almost shit, turning and seeing me standing over him. He turned white and grabbed his chest. But I thought he was acting; he always did that when he didn't like what was happening. She didn't know what to do. I remember Dad rolled off her, and when I saw her lying there with her crotch wide open, I pictured Mom in the hospital bed."

"Is that when he had the heart attack?"

"No, I don't know what happened, but I got a hard-on watching my old man fuck this young woman. She was petrified, didn't dare move. Dad grabbed his chest again, and I grabbed the young lady by her hair and tossed her and her pocketbook and clothes on the back lawn. When I got back, Dad was lying on his right forearm begging me for help. But I thought he was trying to get out of what he just did to Mom. So I didn't get the pills. I just fucking screamed, 'Die you son of a bitch.' The phone rang but I didn't answer. I remember thinking it was Mom."

"Dr. Levine," Mrs. Kay knocks again, "how much longer do you expect to be?"

Levine couldn't answer.

"Dr. Levine, I have an admission. We need Mr. Farrell's bed. His mother is getting impatient. How much longer before we discharge?"

I stand up and sit down, and Dr. Levine does the same.

"Five minutes, Mrs. Kay. Go away."

I bet Mrs. Kay's pissed. Nobody speaks to her like that. I'm sure Dr. Levine will hear about it later.

"Richard, he died of a heart attack. It doesn't sound to me like it was your fault. He had a history of manipulation. You thought he was faking."

"But at the end, he was blue. I pulled a kitchen chair up close to him. I remember his eyes bulged, and just before he took his last breath, he reached out and took hold of my hand. He squeezed it like a vice and said he loved me. I could have stopped it. I could have run down the corridor like I had so many other nights and slipped two or three nitro pills under his tongue. But when I went to get up, I remembered his fucking 'zebra stripes,' how I begged him to stop hurting me. Right at that very instant, I made a conscious decision not to get his nitro pills. I sat down and saw the shadow of his belt and shook all over. I loved him so much and chose to watch him die. The last thing I said to him was, 'Why didn't you love me, Daddy?' And that's when one last tear moved across his face."

Levine stands up, walks over to me, and holds me while I cry.

"Good job," Levine says. "Your dad played the game one too many times. It's not your fault. Nobody could blame you. You didn't kill him. He killed himself."

There, I've told it. No longer is the secret mine alone. I didn't plan to tell him. I promised myself years ago, I'd die with the secret. But the phenomenon of spilling your guts before you leave Lowell Detox is true to form. I'm not sure what it actually is that compels patients to sing prior to discharge. It would make so much more sense if this type of information were delivered early on in the stay.

"Sit down for a minute, Richie. I want to tell you something that I never want you to forget. Times are going to get tough for you. It isn't an easy task turning around a life lived as yours. But it can be done."

I believe him. Others along the way have preached the same words to me over and over. But for the first time in my life I believe it.

"It will take some time. But you must remember the things that your father did to you were not your fault. You didn't deserve to be beaten with a fence post, to be beaten with a leather belt, or to be beaten with his fist."

Levine releases his hold on my shoulder and squats down so his eyes are almost kissing my eyes. He wants me to get it, to understand. I think he really believes I'm redeemable.

"Each and every one of us on this beautiful planet earth have terrible things that happen to us during a lifetime. Death takes loved ones; unthinkable trauma sears itself into our memory patterns and refuses to let go; people we love more than anything desert us when we need them the most."

Levine stops. Silence devours the room. It strangles each and every sound from the outside and hallway. Levine and I sit in a vacuum of sound blackness. I float above my body. My ears ring.

"Listen to me, Richard. Never forget what I'm going to tell you. The only thing that matters is what we do with now. What we do with what's left of us after the pain rips us apart."

I try hard to take it all in. The room becomes bright transparent light. I no longer can see Levine.

"Do you understand, Richie?"

But Levine isn't asking for a response.

"It's what's left of us that matters," Levine whispers into my right ear. "What's left of us."

Chapter 18 ....

April 1, 1987–Discharge
Day: 12:30 p.m.

Levine and I hug; four arms locked together, both of us trembling.

The door glass shakes again and Levine snaps, "Mrs. Kay, we'll be right out."

But it's not Mrs. Kay.

"Richard, it's going on too long. I must leave now. I have many errands," Mom says.

"Okay, Mom, I'm coming right this minute."

I rub the tears off my face and fight to push back the emotion, to pretend again. And then, presto, I'm Richie Farrell, shoulders back, chin out, and full of confidence. When the door opens, Mom looks very impatient. Her lips are moving, as always, in constant prayer for my soul. I pull her close, pick her up, and squeeze her like I did in the old days.

As I step away, my arm still around Mom's shoulder, I

look back into Levine's office. "You think I'll make it, Doc?" But he doesn't reply. Instead he turns his back and watches the young maintenance man outside the window, laughing, flirting with two young, attractive nurse's aides.

Mrs. Kay is waiting at the front desk, acting anxious for me to sign the release papers. Her new admission is an eighteen-year-old boy bouncing off the walls in the next room. My right hand trembles as I scratch my name on the spot marked "X." Mrs. Kay never looks up. What expression I can see is blank and constant.

"Mr. Farrell, one of these days soon you won't be able to make it into a hospital. One day at a time, walk away from this life you're living. It's only going to kill you in the end," Mrs. Kay warns.

The word "kill" forces me to find Mrs. Kay's eyes. I deliberately stop and freeze until she looks at me. Face to face, we stand glaring, like pit bulls at the end of a leash. Both of us hate and love one another in some peculiar way. Both of us want to hug the other, but can't.

Mom's left the building and is waiting in the courtyard. She hates Lowell Detox and everything it stands for. Before I walk out the door, I turn and see Levine's figure standing at the end of the corridor outside his office door. It's too dark to confirm positively, but I could swear he's crying.

The walk down the front stairs is familiar to me. The exhilaration from a giant sucking sound brought on by sensory overload makes me overly anxious. I can hear the butterflies flapping their wings. The balls of my feet create friction on the cement walkway. My knees creak. My peripheral vision is so clear I can almost see behind me.

I flash back to the old football days, the pregame jitters.

The bus ride to the opponent's field, nobody speaking as anxiety finds a way to squash the chatter of teenage boys. I wonder if the ancient Greek gladiators felt the same. Were they frightened to march into the battlefield of the unknown? My favorite book was Homer's *Iliad*, specifically, the scene in which Achilles, the strongman, dies.

"Are you ready, Richard?" Mom asks.

"I'm as ready as I'll ever be, Mom."

"How do you feel?"

"Honestly, Mom. I don't know."

"Well, Richard, if anybody can turn things around—you can. All your life I have watched you beat the odds. Remember, a lot of people are praying for you. God is the only answer, Richard. I wouldn't have survived without Him."

Mom drives along the Merrimack River Boulevard, across the Rourke Bridge, and pulls in to the Market Basket food store. We don't speak at all. I'm thirty now, and there's something surreal about sitting in the passenger seat today. I should be driving, I think. It isn't natural. I'm not sixteen.

What happened to those years? How did this happen?

"Would you like to come in with me? It won't take long if you wish to stay in the car. I'll leave my keys if you'd like to listen to the news or music. But of course, come if you'd like," Mom says.

I sense her confusion. She really wants me to stay but is reluctant to hurt me either way. I help her out by taking the keys and smiling. She knows there is something different about me. We stop for seconds and hold each other's eyes.

"Forget it, Richard," she blurts.

My mother has read my mind. I wanted to confess to her. There was something wholesome about telling Levine. The toll from all the years of keeping secrets had added up. The price was too high. Mom opens the door fast and steps out of the car.

"Mom!" I yell.

Mom freezes and in slow motion turns her head back but keeps walking forward. She doesn't want to hear what I have to say. I reach for my door handle, exit the car, and run to catch up to her.

"I gotta tell you something about Dad."

"What?"

"About the way he died, Mom."

"Richard." She stops and squares herself to meet my eyes. "He's dead; everybody dies. Now, let us get on with living."

I can't help but notice Mom's tarnished beauty. Her cheeks flush and the long flowing, gray-white hair still pulled back into a ponytail. She winks and steps out with the same vigor that made me proud as a young boy. But I have to tell her the truth.

"I killed him, Mom!"

She stops, spins around, shakes her head, and speaks to me with undeniable conviction.

"No," she says, "he killed himself."

Mom's right hand flashes back for my hand and together we walk into the supermarket. Her touch brings to me an immediate realization: Mom knew all along. There wasn't any reason to dig up the graphic details. My mother wanted her husband's affair to die with my dad. She had accepted it, considered Dad's infidelity a human condition he couldn't control, and loved him anyway.

I push the cart down the produce aisle as she checks the strawberries for mold and juggles apples until she finds fruit

with no bruises. I watch her, shoulders back, almost reaching
for the high ceilings. The old smile lines on her cheeks have
become overrun with small spider veins. She's proud, defiant.
We were once warriors. The two of us have survived.

But is the final price the both of us have paid everything
we have inside of us? How would Mom continue without
the madness in her life? I know it's crazy but after a while
you thrive inside turmoil. In fact, in detox I learned peace
and quiet were abnormal. I watch Mom turn the corner to
another aisle without signaling me to follow and wondered
what's ahead for me.

I'm thirty years old and nothing about me seems real.
My heart begins to beat outside my chest when I realize that
the Richie Farrell pushing a shopping cart full of groceries
up and down DeMoulas supermarket in Lowell, Massachusetts, on April 1, 1987, was created by a pack of lies. I'd lied
about everything. I was a ghost.

At the cash register, Mom carefully checks the young
girl's work as she enters the price of each and every item.
My dad had taught her that. He'd said most of these young
girls were stupid and didn't care if they screwed us out of
money.

I just can't take my eyes off the girl's lips. She's all of
eighteen, blonde, with aqua-green eyes and red, delicious,
plump lips. The bottom lip is slightly larger and shiny with
gloss that reflects the fluorescent overhead lights. I smile at
her and my mind immediately leaps to what those lips could
do. I guess Mrs. Kay was right when she said, "First things
first."

Outside in the parking lot Mom steps out a few feet in
front of me and finds the car. She sits waiting as I neatly

place about a dozen paper bags into the trunk. I remember how I loved to shop with her when I was ten and eleven. Back then, she stood outside the car to make sure I didn't break the eggs or squish the bread.

On weekends my dad would come with us. We'd wait in the car while Mom shopped. Dad would always remind her to hurry. But if the Yankees were playing he wouldn't care how long she took. I'd sit in the backseat, directly behind him with my right hand on his shoulder. Mickey Mantle and Roger Maris would always hit home runs. Dad would scream like he was the only person on the planet. Passersby would make eye contact with me to confirm everything was okay. It was wonderful when the Yankees won. But if they lost the entire fuckin' world would be screwed.

I remember a Saturday when the Yanks were down by three in the bottom of the ninth. Dad had turned inward; it seemed as though the heat inside his belly was now trying to escape through his neck. My hand slid slowly off his shoulder; the slightest jerk or increase in pressure would spell disaster for me. Dad removed his glasses—a sign of bad things to come. I pressed my shoulders as deep as humanly possible into the backseat upholstery.

There were two outs, the bases were loaded, and Joe Peppertone was at bat. Dad said he wasn't the greatest hitter. I thought about telling him I was heading to the bathroom when the count got to three balls and two strikes. The next pitch was a foul. "Fuck." Dad pronounced it like the word had four syllables. Three more fouls followed; each one paralyzed the air inside the car further. And then the entire car began to rock. Peppertone hit the ball out of Yankee Stadium. "A fucking grand-slam, Richie boy!" His arms extended out of his shoulders like rubber and he pulled me into his lap in one movement. Air immediately rushed the inside of the car with such speed I began to choke.

"I love you more than all the telephone poles in the whole wide world!" Dad screamed.

Several years earlier Dad had told me there were more telephone poles in America than any other object. One day he brought me to a forest in Dracut, Massachusetts. The entire place was being razed for telephone poles. It was amazing—side by side, two or three feet apart, no branches for twenty feet straight up, and an umbrella of green blocking out the sun. Back then, it was mind shattering to think he loved me more than the sight of those wonderful trees.

"You ready, Richard?" Mom's getting impatient.

We drive through the old neighborhood on the way home. Mom doesn't speak but I can tell she's anxious by the way she increases her grip on the wheel. As we approach Adam Street, St. Patrick's Church steeple looms over our front windshield. She knows and I know there's no way to escape Adam Street. Mom had married Dad here. Sean and I had marched the sidewalks in procession wearing bright white suits for our First Communion. I started lying in Confession directly under the steeple my great-uncle Joe had erected shortly after he'd arrived from Ireland.

Mom's knuckles turn red and then white. Out of respect for her, I never look out at the drug dealers peddling heroin. But Hector sees me and yells, "Richie!" with a strong Puerto Rican accent.

"Go, Mom. Go!"

Mom hits the gas pedal and we rocket forward. I turn

sharply to see if Hector is following. It's worse. Two of his friends, Puerto Rican guys I recognize, are running full stride. I swing my head around to check out the traffic and realize the lights at School Street have just turned red.

"Run the red light, Mom!"

"What? I can't. It's against the law, Richard."

"See those guys running? They aren't part of a welcoming home committee. Mom, I'll spare you the graphic details, but I robbed those guys and they're bad, bad dudes."

She presses her gaze forward like she's been trained. Dad had taught us to never look behind us. He said the only things that counted were in front of us.

"I thought the guy was still in jail. He's killed guys in Puerto Rico and doesn't give a shit about you having white hair. Run it!"

Mom slows, looks to her right and left, and floors it. Hector and his partners become smaller and smaller in the rearview mirror. Mom's eyes begin to fill with water. I've spent the last three years of my life down here in the Acre; the section of Lowell where it all began for the Farrells.

When Mom pulls into our driveway I step out of the car and am taken aback by the size of the backyard. It's shrunk. I want to ask Mom what happened, but I don't even have to shut my eyes to see the bloody noses and swollen ankles from the Sunday-afternoon football games. It happened here. We were young. The yard was huge back then.

I carry the groceries up the stairs for Mom and place them on the same kitchen table in the same room where Dad died. Mom hasn't changed a thing since that night. Suddenly, my legs crumble; everything begins to spin. I pull a chair out in order to steady myself. Mom has already headed down the corridor to her bedroom. I'm alone. And I cry. I cry because I've lost so much of my life. I cry because so many of my lies have become reality and now I don't know the truth about anything.

But one thing is certain, Dad's dead.

If only I could believe that in my Dad's final moment, before his brain shut off, he understood two truths.

I loved him, and I loved him and I let him die.

Epilogue

The first year I went to AA meetings twice a day. I also became very involved in the nondenominational church Robert Billson had first brought me to and soon after began to speak about the hazards of drug addictions in schools and organizations around New England.

I've been straight now for more than two decades. I went back to my wife and kids, and tried to keep it together. Fifteen years later my marriage went up in flames. I became a journalist. Covered a war in Bosnia and worked for HBO. I won the du Pont–Columbia award in 1996 for an HBO *America Undercover* documentary I directed titled "High on Crack Street: Lost Lives in Lowell." I went to Hollywood and wrote dialogue for Brad Pitt. I wrote a *Boston Globe* best seller about the Boston mob's connection to the Irish Republican Army.

Not a day goes by that I do not hear my father's voice.

A Note to the Reader.......................................

I wrote this memoir as a direct response to James Frey's *A Million Little Pieces*. I'm angry he lied. But let me explain, the fact that he made up certain events that were discovered by the media is irrelevant to me. Frey is a wonderful writer with a fascinating story.

What makes me furious is that James Frey lied to hundreds of thousands of people who struggle every day to fight off their addictions. Nobody goes to a bar the day they're discharged from a rehab hospital, sits on a bar stool, orders a shot of alcohol, stares it down, and walks away. That's bravado nonsense, make-believe ridiculous, and frankly, it is a damn shame Frey had the balls to lie about something that important to all of us in recovery.

Frey's memoir takes root in one of the most luxurious rehabilitation hospitals in America. Mine is narrated from a dilapidated state-funded detox where the windows are being held together with duct tape. He's a tough guy in his story. All the tough guys have died or gone to prison in mine. But the differences between Frey's work and this memoir are of no importance here. All that should matter after reading

275

Frey's memoir or this memoir is the bottom line: recovery from alcohol and drug addiction is insidious and most times emotionally crippling. Yes, it can be done, but not a man or woman alive recovers fully without reaching out for help. At this standard, Frey fails miserably. I'll let the reader be the judge of mine.

Please understand, I'm not condoning the other facts he may have fabricated. But to be honest and fair, while judging Frey's work as a whole, truth and reality lies someplace in that dead-black space between memory and imagination. Medical science has recently discovered that traumatic events are recorded in a specific section of the brain completely separate from where normal memory is stored. How individuals access traumatic memories is still very much a mystery.

Now, I understand facts aren't a game we make up as we go. But perception of a past event is something uniquely held by each individual. For example, the process of writing this memoir forced my memory to retreat twenty, thirty, sometimes forty years. At one point during recall, it became apparent that my childhood was like the bombed-out villages I walked through as a journalist in Bosnia. Of course, the village had a history. You know it was there. Now, it's just full of crater.

Tragically, my memory is the same, shell-shocked. I found it difficult to separate the story truth from the happening truth. You see, when my dad beat me with a fence post, I was twelve and looked away. And when my dad caught me thumbing, duct-taped me to a kitchen chair, and turned on Mom's electric carving knife, I closed my eyes, pissed myself, and floated away. Now, four decades later, I'm left with nothing but faceless truth.

My memory's pictures got all jumbled up. At times while I was writing this memoir, I felt like I was trapped inside an oversized traffic rotary spinning around and around until a major collision between my memory and imagination forced me to write the truth as I saw it now, happening back then.

But this is a true story. Nothing in my memoir is invented. Therefore, I want you to be perfectly clear about what I mean when I speak of story truth and happening truth. During the early '90s, I witnessed many soldiers and civilians die in a war over political control of the former Yugoslavia. One morning, during a United Nations bartered cease-fire to remove those deemed gravely wounded, a sniper's round rang out and killed a man five feet away from me.

Here is the happening truth.

Frano was a soldier. He was Croatian. I had spent forty-eight hours with him in a bunker near Marshal Tito Boulevard in Mostar, Bosnia. One morning, he stood up, a shot rang out, and he was dead. Terror paralyzed me. To this day, I struggle with actual events. Sometimes, in my dreams, I see him die. Other times, I see myself face down, unresponsive, afraid to look up and find the truth.

Here is the story truth.

Frano's hair was dark as an undertaker's hearse. His coffee-black eyes smiled first and his jaw was thick and square like most of the Bosnians. The Serbs had surrounded the city for two days, sending one shell after another into the civilian population. Frano was a Croatian soldier only because in Mostar at the time there was no such thing as a male non-combatant.

One morning during a cease-fire, Frano stood up to stretch. He dusted off his green-brown fatigues and *whack!*

the sound exploded, sniper, panic. Frano winced, his eyes rolled inward, and a chunk the size of my fist painted the bunker red. Dust flew off his pants and the impact or the response to impact blew him right out of his left boot. Frano was dead.

For years, I've fought with the reality of Frano's death. Nothing I write satisfies my thirst for the truth. The only resolution lending any comfort is the fact that Frano's dead and I witnessed it. The noise, the fear, the confusion that followed the sniper's shot can never be perfectly described. Ten people were in that bunker that morning and each and every one had a different account of what took place.

In closing, these pages contain my story and how I saw it, to the best of my God-given ability. Some may have seen it differently and that is their perception of reality. From my perspective, I wrote this memoir without fabrication. I have changed the names, locations, and identifying characteristics of a number of individuals in order to protect their privacy. In many cases, I borrowed names of people I met in my recovery to take the place of actual characters from my past. For example, Dan Callahan was the attorney who represented world-class, professional boxer Dickie Eklund, while I was filming a documentary film for HBO's *America Undercover*. He was not the attorney who represented me. I have no recall of that attorney's name. I have absolutely no memory of what he looked like.

And one final word to all my brothers and sisters attempting recovery: If I can make it, anybody can.